RELATING

A modern classic in which astrology and psychology are
brought together to show how people relate to each other
on both conscious and unconscious levels.

The meeting of two personalities is like the contact of two chemical substances: if there is any reaction, both are transformed.

— C. G. Jung

RELATING

An Astrological Guide to Living with Others

Liz Greene

Preface by Gerhard Adler

Aquarian/Thorsons
An Imprint of HarperCollinsPublishers

The Aquarian Press
An Imprint of HarperCollins*Publishers*
77–85 Fulham Palace Road,
Hammersmith, London W6 8JB

First published 1977
This edition 1990
2 5 7 9 10 8 6 4

A catalogue record for this book
is available from the British Library

ISBN 0 85030 957 3

Printed in Great Britain by
Mackays of Chatham PLC, Chatham, Kent

Contents

Acknowledgements

For permission to use copyright material, the author gratefully makes the following acknowledgements:

Alfred A. Knopf Inc. for permission to quote from Khalil Gibran's *The Prophet*.

Hutchinson Publishing Group Ltd. for permission to quote from M. Esther Harding's *Woman's Mysteries*.

W. Foulsham & Co. Ltd. for permission to quote from Vivian Robson's *Astrology and Human Sex Life*.

Prentice-Hall Inc. for permission to quote from Frances Wickes' *The Inner World of Choice* and Jung's introduction to *The Inner World of Childhood*.

Souvenir Press Ltd. for permission to quote from Joseph Campbell's *Creative Mythology*.

Worldwide Media Services Inc. for permission to quote from Franz Hartmann's *Paracelsus, Life and Prophecies*.

Simon & Schuster for permission to quote from Nikos Kazantzakis's *The Rock Garden*.

Anchor Books for permission to quote from June Singer's *The Boundaries of the Soul*.

G.P. Putnams Sons for permission to quote from Edward Whitmont's *The Symbolic Quest*.

Macmillan Inc. for permission to quote a passage from 'Among School Children' from *The Collected Poems of W.B. Yeats*.

Lucis Publishing Co. for permission to quote from Alice A. Bailey's *Esoteric Astrology*.

Routledge & Kegan Paul Ltd. for permission to quote from the following works by C.G. Jung: *Modern Man in Search of a Soul; C.G. Jung Letters, Vol. II; The Collected Works of C.G. Jung Vol. 12, Psychology and Alchemy; Vol 10, Civilisation in Transition; Vol. 6, Psychological Types; Vol. 9(ii) Aion; Vol. 7, Contributions to Analytical Psychology; Vol. 9(i) The Archetypes and the Collective Unconscious*.

Preface

by

Gerhard Adler

Perhaps it is best to say what this book — written by a highly expert astrologer with a worldwide reputation — is not. It is not an ordinary astrological tract on relationship, nor does Dr Greene identify generally with many of the traditionally accepted astrological interpretations. Her approach is utterly individual, in more than one sense. First, she has a highly original approach; and second, she puts the individual and his individual choice in the centre of her deliberations.

In this approach, she is greatly helped by her profound knowledge of psychology, being a highly trained psychotherapist herself. As a matter of fact her approach is characterized by the successful attempt to bring psychology and astrology together, always using both methods to clarify her arguments. I, as an analytical psychologist, was impressed by her comprehensive knowledge of psychology — in particular that of C. G. Jung — which she applies to all aspects of individual problems, be they the problem of the shadow, anima and animus, or the self. In a happy way she connects these psychological topics with her astrological material.

What impressed me most about her approach is her refusal to use astrology as a fixed map, firmly predicting the events of life; and her insistence on astrology being more in the nature of an indication, outlining the potentials of a person, making the final result dependent on how the individual deals with and uses these potentials.

As just one example of her careful and creative approach I would like to mention the astrological use of synastry, the comparison of two individuals' charts. Here traditional astrology, comparing the horoscopes of two people, is too inclined to draw final conclusions — and giving according advice — about the compatility of two individuals for a relationship. Instead Dr Greene is careful to point out that one can never base such a decision on just two birthcharts, as if they were divinely pre-ordained, but that one has to get away from statements such as 'suitable' or 'unsuitable', 'good' or 'bad' auspices. A 'good' marriage may easily become sterile, whereas a 'bad' marriage may by its conflicts and their conscious acceptance prove highly creative. Here the synthesis between her astrological and psychological approach proves most helpful when she relates certain astrological aspects to the individual's inner image of the partner in question, aiming at a transpersonal experience of the inner marriage, the *coniunctio*.

This leads her to emphasize how outer and inner worlds are images of each other, how both concrete and symbolic realities have to be understood and lived. In this connection she makes interesting and informative comments on the next astrological (and astronomical) era, when the vernal equinox leaves the constellation of Pisces and progresses into the constellation of Aquarius. A great deal has been written of the presumed nature of this Aquarian Age. But here again I find Dr Greene's interpretation most helpful, once more combining astrology and psychology. I can do no better than quote her own words: 'Aquarius symbolizes an attitude of consciousness which is interested in knowing and understanding the laws by which the energies which stand behind manifested life operate', implying a new attitude of science which more and more is going in the same direction as religion — toward the mystery of life.

Much more could be said about the book, but there are so many valuable insights that I feel I have done no more than mention a few personal reactions. To sum up, I would like to say that I found the book, written in beautiful language, most rewarding. It makes a truly creative contribution to the understanding of psychic dynamics, treading new ground in an — in the best sense of the word — unorthodox way. I have tremendously enjoyed reading the book and I am sure that everyone studying it will find himself or herself greatly enriched by it.

GERHARD ADLER

Foreword

Almost ten years have passed since *Relating* was first published, and during that time the study of astrology has slowly and inexorably widened, deepened, and found its way into sectors of society which once would have considered such a subject mere occult nonsense. This gradual increase in the serious study of astrology may be due to a number of factors, some explicable and others more mysterious. On the one hand, the indefatigable efforts of individuals such as Michel Gauquelin have produced a body of statistical evidence in favour of astrology's validity which has begun to influence the more pragmatic-minded sceptic in fields such as behavioural psychology — once a bastion of the most rigid kind of rational thinking. The scientific justification of astrology has become an important issue, even a crusade, for many astrological students and practitioners who have become fed up with the blind rejection of what they know to be their own affirmative experience; and their efforts have begun to yield fruit.

In conjunction with the more scientifically acceptable face of astrology being made available to the interested layman, there has also been an increase in good — as well as not so good — literature written on the subject. The selection of astrological works available to the reader has increased dramatically in the last decade, and so too, for the most part, has the standard of the writing. Where once a curious individual had to content himself or herself with three or four rather spiritually weighted tomes which often did more to obfuscate than to clarify how astrology works, now we may progress from a variety of excellent textbooks written from a number of different perspectives, without feeling that we are also being groomed for a particular esoteric or spiritual viewpoint. Astrology has spread in part because of the efforts of individual astrologers to express and explain their art (or science, depending upon your viewpoint) as clearly as possible to the layman.

But there may also be a subtler and deeper issue at work behind the increasing interest in astrology as a subject fit for a sane individual to study. For astrology belongs to a wider field, that of the study of the human psyche; and as we become more psychologically aware and sophisticated, so too we begin to explore older and more imaginal approaches to understanding as well as availing ourselves of modern psychology's formulae. Words which once belonged almost exclusively to the domain of the practising analyst and psychotherapist — such as 'archetypal', 'extroverted', 'introverted', and 'complex' — have now begun to find their way into ordinary language, and this reflects an increasing subtlety in our perception of human motives and human behaviour. While Freud's *Interpretation of Dreams* may never become a best-seller, most of us now know what is meant by the Oedipus Complex, albeit often inaccurately; and we have even begun to throw around the term 'unconscious', although all too often being unconscious of its real meaning. Perhaps it is because Jung's belief that there are no longer any new frontiers to explore save that of the human soul has begun to occur to us at last. Or perhaps it is that somehow we sense, on some level, that — once again paraphrasing Jung — if there is something wrong with the individual, and if there is something wrong with the individual then there is something wrong with me; and if I want to help to make the world a better place then I must begin at home, in my own psychic garden.

Thus, along with an increasing interest in the inner world, there has also been an increasing interest in what has come to be called 'psychological' astrology; for this approach to astrology has more or less abandoned the old fortune-telling exercise (what is going to happen to me next year?) in favour of seeking, through a combination of astrology's ancient symbolism and the lens of depth psychology's insight into human motives and behavious, why we create the lives we do and how we may express what is in us more creatively. This is largely so that we need no longer feel that life will happen to us, but rather that we are participants in life. This psychological approach to astrology — or, if you prefer, this astrological approach to psychology — has now begun to find its way into the helping professions as a most effective tool for quick and deep insight into the individual. Here the increasing influence of astrology is not so much due to statistical research, but perhaps due more to an increasing number of individual astrological students combining their study with training in one or another of the psychotherapeutic schools.

My original intent in writing *Relating* was to approach the vast and complex dilemma of human relationships through a combination of astrological symbolism and depth psychology — chiefly the psychology of C. G. Jung — because it seemed obvious to me through my experience of working both as an astrologer and a psychotherapist that what we meet in outer life ultimately reflects what lies within ourselves; and that relationships are our greatest mirrors and teachers of the stuff of which our own souls are made. This is not a new idea; it is implicit in much of Greek philosophical thought, as well as in the Hermetic teachings of the Renaissance. But it was relatively new in the astrological literature of a decade ago, although Jung — who regularly utilized the insights of astrology — wrote extensively on the subject. Astrology, however, found its entry into England via Theosophy, which as a philosophical system is benign but nonetheless shies away from that 'lower nature' which depth psychology has made so much effort to restore to its merited place in the wholeness of the individual; and even with the more enlightened approaches of Charles Carter, Margaret Hone, and the early days of the Faculty of Astrological Studies astrology still retained its unmistakeable antecedents in its talk of higher and lower natures, benefic and malefic plants, good and bad aspects, and a rather fatalistic approach to relationships (Venus in the second house in trine to Jupiter means you will marry money). Because Jung's psychology is round rather than vertical, and gives value to all dimensions of the psyche, this approach to the horoscope has always seemed to me to be a healthier one, and in the years since I wrote *Relating* my work as a Jungian analyst has proven to me over and over again the importance of recognizing and integrating the unconscious dimensions of the psyche if any psychological balance, health, and equalibrium are to be maintained — not to mention being able to let other people be other people and not extensions of our own unlived and unrecognized selves.

The connections between certain of Jung's models of the psyche and certain astrological classifications which I made when writing this book have been vindicated to me many times over in the last decade. I feel now, even more strongly than I did then, that the four elements of astrology are the essential building-blocks of the horoscope, just as the four functions of consciousness are the essential building-blocks of the personality; and if one begins an assessment of the horoscope with the peculiar individual balance of elements then the essential spinal column of the chart is depicted and the overall story of the individual's development pattern is displayed. The dilemma of the undeveloped functions of consciousness and their habitual projection onto partners, parents, children and friends remains to me one of the most fascinating, problematical and potentially enriching dimensions of human relationship.

Likewise, the more I have studied transits and progressions in the light of the emergence into consciousness of previously unconscious aspects of the psyche, the more I am intrigued by the remarkable way in which we appear to 'manifest' in outer life what is just coming to the boil in the inner world. This issue of externalized 'soul' came to preoccupy me so much that I eventually wrote about it in depth in *The Astrology of Fate;* but the seeds of this later exploration lie in the chapter in *Relating* which is devoted to the 'infallible inner clock' of transits and progressions. I do not feel it is possible to understand why, now, and for what purpose another individual enters one's life — be the context love, sex, friendship, enmity, professional help, or whatever — except in terms of one's own psyche and what is emerging, needing to be integrated, and wanting to be lived. For this, it seems to me, is what our journeys with our fellow travellers are truly about, and behind the frequent problems, pains, quarrels, disappointments, and betrayals, as well as the joys of relationship, lies an awesome mystery, of whatever it is — within or without — that possesses the intelligence and the creative power to draw us so unerringly to those who reflect our own fates and our own Selves.

LIZ GREENE
London/Zurich, 1986

Introduction

Knowest thou not that heaven and the elements
were formerly one, and were separated from one
another by divine artifice, that they might bring
forth thee and all things? If thou knowest this,
the rest cannot escape thee. Therefore in all
generation a separation of this kind is necessary.
... Thou wilt never make from others the One
which thou seekest except first there be made
one thing of thyself ...

— Gerhard Dorn

Princes and princesses, as every child knows, always live happily ever after. Even in the face of magic spells, wicked stepmothers, ogres, giants, and malevolent dwarfs, love triumphs, evil is overcome, and the happy couple disappear into the mists of imagination with hands linked and no hint of divorce courts or maintenance payments to cloud the ever after.

The process of "growing up", as every child is told, with its increasing maturity and capacity to face "life as it is", naturally teaches us otherwise. Princes and princesses, along with Santa Claus, the Easter Bunny, imaginary playmates, and other relics of the fantasy life of childhood, are not suitable stuff for adults to dwell on. No one, we begin to learn fairly early in life, lives happily ever after; we must make relationships "work", and they are a matter of responsibility, commitment, discipline, obligation, self-sacrifice, communication, and other terms that are used so often their meanings should be fairly clear. But somehow, in the experience of living, these terms become increasingly ambiguous as we realise that this other, this stranger who stands before us, whether husband or wife or son or lover, friend or teacher, business associate or enemy, is still a stranger.

Relating is a fundamental aspect of life. It is archetypal, which means that it is an experience which permeates the basic structure not only of the human psyche but of the universe in its entirety. In the final analysis all things are built upon relating, for we would not be conscious of any aspect of life without recognising it through its difference from every other aspect. We recognise day because there is night, and the relationship between the two defines and identifies each of them. And if some minimal thought is given to this idea, it becomes increasingly apparent that we human beings can only conceive of ourselves as individuals through comparison with that which we are not.

For a number of reasons, some obvious and some very much more subtle, there is a greater emphasis now on the experience of relating than there has been during other periods of our history. Relationships have always been an important facet of living, but we have not always called them relationships, nor have we recognised any purpose to them other than the obvious ones: alleviation of loneliness, satisfaction of desire, continuity of the species, protection for the individual and for society, experience of love (a thoroughly ambiguous word, as every adult knows), and furthering of material gain. These are all valid enough reasons for us to make the often rewarding and equally often painful effort necessary to live with our fellow human beings. Primarily through the work of psychology during the last seventy-five years, however, it has become apparent that relationships are not only a means to personal satisfaction of one kind or another. They are also necessary for the growth of consciousness and the individual's understanding of himself. A man does not know what he looks like until he sees himself reflected in the looking-glass, and this simple truth applies not only to physical reality but to the reality of the psyche as well.

In innumerable esoteric as well as psychological writings

we are told that man is about to enter a new age. The German word *Zeitgeist* aptly describes this concept, although it does not lend itself readily to translation. Very roughly, it means a spirit of the times, a new wind which blows through an era and heralds alterations of a significant and dramatic kind in man's consciousness. One might say that the great changes which occurred in man's outlook at the time of the Renaissance, in religion, science, the arts and all other fields of human endeavour, were the manifestations of a *Zeitgeist*. Something new was born which enabled man to see a different kind of reality, or more precisely, to see a larger chunk of reality than he had perceived before. The changes in consciousness which occurred at the dawn of the Christian era might also be considered the manifestations of a *Zeitgeist*, for it is characteristic at the beginning of a new aeon that old gods die and new ones are born. It would appear that we are experiencing another *Zeitgeist* at this time in history, although its dim outlines are apparent now only to those who have studied the language of symbolism.

It is possible that this shift in consciousness, to which astrology has given the symbolic name of the Aquarian Age, has, as one of its central motifs, a striving toward inner knowledge — a knowledge that would complement the emphasis on external knowledge already very familiar to us. Our current time-spirit appears to be deeply concerned with self-understanding, and with a search for meaning. And although one can attribute this search to economic and political changes which inevitably create tension, stress, and self-questioning, it may also be possible to view these two concurrent trends — socio-economic upheaval and what can be simply described as a spiritual quest — as synchronous events. That is, one need not be the cause of the other, but both may be symptomatic of a deep inner change occurring in the collective psyche of man.

It may seem that such weighty matters as the changing of man's consciousness, and the entry into a new age, have little to do with the very subjective upsets and problems which drive so many people to seek counselling for their difficulties in relationships. If a man's wife has left him for a lover, or a

woman is struggling with feelings of sexual inadequacy which
cripple her potential for a fulfilling marriage, it may seem
irrelevant to be told that there is a *Zeitgeist* afoot. Yet the
relevance exists. We are told often enough that divorce
statistics are on the rise, that the time-hallowed values and
moral standards which have propped up our relationships for
many centuries are crumbling and becoming meaningless to
younger generations, that current sexual behaviour has taken
new twists and turns unrivalled even by the declining Roman
Empire. Something definitely appears to be happening to our
criteria for evaluating relationships, and something is also
happening to the ways in which we are dealing with our
problems. Once upon a time, we suffered in silence. Yet now
there is a steady increase in the number of published
volumes, as well as magazine and newspaper articles, dealing
with the difficulties of getting along with other people. There
is also a steady increase in the marriage counselling business,
in "growth movement" workshops and groups, and in
individual therapy and analysis — all of which attempt,
among other things, to deal more or less successfully with
each person's needs, desires, conflicts, fears and aspirations
in relationships. One need hardly mention such phenomena
as the Women's Liberation Movement and the Gay Liberation
Movement, both of which attempt to confront in their own
ways certain aspects of the problems of relationships. Even
the controversy around sex education in schools is an issue
which centres around relating, as is the question of abortion.

All this re-evaluating of relationships is as much a part of
the overall search for more meaningful values and greater
understanding of the psyche as the more surprising
emergence of interest in ancient esoteric studies such as
astrology, alchemy and other apparent oddities. They are
all aspects of the same quest, and the sooner we realise this
the greater perspective we will have on the broader context
behind our personal problems.

Science, which has had the last word about reality for a
long time now, is surprising herself in approaching the
domain of what used to be called the arcane studies. To our
dismay we are being told by people with respectable letters

after their names that plants respond to human emotion and enjoy music, that the sun, moon and planets actually appear to emit energies which affect human life, that the mind of man is capable of such feats as telepathy, telekinesis and clairvoyance within the strictly controlled and monitored enclosure of the laboratory, and that God may in fact be alive and well after all, hiding secretly in matter. At this point it is not only dogmatic narrow-mindedness but fear as well which keeps people clinging tightly to their old concepts of what is real and rational, because even science is standing at the threshold of a universe which bears a startling resemblance to the magical and mysterious world of fairy tales. It is difficult when one thinks one is standing firmly on solid rock, to discover that the rock has begun to shift, dissolve, and reform into something else. In this new landscape into which all of us, whether we care for the idea or not, are being thrown, we are in desperate need of maps. We have so few guidelines, for we are learning at an alarming rate that we know really very little about the nature of man.

Under its present name psychology is a very new science, and in many ways it is primitive and inexperienced in the same way that everything is in its infancy. Yet psychology is one of the few reliable maps we have, even though we are drawing the map while in the very process of exploration. Psychology in its deepest sense, however, has existed for a long time under other names, the earliest of which, perhaps, was astrology. This may be more surprising to psychologists than to anyone else, but our word psychology comes from two Greek words — *psyche*, which means soul, and *logos*, which means wisdom — and the study of the human soul was the province of astrology long before it became the province of anything else.

In certain circles the oldest science and the youngest appear to be forming a most curious marriage. Astrology has lately been enjoying a renaissance, although its real value is not in the popular and misguided conception of magical prognostications of the future, but in the much more important role of becoming a tool of immense power in the exploration of the human psyche.

Although psychology and astrology use different languages and different methods of research and application, their subject of investigation is the same, and they are potentially very fruitful bedfellows. The fruit of such a coupling has yet to be fully recognised, but it constitutes the subject of this book. And if we consider the idea that relationships are, among other things, a path toward individual self-discovery, it is probable that the ancient wisdom of astrology and the modern insights of depth psychology jointly have something to tell us about the ways in which we relate to other people.

A properly erected astrological birth chart is a symbolic map of the individual human psyche. This map is like a seed because it contains in microcosm the potentials existent within the individual and the periods of his life when these potentials are likely to be brought into actualisation. Although the imagery of astrology is different from psychology's more precise terminology, the astrological birth map may be likened to those models of the psyche which have been offered to us by men of genius and insight in the psychological field, such as C.G. Jung and Roberto Assagioli. But models are only models, and are not reality; nor are they intended to be interpreted as reality. A model is really a hint, an inference, a lens through which, if we look carefully, we may glimpse that which cannot be articulated in words or expressed in concepts. The heart of each human being is a mystery, and the essence of attraction and repulsion between individuals is equally a mystery, no matter how much we attempt to pin it down in conceptual terms. But given useful maps, we can begin at least to fathom the mystery with the heart, even if we cannot grasp it with the intellect.

No attempt will be made here to prove or disprove the validity of astrology. There is already a quantity of excellent literature available to the interested enquirer which deals specifically with factual evidence on the subject, and a complete bibliography will be found at the end of this book. Each individual must in the end form his own opinion about astrology; but one cannot genuinely form an opinion until one knows something about the matter and has some experience at his disposal rather than popular conceptions and misconceptions. We should have learned by this time that such conceptions and misconceptions are extremely fallible; it is not so long ago that we believed the earth was flat and held up in the heavens by a giant tortoise, and this with the full approval of the scientists of the day. The proverbial proof of the pudding is in the eating, and can only be determined when the individual has his own direct experience and knowledge to help him crystallise a judgment of his own — not one accepted at second-hand.

If this book is not an attempt to justify astrology, neither is it a manual on how to cast your own horoscope — partially because that would entail a volume in itself, and partially because there are already many such volumes available. All of the astrological material offered here, therefore, is interpretive rather than mechanical. In order that it be used to the best advantage the reader should obtain, either through his own efforts or from a professional source, a correctly drawn horoscope for himself and for those with whom he is involved.

There are many ways of looking at reality, some of which are valid for some people and not for others. It is entirely possible that no one sees the whole, because we can only see through the perspective of our own psychological colouration. Reality is, therefore, subjective even to the most "open-minded" and "detached" among us. We have recently learned that even sub-atomic particles may alter their behaviour according to the observer, and the once safe field of inanimate matter is no longer safe to us as the last bastion of "objective reality". And this recognition of our one-sidedness is perhaps the beginning of wisdom.

It might even be time to dust off our old fairy tale volumes, because Jung's work has shown us that fairy tales, like dreams, are not what they seem to be. There is a wisdom in myths and fairy tales which speaks to something in us other than the intellect. The reasons for this lead one into direct confrontation with the reality of the unconscious psyche and the world of symbols. If the fairy tale tells us that the prince and the princess live happily ever after, there is some meaning to that resolution, for as even a child knows, fairy tales do not belong to the ordinary world and are not meant to be taken so. They belong to the world of the unconscious, and they are symbolic. If the fairy tale tells us that the prince, in order to win the princess, must challenge the dragon, slay the evil sorcerer, and destroy the power of the wicked stepmother with the aid of his helpful animal companion, this too has meaning, and we can learn much about the paths which lie open to us when we look at the prince's quest with different eyes. Myth and fairy tales are yet another map into our strange country. In their portrayals of the vicissitudes and struggles of the hero who seeks his beloved, they mirror an inner journey which each one of us must make in order to become whole. And only in a recognition of our own wholeness is it possible to recognise the stranger, the other. Perhaps only then can we begin to truly relate.

Perhaps we need to grow down, rather than up, so that we can look at our so-called reality with a child's eyes and recognise that truth can exist in the world of the psyche independent of material correlatives. "Facing life as it is" may in fact be an attitude which contains tremendous arrogance and very little wisdom, since none of us really knows what life is; we only know how it appears to us. Our lives have exactly as much meaning, or as little, as we infuse into them. We are all apparently alone, but whether this should necessarily be so, or whether aloneness should mean what we think it means, is questionable.

Most of all we need the courage to experiment with new tools, and to do so without prejudice. Jung had the courage, as a physician and a researcher, to learn astrology and to use it in his exploration of the psyche. If, thanks to his work, there is any truth to the greater understanding of ourselves which we now possess, it makes sense for us to have the courage to explore ourselves with similar tools — especially when those tools may help us to live more meaningful lives and enjoy more meaningful relationships. The prince's quest contains many surprises, and one of the greatest is the realisation that each of us is at once the prince, the dragon, the wicked stepmother, the helpful animal, and the beloved; and we are also the quest, and the storyteller, all at the same time.

1
The Language of the Unconscious

The world and thought are only the spumes; of menacing cosmic images; blood pulsates with their flight; thoughts are lit by their fires; and these images are — myths.
> — Andrei Bely

All that passes is raised to the dignity of expression; all that happens is raised to the dignity of meaning. Everything is either symbol or parable.
> — Paul Claudel

Most of us who believe ourselves to be thinking individuals like to assume that we know a good deal about ourselves. We very probably do, from the standpoint that we can list our virtues and vices, catalogue our "good" and "bad" points, and assess our likes, dislikes and goals. But even a self-conception of this limited scope is too great for many people, who appear to wander through life devoid of any sense of identity other than a name which they did not choose, a body over whose creation they exercised no control, and a place in life which is usually the result of material necessity, social conditioning, and apparent chance.

Yet even if we take an individual who has the perspicacity to "know" himself in behavioural terms, a very curious phenomenon occurs. Ask him to describe himself, and, if he is honest with you and with himself — a rare enough premise to start with — he may give you a very comprehensive picture of his personality. But ask his wife to describe him, and one might think she was speaking of another individual. Character traits appear of which the man himself appears totally ignorant, goals are attributed to him which are the least important of his values, and qualities are often conferred upon him which are diametrically opposed to those which he believes constitute his own identity. One begins to wonder who is deluding whom. Ask his children what they think, and you will get a totally different picture; his fellow workers will contribute still further information, and his casual friends will portray yet another man. We can all attempt this simple investigation, and through it see that the most observant of us, the most introspective, sees only what he chooses to see through the lens of his own psyche; and as our conceptions of reality, both about ourselves and about others, are always seen through tinted lenses, it is inevitable that we will know far less about ourselves than we suspect.

> We must admit that what is closest to us is the very thing we know least about, although it seems to be what we know best of all.[1]

Whatever anyone may have to say about Freud's theories on the unconscious, we cannot avoid the fact that man contains far more within his psyche than is accessible to the limitations of his conscious awareness. Whether we are really motivated by biological needs, as Freud suggested, or by the will to power, as Adler suggested, or by the urge toward wholeness, as Jung suggested, one thing is clear: we are usually not aware of our deepest motivations, and, given this degree of blindness, are hardly in a position to be aware of anybody else's.

The concepts of conscious and unconscious are difficult

1 *Modern Man in Search of a Soul*, C.G. Jung, Routledge & Kegan Paul, London, 1961.

terms to explain because they are living energies which, unlike the organs of the physical body, do not lend themselves to categorisation. Nevertheless the psyche of man contains a vast field of hidden material which is usually communicable only through channels which are ordinarily rejected or overlooked. Most people do not understand their dreams, and frequently either make no effort to remember them or consider them meaningless; fantasies are considered to be childish unless they are erotic, in which case they are considered to be sinful; emotional eruptions are felt to be embarrassing, and are cloaked with excuses ranging from ill health to business difficulties.

In terms of the subject of relating, perhaps the most important mechanism we possess that enables us to see into the psyche is that of projection. We often use the term in connection with the cinema, and its meaning in this context can help us to understand it in a psychological sense as well. When we see an image projected upon a screen, we look at the image and respond to it, rather than examining the film or transparency within the projector which is the real source of the image; nor do we look at the light within the projector which makes it possible for us to see the image in the first place. When a person projects some unconscious quality existent within himself onto another person he reacts to the projection as though it belonged to the other; it does not occur to him to look within his own psyche for the source of it. He will treat the projection as though it existed outside him, and its impact on him will usually trigger a high emotional charge because it is, in reality, his own unconscious self that he is facing.

This very simple mechanism is at work whenever we have any highly coloured or irrational emotional reaction, positive or negative, to another person. It is a lifetime's work to introject, to recognise and bring back into ourselves, these unconscious qualities, so that we can begin to perceive the dim outlines of the other's identity. And we certainly do not come closer, but only move further away, when we make or break relationships according to responses based on our own projections.

> Psychic projection is one of the commonest facts of
> psychology ... We merely give it another name, and as a
> rule deny that we are guilty of it. Everything that is
> unconscious in ourselves we discover in our neighbour,
> and we treat him accordingly.[1]

Why should we attribute to others that which belongs to
us? It is understandable if we consider "bad" qualities. If I do
not like a particular trait in myself, if in fact it is so painful for
me to acknowledge that it remains unconscious, this
unrecognised piece of me will torment me in its impetus
towards expression by appearing to confront me from the
outside. It is more difficult to understand why we should
disown positive qualities. To do so, we must learn something
about the structure and laws of the psyche — always bearing
in mind that anything psychology has to say about the psyche
is really the psyche talking about itself, which renders
"complete objectivity" impossible. We can then return to our
subject of projection.

The ego is the centre of the field of everyday, rational
consciousness; very simply, it is what I know — or think I
know — to be myself.

> Consciousness consists primarily of what we know, and
> what we know we know.[2]

For most of us, the ego is all we know of ourselves, and as we
stand at this point and survey the world, the world appears to
us coloured by the particular viewpoint of the ego. Anybody
who sees something different we assume to be stubbornly
narrow-minded, deliberately lying, or possibly abnormal or
insane.

The ego appears to develop along particular lines from
birth. If we were wholly the product of our heredity,
conditioning and environment, children born into the same
circumstances would be exactly the same psychologically —

1 *Ibid.*
2 *The Boundaries of the Soul*, June Singer, Anchor Books, N.Y., 1973.

which of course they are not.

> The individual disposition is already a factor in childhood; it is innate, and not acquired in the course of life.[1]

Astrology also suggests that the individual's temperament is inherent at birth, and an understanding of astrology may be of help in perceiving the nature of this seed which develops into the adult ego. It can not only tell us about the self we know, but also about the one we do not know. The symbolism of the birth chart also reflects the natural human tendency to experience and evaluate life through the ego, for the horoscope is a mandala with the earth, rather than the sun, at its centre. It shows, in other words, how life appears and is likely to be experienced by the individual consciousness rather than what life truly is.

As we grow into adulthood, there are many qualities in our natures which are not incorporated into the developing ego, although they belong to us nonetheless. These things must be allowed to live, but they may be unacceptable to parents, may contradict religious doctrines, may violate social standards, or, lastly and most importantly, may simply conflict with what the ego values most. Some of these rejected qualities may be "negative" in the sense that they are destructive; some may be "positive" and may be of far more value, individually and socially, than what the ego has made of itself. An individual may, in fact, value mediocrity — without realising that he is doing so — and may stifle the emerging seeds of individual uniqueness and creativity within himself; or his self-image may be an overly modest one, and the more outstanding qualities are then relegated to the unconcious. All of these things will be projected onto a suitable object.

The object of a projection is not limited to individuals. It may be an organisation, a nation, an ideology or a racial type which becomes the focus for one's projection of the

1 *Modern Man in Search of a Soul.*

unrecognised dark side. A man who is violently and irrationally opposed to capitalism may be projecting as strongly as a man who is equally violent and irrational in his reaction to communism. The hallmark of projection is not the viewpoint, but the intensity and high charge of the reaction. One can stand in the middle of an argument between two people and listen with astonishment as each accuses the other of what they are both doing. When one is not a participant, it is laughable and at the same time tragic, as most marriage counsellors can attest. But when one is involved, in the spell of one's own projection mechanism, with the unconscious aroused, one is absolutely convinced of one's rightness. To accept the painful and omnipresent possibility of being mistaken is distasteful, because it means surrendering long-cherished illusions about ourselves. To live life without these illusions requires courage and a moral sense which has no resemblance to the common societal conception of black-and-white morality. It is no wonder that we project, for only by doing so can we continue to blame others for our pain instead of recognising that the psyche contains both dark and light and that our reality is the one we ourselves have created. Yet in projection and its subsequent discovery lies an enormously important vehicle by which we can come to know what is hidden in ourselves, and what we do not see in others.

It is usual to focus projection on a screen which bears some slight resemblance to the projected image, although it is common enough for the resemblance to be misinterpreted as identity. A person must be a good "hook" on which to hang the thing, if we are to get away with it; and we desire, moreover, some selectivity in our relationships. (Here also, as we shall see, astrology provides an important key to what we are likely to project, and what kind of individual we are likely to honour or insult with the bestowal of our projections.) But in spite of the resemblance between the screen and the image, they are never the same, and the projection is almost always a gross exaggeration of some quality which, left alone, might be harmoniously integrated in the nature of the other person or of oneself.

There are certain unpleasant aspects of projection that enter into relationships. If a person is perpetually the target for someone else's unconscious qualities, and if he lacks the self-knowledge to discern what is happening, he will, in time, begin to resemble the projection. We all know of seemingly inexplicable situations in which, for example, a woman apparently has the misfortune to attract one painful match after another. Each of her lovers may beat her, even if he has had no history of such behaviour before; and we shake our heads sadly and say something about woman's lamentable plight, never recognising the unconscious collusion her situation has entailed. Through our projections, we have a knack of drawing from other people qualities which, left alone, might have remained seeds which would never have sprouted; and there is not one of us who can say that his own psyche does not contain the same possibilities for both good and evil. None of us is in a position to judge seeds. But with the careful watering and sunlight of our projections, we evoke these responses from each other in a manner which sometimes seems like demonic possession.

The man who believes women to be devouring, manipulative and destructive, because there is some unconscious part of him which contains these qualities, may mask all this under a conscious attitude of attraction for the opposite sex; yet he may be horrified to discover that every woman with whom he becomes involved turns out in the end to attempt to devour, manipulate and destroy him. He may believe that he has perceived a general truth about womanhood, yet it is possible that he has himself evoked these qualities in women who might otherwise never have displayed them. In another relationship the same woman might behave completely differently; and since the collective opinion of the male sex is not unanimous in misogyny, we may safely adopt certain suspicions about our poor devoured gentleman.

But who is to blame here? Can we say that one is responsible for the unconscious? Is it not more realistic and more charitable to admit that we cannot control that of which we are ignorant? Even the courts will concede that a crime committed in a state of insanity merits psychiatric treatment rather than punishment. What, then, about our unconscious projections of hostility, anger, stupidity, destructiveness, possessiveness, jealousy, meanness, pettiness, brutality and the myriad other aspects of our own shadowy sides which we perpetually think we see in the people whom we feel have disappointed us?

Although we are not responsible for the unconscious — after all, the ego is only a latter-day outgrowth of the matrix of the unconscious — we are responsible for trying to learn a little about it, as much as is possible given the limitations of consciousness. Perhaps this is a challenge which is part of our *Zeitgeist*. After so many thousands of years of history we are no longer children, and must accept the responsibilities of psychological adulthood. One of these responsibilities is to bring home our projections.

We do not know very much about the unconscious, and this is obvious since it is, after all, unconscious. We know that this limitless sea, out of which our small lighthouse of awareness springs, appears to work in accordance with different energy patterns and different laws; it has a different mode of communication and a different language, and must be explored with a respect for these differences. If an Englishman travels in Germany, he cannot expect to be understood if he stubbornly persists in speaking only English; and the same applies to the relation between the ego and the unconscious. The ego unfortunately often has the same attitude as the Englishman, and is astonished that it should be expected to make this sort of compromise. But if we seek to explore ourselves and fulfil our real potential, we must first learn the language of the unconscious. And it is unquestionably alien, so alien that we laugh nervously or shy in fright from its face in dreams, fantasies, emotional eruptions, and all those areas of life where a magical or strange quality permeates our perceptions and blurs the edges of what we thought was a sharp and clear-cut reality.

> We only believe that we are masters in our own house because we like to flatter ourselves. Actually, however, we are dependent to a startling degree upon the proper

functioning of the unconscious psyche, and must trust that it does not fail us.[1]

One of the most important postulates that Jung established about the unconscious is that it is compensatory to consciousness.

The psyche is a self-regulating system that maintains itself in equilibrium as the body does. Every process that goes too far immediately and inevitably calls forth a compensatory activity.[2]

Everything, in other words, which is not contained or expressed within the ego's life is contained within the unconscious, in a nascent and inchoate form. One of the characteristics of man's conscious ego is that it specialises and differentiates; the unconscious, on the other hand, is a fluid, shifting, undifferentiated sea which flows around, under and above the clear shell of the ego, eroding certain parts and depositing fresh ones, in the same way that the sea itself flows around a rocky promontory. The psyche as a whole contains all possibilities; the ego can only work with one possibility at a time, as its function is to order, structure and make manifest a particular fragment of the limitless experiences of life. It is no wonder that in myth and fairy tales, this world of the unconscious is so often symbolised by the sea, and the hero's journey into the depths is the ego's journey to the depths of the psyche. The unconscious is an underwater world, full of strange and magical creatures; and for human lungs used to breathing air, total immersion is of course a psychological death. This death we call insanity.

In the light of all of this, one can begin to understand why the man who has grown into a lopsided shape, whose ego has developed along a narrow path and denied all other possible expressions, is also the man who is most likely to be plagued with intense projections on others and who seems most beset

1 *Ibid.*
2 *Ibid.*

by the apparent shortcomings of his fellow human beings.

The primary mode of expression of the unconscious is the symbol. We are surrounded by symbols all our lives, from our own inner life, from the lives of others, and from the world around us, but we are often oblivious to their meaning and their power. A symbol is not the same thing as a sign; it is not simply something which stands for something else. The various signs which we see on the road, for example, have specific meanings: no right turn, or no parking, or construction work ahead. But a symbol suggests or infers an aspect of life which is inexhaustible in interpretation and ultimately eludes all the intellect's efforts to fix or contain it. One cannot ever fully plumb the depths of its manifold meanings, nor can one catalogue these meanings in intellectual terms because they frequently contain antitheses which the conscious ego cannot perceive simultaneously. Moreover, a symbol's meanings are linked not by logic, but by association, and associations can radiate out in a multitude of contradictory directions. We cannot be conscious of all associations at the same time; nor can we establish a perimeter for the ripples of association in the same way that we can for the clearly defined path of logic. A symbol is like a stone dropped into the pool of the psyche. We are in the middle of the pool, so to speak, and cannot have eyes at the backs of our heads.

A symbol evokes a response from us at an unconscious level, because it brings together associations which are not logically connected, and fuses them into a meaningful whole. A simple example would be the flag of a particular country. To a patriot, that flag is a symbol of everything his country means to him; when he is confronted with it, all the emotional and religious values it embodies, the sense of freedom or lack thereof, his home, his roots, his heritage, the possibilities of the future, and a myriad other associations which he could never fully explain burst upon him in one instant with a high emotional charge. One can see in this simple and inadequate example some of the power of the symbol. A flag can evoke hatred, violence, passion, love, sacrifice, self-destruction or heroism, and can plunge an individual — or a nation of individuals — into an emotional reaction over which there is no conscious control. The symbol of the swastika, used with cold intelligence and full knowledge of its power, helped throw the world into chaos only forty years ago; and even now, when one sees it scrawled on a subway wall or the side of a building, it has the capacity to evoke powerful emotional reactions and a host of powerful associations. In much the same way, conventional religious symbols can have immense power. The silver crucifix about the neck of the devout Christian, or the Star of David about the neck of the Jew, has a meaning which can never be communicated in words yet which affords a glimpse of what to many is the highest and holiest of mysteries, embodied in a simple geometric form.

The flag, the swastika, the Star of David and the crucifix are symbols which we can readily identify as symbols. But there are symbols around us which we do not identify so easily, because they are expressions of the underlying energy patterns which shape life itself. These basic lines of energy Jung called the archetypes, and although an archetype has no form, it communicates itself to us through many symbols of a nature so vast that the conscious ego backs off in awe. Nature itself, like mankind, functions in accordance with archetypal patterns, while at the same time embodying them. In the cycle of the seasons, for example — with new life emerging in the spring, maturity and fruitfulness of summer, gradual disintegration and harvest of autumn, barrenness and secret underground germination of winter — we may see the cycle of our own lives, from birth to maturity, decay, death and rebirth. The cycle of the sun in the heavens, rising in the east, culminating at the midheaven, setting in the west, and vanishing during the night only to rise again, seemed to the ancients to be the face of God because they saw reflected in the solar journey the entirety of life. Unlike our forefathers, we no longer worship the sun, but we still respond unconsciously to the symbol. The growth of a plant, from seed to leaf to flower and again to seed, again symbolises this life process — as does the waning and waxing of the moon, the cycles of the planets and constellations. Here we can begin to see why astrology was, to the ancients, an eye opening into the workings of the universe — because every experience of which a human being is capable, if seen symbolically, may be found to correspond to one of these natural cycles in the heavens. The language of literature abounds with similar correspondences, as does that of myth and fairy tale; and we even use them in our daily speech, when we speak of the ebb and flow, the waxing and waning of life, of desire, and of love.

These things need to be meditated on and felt, rather than analysed, for the natural symbols of life tell us about our wholeness and our connection with each other and with the flow of life itself; but they cannot be discerned if we see only with the intellect. One could stretch it all even further and suggest that we human beings are ourselves symbols; for all the universe is energy, and there are certain basic underlying energy patterns, formless yet with definite qualities, which embody themselves as man.

Freud spent a great deal of time trying to demonstrate that everything in dreams is a symbol of either the male or the female sexual organs. What did not occur to him was the possibility that he had things the wrong way around, and that male and female organs are themselves symbols for the mysterious archetypal energies which the Chinese call *yin* and *yang*. As Jung was once reputed to have said, even the penis is a phallic symbol. Those qualities which we associate with masculinity — directness, will, one-pointedness, clarity, openness, force — are mirrored in every man's body, and those qualities which we associate with femininity — subtlety, hiddenness, delicacy, gentleness and softness — are also mirrored in the body of every woman. As a result of Jung's life work, we have reason to believe that the archetype, the basic energy itself, exists before there is a form through which it can manifest. Or, as the Bible expresses it, in the beginning was the Word.

When we look at each other's faces, we see there the symbols of inherent character traits. We express this instinctually in our talk of weak chins and determined jaws, scholarly foreheads and predatory noses, penetrating eyes and artistic hands. We are putting into words our unconscious perception that the body itself may be a symbol of the individual, and we see in physical form a crystallised, concretised distillation of the other standing before us. This is a most important principle to contemplate, because it tells us something about what sexual attraction and repulsion really are.

A very different world opens to us if we assume that manifest reality itself is a symbol. On this basis all religious doctrines are established; and all esoteric thought, the secret wisdom tradition of centuries, stems from this miracle of symbol which the Emerald Tablet crystallised in the phrase, "As above, so below." Jung hints in the same direction in his work; but as a scientist, he was obliged to base his ideas on empirical observation rather than intuitive vision — or at least, to back up his vision with verifiable facts.

> The psyche arises from a spiritual principle which is as inaccessible to our understanding as matter.[1]

The same archetypal patterns underlie both.

We can begin now to glimpse what the unconscious really means. Freud thought it was a dustbin into which the private accumulation of each man's rejected debris was poured; he believed that its contents were composed almost exclusively of repressed desires which were unacceptable to the conscious ego and to the society in which man lives. There is undoubtedly an accumulation of filth in the unconscious of each man — probably in direct compensatory proportion to the "cleanliness" of the conscious ego. At the same time, there is also an accumulation of treasure. Moreover, filth is also relative; it is not very appetising on the kitchen table, but every gardener knows that without his compost heap he would have a very poor garden. The unconscious opens out below and above us as a repository of immense creative energy, a matrix from which all things spring; and it does not stop at the individual level, but merges into a great collective

1 *Ibid*.

sea beyond human bounds which extends to the unknown. It is possible that what modern psychology calls the unconscious was once known to the ancients as the gods, or God; and it is no wonder, when we ponder these things, that science and religion, having thrown stones at each other for so many centuries, are beginning to discover that they are travelling in the same direction, toward the same mystery — however different their vehicles.

From this excursion into the world where psychology and religion meet, let us go back to the practical problems of relationships. We can now see that most of what goes on in a relationship is unconscious, because most of what a man is remains unconscious. The mystery of why a man is attracted to a certain type of woman, why he begins his relationship in a particular way, why it takes the course it does and why he encounters the particular problems he must cope with, is less a mystery when we realise that much of what we call attraction and repulsion is really attraction or repulsion pertaining to unconscious qualities within the man himself. It is a rare man who can say there is no element of projection in his relationships, for there is probably a good deal in the unconscious which can never become conscious and which we will eternally project. It may be that we even project God. Who then is the beloved, and where is she to be found? Within or without? Or both?

II
The Planetary Map
of Individual Potential

What is below is like what is above. And what is
above is like what is below, so that the miracle of the
One may be accomplished.

— Tabula Smaragdina

Fate and soul are two names for
the same principle.

— Novalis

The Birth Chart
Any understanding of the language of astrology must
commence with a realisation of what the birth horoscope can
and cannot tell us. The horoscope is a highly complex
astronomical map, based not only on the date of birth but on
the time, year and place as well. We must first, therefore,
discard all preconceptions and prejudices based on popular
magazine astrology, which has virtually nothing to do with
the real study.

The birth map does not plot the fate of the individual in a
predestined way. Rather, it symbolises the basic lines of his
character's potential development. It takes a minimum of
thought to realise that a man will act and shape his life
according to his needs, fears and abilities, and that these
needs, fears and abilities stem from his inherent disposition.
In this sense character is fate, and if we are ignorant of our

own natures — as most of us are who have never explored the unconscious — then the stars cannot be blamed for the fact that we run headlong and blind along the course we ourselves have chosen. This fundamental point is critical to an understanding of the entire study of astrology. The more shallow interpretation of fate and free will — fate is what I am "destined" to do, while free will is what I "choose" to do myself — makes it impossible for us to see the subtle paradox that these two opposites are one and the same.

We know that behind all life, whether psychic or material, lie the archetypal patterns, the bare bones of the structure of existence. We do not yet know whether there is any material basis for the fact that astrological data correlate with human behaviour, although through our research on biological clocks and sunspot cycles[1] it will not be long before we have our evidence. Michel Gauquelin's labourious and thorough statistical research has demonstrated in a dramatic way that such correlations are valid[2], but the reason for their validity still eludes us. The material facts pertaining to astrology, however, such as the possibility of energy emanations from the planets which affect the energy field of the sun, are only one end of the spectrum of the archetype. The other end is symbolic, and the positions of the heavens at a particular moment in time, by reflecting the qualities of that moment, also reflect the qualities of anything born at that moment, whether it be an individual, a city, an idea, a company or a marriage. One does not cause the other; they are synchronous, and mirror each other.

So far as the reason for this synchronicity is concerned, we are left, on the one hand, with Jung's archetypes of the collective unconscious and, on the other, the teachings of esoteric doctrine. These two viewpoints seem to disclose the same truth, which the findings of quantum physics and biology in the last twenty-five years are beginning to affirm. Life is really one organism, and the various parts of that organism, although different in form and apparently separate,

1 See Lyall Watson's *Supernature*, Hodder & Stoughton, London, 1972.
2 *Cosmic Influences on Human Behaviour*, Michel Gauquelin.

partake of the same whole and are interconnected with every other part.

Paracelsus, writing on astrology in the 16th century, says:

> If I have "manna" in my constitution, I can attract "manna" from heaven ... "Saturn" is not only in the sky, but also deep in the earth and in the ocean. What is "Venus" but the "artemisia" that grows in your garden? What is "iron" but "Mars"? That is to say, Venus and artemisia are both the products of the same essence, and Mars and iron are both the manifestations of the same cause. What is the human body but a constellation of the same powers that formed the stars in the sky? He who knows what iron is, knows the attributes of Mars. He who knows Mars, knows the qualities of iron.[1]

The solar system is not only an arrangement of physical sun and planets bound together by the force of gravity and orbiting through space. It may also be seen as the symbol of a living energy pattern, reflecting at any moment the smaller forms of life which are contained within it.

In attempting to understand the symbolism of the birth horoscope, it is useful to consider what we know of the psyche, for the chart at birth is really a model, in symbolic terms, of the various energy patterns or psychic components which make up the individual. We know that the ego, as the centre of the field of consciousness, is a regulating centre which serves the function of illuminating those areas of the unconscious, both personal and collective, which are striving for light; and we know as well that the ego is the surrogate or reflection of that mysterious centre which Jung calls the Self, and which esoteric teaching calls the Soul. We know too that as an individual develops it is likely he will block from his field of awareness those aspects of his nature which in reality belong to him, yet which for one reason or another are incompatible with his values or with the values of his family

1 *Paracelsus, Life and Prophecies*, Franz Hartmann, Rudolph Steiner Publications, N.Y., 1973.

or society. Finally, we know that it is extremely important, if one seeks self-fulfilment and a meaningful life which fulfills also the larger purpose for which one has been born, to bring these aspects of his own nature to light, rather than condemning them to the perpetual darkness of the unconscious. As it is ideally projected from the early days of childhood, the personality is almost never fully expressed; only a part is enacted, and for many people this part is far smaller than that which constitutes their real birthright. In such cases, we say that a man has not really fulfilled his potential, that he has wasted opportunities or talents, or that he has never really been "true to himself"

The birth chart is a seed or blueprint of all that potentially belongs to a man's personality — if it were in full flower, and fully conscious. It is a road map in the truest sense, for the object of studying it is not to "ovecome" the "influences" of the planets, but rather to allow room in one's life to express all those qualities and drives of which the chart is a symbol. Only then can the individual approximate the original plan for his life's development as it is "conceived" — for we must in the end infer intelligent, purposeful development — by the Self.

If this seems too abstruse or lofty a definition of the birth horoscope, it is pertinent to remember that astrology, before it became the property of popular magazines and newspaper columns, was once a sacred art. Through it, the student had access to an intuitive perception of the workings of the energies behind life, which no other ancient system — except perhaps its Eastern equivalent, the *I Ching* — could offer. The great is reflected in the small, and the fact that astrology can also be used to illumine more mundane problems is not a repudiation of its deeper psychological value. It is only a reflection of the fact that even in the minutest details of our lives, we reflect that which is our essence.

When seen in this light, it will be apparent that an understanding of the birth horoscope affords a new dimension to the understanding of one's life path. Likewise the comparison of two horoscopes will provide considerable information about the interworkings of two lives; and it is from this art of chart comparison that synastry — the use of chart comparison to explore and evaluate relationships — has developed.

Astronomically, the birth horoscope is simply a map — accurately calculated so that it cannot be faulted by the most pernickety astronomer — of the heavens as they appear from the exact time and place of the individual's birth. The circle of the twelve zodiacal signs is a symbol of totality, and in its totality it represents all life's possibilities. In this respect, the zodiac is like any other universal symbol of wholeness, such as the egg, or the urobouros (the serpent devouring its tail), or the equal-armed cross. It is a mandala, and as Jung as shown, mandalas are the symbolic expression of the potential wholeness of life and of the human psyche. They are at the same time symbols of the Self, and symbols of God, for these two are, in terms of human perception, the same.

Against the backdrop of this circle of the zodiac (which is called the ecliptic and which is in fact the apparent circle of the sun traversing the heavens) lie the sun, the moon and the eight known planets. The positions of these planets as they are placed around the zodiacal wheel at the moment of the individual's birth form the internal pattern of the birth chart. Thus we have a symbolic picture, with the wheel of wholeness around the outside and the individual combination of psychological components on the inside. Every chart is made up of the same ingredients: twelve zodiacal signs, eight planets, and the sun and moon. Yet every chart is different because at any given moment the arrangement of all these factors is different, both within the planetary pattern and in the relationship between the planets and the horizon of the earth itself.

In other words, human beings are built of the same raw stuff, the same drives or energies, needs and possibilities; but there is an individual arrangement of these energies which gives the stamp of uniqueness to the pattern. The same forces are present in all of us, a fact with which one is confronted endlessly in any work involving counselling or therapy. But there is a creative individuality which makes of these basic energies a unique work of art, which is the individual life.

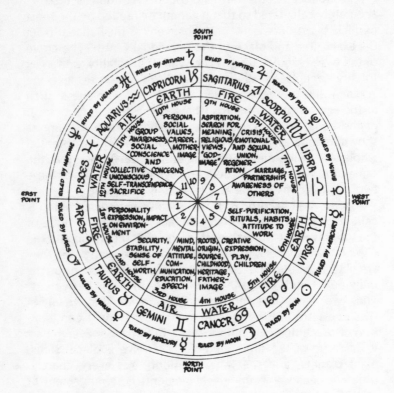

The Structure of the Birth Chart

This creative shaping does not, we must assume, stem from the ego, which is hardly capable of such a feat; it stems from the Self, and the Self, as such, is not mapped out on the birth chart. It is the entire zodiac. Nor can the chart show the individual's decision at any point in his life to voluntarily cooperate with his own psyche's endeavour to achieve greater consciousness, and therefore to make fuller use of those potentials which are his from the beginning. In this decision lies the deepest meaning of individual free will.

The Planets

The basic building blocks in astrological symbolism are the eight planets and the sun and moon. In astrological jargon, the sun and moon are also referred to as planets, because doing so makes things easier. In astronomy, these ten heavenly bodies are the components which form the organism of our solar system. Symbolically, they form the organism of the human psyche. In ancient esoteric teaching, it was believed that space was not "empty", but was in fact the living body of a gigantic life, an organism which possessed the attributes of consciousness and purpose. Its physical form was the solar system, and the sun expressed the heart, around which the moon and eight planets served as organs or centres of energy — in the same way that the organs of the human body serve the primary function of the life-giving heart. Prior to the discovery of Uranus in 1781, only five planets were known; but we may see shadowy intimations of the other three in mythology, where they are invariably symbolised as gods who are invisible, who live beneath the waters or the earth. Although we may find this esoteric concept of the solar system abstract and difficult to imagine, it is an indispensable symbol for any attempt to understand how the planets function in the birth chart.

Astrology, like the collective unconscious with which psychology is concerned, consists of symbolic configurations: the "planets" are the gods, symbols of the powers of the unconscious.[1]

We can now proceed to explore the meaning of each of the heavenly bodies in accordance with the basic urges or archetypal patterns they symbolise in the individual.

Sun and Moon

The sun, which is the heart of the solar system and the single most important symbol within the birth chart, suggests by its pictorial representation — a point at the centre of a circle — that it reflects the individual's urge to become himself. Although this sounds simple enough, it is a lifetime's task. The circle is the ancient symbol of wholeness, of divinity, and of the eternal oneness of life, because it has no beginning and no end; the dot at the centre suggests that spirit, or life, or the Self, manifests itself (at a particular place and a particular point in time) as an individual ego which possesses, as one of its atrributes, the impulse towards self-realisation. Like any other living symbol, the sun on the birth chart cannot be reduced to a few well-chosen keywords. But we may obtain some hint of its meaning if we know that it suggests the path which the individual must follow to fulfil his basic urge for a sense of identity. We could say that the sun symbolises the urge for self-expression, self-realisation, self-awareness or any of a number of other terms which do not really make sense unless one is conscious of the underlying need within oneself to be oneself — and unless one can see this need at work in all the creative acts one performs not for any ulterior motive, but as a genuine reflection of the essence of individuality.

The planets on the birth chart symbolise the archetypal experiences of life, and astrology is only one way of portraying them. Another, as we have seen, is myth and fairy tale, and the sun may be considered a reflection of the same principle which is expressed as the Hero. The Hero's Quest is

1 C.G. *Jung Letters*, Vol. II, edited by Gerhard Adler, Routledge & Kegan Paul, London, 1976.

the same journey that is expressed through the symbolism of the birth chart; and the Hero always and forever seeks first his other half, so that he may be whole, and then his source, so that he can truly recognise his parentage and his purpose. We might say also that the sun on the horoscope is a symbol of the urge within the individual to recognise that life force or centre of which his conscious ego, his personal "I", is a reflection.

The sun, then, is a symbol of the ego, in the sense that Jung employs the term. Ultimately, it is the vessel or vehicle for the totality of the psyche, the Self, to become manifest. As we have already noted, the chart does not show the Self, which is symbolised by the zodiacal wheel as a whole. The birth chart is only the route the ego takes, the particular quest of the individual Hero; and those qualities which the individual can potentially actualise in consciousness — his little share in the larger spectrum of life — are symbolised by the sign in which the sun is placed at birth.

Much unintentional damage has been done to astrology by sun-sign columns in newspapers and popular magazines, and unfortunately even the more serious astrological student is often caught in the same trap as the reader of such columns: the sun-sign is generally interpreted as a set of pre-existent and crystallised behaviour patterns. We may read that if one is an Aries, one is headstrong, impulsive, rash and fond of challenge. If one is a Taurus, one is stable, reliable, sensuous, stubborn and fond of material well-being. And on and on. But it would be much more meaningful and more in keeping with the understanding of the psyche afforded by the work of analytical psychology, to see the sun not as a mere catalogue of character traits, but as that which one is striving to become, and what one is in potential, in essence. In fact, this symbol of the fully integrated ego is rarely attained before the first thirty years of life are over; and the dawning of some real self-questioning usually follows on the heels of the 29-year crisis point called the Saturn return. Living out the full potential of the sun is a lifetime's journey. So we may say that your sun-sign does not "make" you anything in particular; rather, it symbolises those energies, that particular myth, of which you are trying to learn how to become conscious, and trying to express in a creative way. It is each individual's task to make conscious and bring through the channel of his own unique individuality the meaning of the sun-sign symbolism, so that it is stamped with the mysterious essence of one's own Self. Being born with the sun in Aries may not make a man headstrong and impulsive; but it suggests that he needs to cultivate a sense of the vitality of life, an ability to assert himself in the outside world, a capacity to initiate change and meet challenges creatively, if he is to become whole. At risk of oversimplifying, we may say that in a similar fashion the Taurus must learn to relate to the earthy world and build a sense of permanent worth in it; the Gemini must learn to develop his powers of intellectual discrimination so that he can learn more about the world around him; the Cancer must learn to open the flow of his feelings to others so that he can nurture the budding consciousness of those he loves; the Leo must learn to recognise through his creative efforts that centre within himself which is the true creator and to which he must offer allegiance; the Virgo must learn to perfect and refine himself as a vessel of service so that he can take his part in the transmutation of all that is base or undifferentiated in life; the Libra must learn how to recognise the opposites within his own nature and balance them so that he can relate to others; the Scorpio must learn to love and integrate his own darkness, so that he may heal the darkness around him; the Sagittarius must learn to see the underlying consistency in all human aspiration so that his sense of the meaningfulness of life experience can be taught to others; the Capricorn must learn to master his environment and then himself, so that he shines as an example of the power of human will; the Aquarius must learn to become conscious of the group life of which he is a part, so that he can offer his share in the growth of collective consciousness; and the Pisces must learn how to offer himself as a gift to the larger life, so that he can perform the work of salvaging what has been lost. The sun-sign is hardly as personal as a set of behaviour patterns, and will not make anybody anything. It is a symbol of that which needs to be attained. Most probably the individual will only attain it with difficulty.

It is well to bear in mind that the sun is not a personal point on the chart, in the sense of pertaining to personality behaviour. It symbolises the path, the goal, not the machine in which one travels — until such time as these become one thing. The sun is the heart of the human being, and how many of us truly know our hearts?

The planets, like all the symbolism in astrology, fall into two groups of masculine and feminine energies. The sun is considered to be a masculine planet, because it is associated with that side of life which concerns will, consciousness, decision, and impact on the environment — in other words, an active principle. As might be expected, it is more "accessible" to men than to women because it reflects an easier impulse for a man to make conscious. By the time they turn sixteen, most men are well aware of the necessity of having an individual identity; many women, on the other hand, are content to find their identity, during the first half of life, through their partners and family. The principle of self-fulfilment through radiating the light of the ego into the world is much more a prerogative of masculine consciousness than of feminine. In a woman's horoscope, therefore, the sun often suggests what she seeks from the masculine side of life, and from her men, in order to complete herself. But ideally, of course, both the masculine and feminine polarities of the chart need to be expressed by each individual. This is part of the challenge of our growing consciousness.

The sun reflects the urge within every human being to express himself, and to grow into what he potentially is. The moon, in contrast, symbolises the urge towards unconsciousness, towards the past, and towards immersion in the flow of feeling which allows the individual to be part of the mass currents of life without undertaking the struggle required for self-consciousness. The moon is also a symbol of the mother, both personal and archetypal, and it is to this womb with its blessed security and safety that the lunar side of us longs to return. The moon portrays the urge to sink oneself into the

experience of living, without having to evaluate or understand the experience; it also symbolises the urge for comfort,
and for the satisfaction of emotional needs. While the sun
strives for differentiation, the moon strives for relationship
and merging of identity. The sun eschews personal relationships in favour of developing the independent ego; the moon
eschews identity in favour of relationships, and longs for the
peace of the night in which all colours blend and everything
sleeps. Esther Harding, in her book on the psychological
meaning of moon symbolism, states:

> In the days of moon worship, religion was concerned
> with the unseen powers of the spirit world, and even
> when the state religion was transferred to the sun, a god
> of war, of personal aggrandisement, and of the things of
> this world, the spiritual qualities remained with the
> moon deities. For the worship of the moon is the worship
> of the creative and fecund powers of nature and of the
> wisdom that lies inherent in instinct and in the at-one-
> ness with natural law. But the worship of the sun is the
> worship of that which overcomes nature, which orders
> her chaotic fullness and harnesses her powers to the ful-
> filling of man's ends.[1]

Sun and moon comprise a dyad of male and female on the
birth chart which symbolises the polarity of male and female
within each individual, and the tension implicit between
them is necessary. Without it there could be no consciousness and no life. Sun and moon are akin to the other paired
symbols such as dark and light, spirit and matter, active and
passive, mother and father, life and death, and every other
pair of antitheses which constitute the great pillars sustaining
the organism of life. These opposites encompass everything
from the sublime to the ridiculous: the sun not only infers in
a very broad and deep way the individual's path to fulfilment,
but also says something about the image he will project to
the crowd; and the moon not only infers the path through

1 *Woman's Mysteries*, M. Esther Harding, Rider & Co., London, 1971.

which a man may re-establish contact with the life of nature that lies at the roots of his being, but also says something about the way he maintains his house and the sort of personal habits he displays. This spectrum of meaning often confuses people about astrology: how can one symbol mean something so significant and so seemingly insignificant at the same time? But every symbol, by its very nature, always does; and moreover, we are dealing here with the archetypes, and the planets which symbolise them are the basic scaffolding of the individual's experience. Everything which belongs to them, from the shallowest to the most profound, will conform to the pattern.

We may discern in the moon's sign at birth something of the way in which the individual expresses himself when *not* an individual, but a creature of instinct. In other words, the moon symbolises the instinctual or non-rational nature. It also suggests by its placement on the birth chart that sphere of life wherein the individual seeks a symbolic sleep, an unconsciousness, an escape or refuge — which is most likely to be dominated by his needs rather than able to rely on his own will and his capacity for decision-making. One may observe the moon when the ego is not striving towards something — when a person relaxes into his instinctual response patterns.

An example may help to clarify the polarity of the sun and moon on an interpretive level. With the sun placed in a particular birth sign, the goals which are symbolised by that sign become part of the individual's aspirations in life in some way. When the moon is placed in a particular sign, the instinctual needs symbolised by that sign become part of the individual's requirements for emotional well-being. So, for example, we may see the man with the sun in Leo striving towards creative self-expression as a major goal in life, with a conscious valuing of honour, loyalty, integrity, and individual uniqueness. We may on the other hand see a man with the moon in Leo responding to life in an intuitively dramatic manner, with a less conscious need for show, acceptance, adoration and a stage on which to perform — not because he values these things, but because he requires them to feel

secure. The man with the sun in Leo will, if he is truly
following his path, strive to become the highest and best that
the figure of the Hero has to offer; the moon in Leo simply
feels special and reacts accordingly, with a somewhat less
discriminating — but more natural and relaxed — assortment
of Leonine qualities to offer.

In general, the sun is a symbol of consciousness and the
moon of the unconscious in a man's horoscope; and in a
woman's the moon symbolises consciousness and the sun the
unconscious. There are exceptions, of course. They usually
occur, for example, when a woman has a strong masculine
bias, whether because she has a powerfully developed mind
or because she is rebelling against her instincts. They also
occur when a man has a strong feminine bias because he has
powerfully developed feelings, or because he is rebelling
against the necessity to struggle for individuality. But the sun
and the moon are two halves of the same unity, and both are
necessary in their appropriate places. It is the harmonious
integration of these two symbols which the alchemists
described in their *coniunctio* or sacred marriage, and which
in fairy tales is the end of the story, the hero and his beloved
living happily ever after. As we have seen, however, it is a
rare individual who can include all of himself in his
actualised experience. Instinct usually clashes with life's
goals, because the goals are either too narrow or too difficult
to achieve, or forbidden by society or one's own values; and
the individual often feels he must choose between them,
when what is really needed is a marriage between them so
that both can be expressed as a living unity. If he cannot
accomplish this inner marriage, how then can he expect to
make a success of an outer one?

Mercury

We come next to the planet Mercury, in astronomical terms
the smallest and fastest planet in the solar system, in
mythology a strange androgynous figure who possesses the
keys to knowledge and who carries messages to and fro
between the gods and between gods and men. Mercury, who
is connected with the Greek Hermes, the Egyptian Thoth and

the Norse or Teutonic Loki, is a symbol of the way in which
we not only perceive, but order our perceptions so that they
can be comprehended and communicated. He is primarily
the symbol of the urge to understand, to integrate
unconscious motive with conscious recognition. This planet
does not represent the intellect, although he has been so
described in older textbooks; for we must remember that
there are other modes of perception besides the rational,
which have not, in the past, been accorded much
recognition. One may perceive and understand through the
feelings, or the intuition, or the five senses. Mercury placed
in Cancer at birth suggests a person who perceives through
the unconscious and evaluates his perceptions through
feeling; Mercury in Capricorn, on the other hand, perceives
through his senses and accumulates facts in his rather hard
head, evaluating his perceptions according to what has
already been tried and proven. The planet is a symbol of the
mode in which the individual becomes conscious of his
environment as well as of himself, and it also might be said to
symbolise the urge to digest experience, to become aware.

Mercury is connected with the strange figure of Mercurius
in medieval alchemy. This suggests that — although he is not
considered to be particularly powerful or significant in
traditional astrology, which generally relegates him to the
definition of "communication" — there may be more to the
planet than meets the eye. In alchemy, Mercurius is the great
transformer; and perhaps we should recall that it is man's
urge to understand which raises him above the other
kingdoms of nature, which drives him to reflect upon his
development and consequently to cooperate voluntarily with
the unconscious in its striving toward further integration.
Then we can begin to see why, in the *Secret Doctrine*,
Blavatsky says, "Mercury and the sun are one," implying
thereby the unity between the little microcosm of man's
understanding and the great macrocosm of cosmic purpose.
As the planet closest to the sun, Mercury is the sun's
messenger, and while the sun is the symbol of the essence,
Mercury is the symbol of that function which enables us to
know the essence.

Mercury's sign position at birth suggests the way in which the individual learns, how he perceives and categorises or digests what he learns: what the method is by which he transmutes experience into understanding. As messenger, Mercury is a symbol of the bridge between the Self and the ego, as well as between the ego and the environment; he is the great unifier, as well as the great destroyer. By his knife edge, the individual may either recognise the inter-connection of all things, or sever himself from all connections through a proliferation of isolated and meaningless data.

Venus and Mars
Venus and Mars, who were lovers in Greek and Roman mythology, are another male-female dyad. They are another way of expressing sun and moon, that is, yin and yang, or male and female. But here the basically feminine urge towards relating, harmonising and adjusting in the sphere of personal relationships, plays a delicate counterpoint to the basically masculine urge towards conquest, towards severing and separating and asserting self over others to fulfil desire. Venus symbolises the need which seeks to share with another, even to the point of being subsumed; Mars symbolises the passion which seeks to expend itself on another, and to reach an objective goal. Mars desires; Venus is the urge to be desired. Venus allows us to recognise that we are in relationship with others and, by comparisons, seeks to discover the similarities; Mars enables us to impose our way despite others, and through self-assertion, exposes the differences.

The ancient astrological glyphs for these planets are now used as the biological symbols of male and female. These two "gods" are expressions of the great sun-moon polarity in a specialised form: they are the cosmic principles of light and dark, active and passive, acting specifically in the field of human relationships.

If the moon is the mother, Venus is the archetype of the lover or hetaira: these are two faces of woman. If the sun is the father, Mars is the conqueror: these are two faces of man. Each of us has all four of these faces, but we will choose to identify with one more than with the others; as D.H. Lawrence says, women are either wives or lovers, men either husbands or lovers. The expression of that urge which Venus symbolises may be seen in the way a person adorns himself, his personal taste, his response to beauty, and his social values; it may also be seen in what the individual values most in relationships, what he seeks in the ideal partnership. The expression of the urge which Mars symbolises may be seen in the way in which a person goes about getting what he wants; the quality or mode of his desire is reflected by this planet, the manner in which he carries out the chase, and the form of expression his passions assume.

Because these two planets are so particularly important in interpersonal relationships, more will be said about them later. The same general law seems to apply here as with sun and moon: for men, Mars is a more accessible energy, while for women, Venus is more accessible. In consequence, as with sun and moon, the planet antithetical in its energy to the sex of the individual will usually be projected upon a suitable object in interpersonal relationships, and the individual will try to live out his transsexual side through his partner. Often the sign in which Venus is placed, on a man's chart, will describe what he seeks in a woman as ideal lover; and the sign in which Mars is placed, on a woman's chart, will describe what she seeks in a man. A woman with Mars in Capricorn, for example, may find the qualities of earthiness, ambition, strength of will and determination sexually attractive in a mate; a man with Venus in Pisces may find the qualities of sympathy, compassion, gentleness, imaginativeness and forgivingness lovable in a woman.

Jupiter and Saturn
With this pair of planets we leave behind the sphere of the personal drives and impulses. Sun, moon, Mercury, Venus and Mars are called personal planets because they symbolise urges which manifest in a personal way; they are ego-

oriented, in terms of the psychic energies they symbolise, and are relatively easily available to consciousness, allowing for the difficulties of integrating the opposites. The realm of Jupiter and Saturn, both kings of the gods in ancient mythology, takes the individual outside the sphere of his personal ego-consciousness, and he begins to establish contact with that which is transpersonal — both inside and outside him. Jupiter and Saturn are the great explorers, the guardians at the gate of the personal world; they are both two-faced, one face looking within and one looking without, and both symbolise urges to transcend the limited confines of the little self. One goes up and the other down; they are, respectively, like the carrot which leads the donkey on by promising him future possibilities of reward, and the stick which drives him to move because it is too painful to stand still. Obviously we tend to prefer the carrot to the stick, and are inclined to value luck more than pain; but both these planets symbolise, in opposite ways, urges towards growth of consciousness. It might be said that Jupiter is a masculine urge, and Saturn a feminine one; this is because Jupiter, a god of the heavens and of the thunderstorm, is connected with the "upper" regions of the intuitive mind, while Saturn, a Titan and a god of the earth, is connected with the "lower" regions of the personal unconscious, the dark side of human nature. Both are necessary and create between them yet another variation on the theme of light and dark, this time transferred to the sphere of realisation of meaning.

As the symbol of Saturn will be more fully covered later, not much will be said about him now. Jupiter, however, merits some further description. This planet is connected with what may be termed the religious urge in man, an urge which Freud and his followers felt was merely a sublimation of the sexual instinct but which Jung has shown to be as basic a drive within the human being as any of the biological impulses. Man needs not only to survive, and to propagate his species; he also needs to know that somehow, somewhere, there is a pattern to life, an intrinsic order and meaning, a whole of which he must have at least some dim intuitive cognisance if he is to maintain any capacity for hope and for growth. It may be that we have created God; but we cannot create that of which we have no experience, even if it is an unconscious one, and Jupiter may be said to symbolise the need to experience the numinous, the divine, through projecting it out of ourselves and into symbolic forms which we then worship and call deity. The sign in which Jupiter is placed on an individual's birth chart suggests the way in which he seeks this experience of meaning in life. An individual with Jupiter in Virgo might, for example, seek to experience a sense of meaning through his work, because his work may provide a kind of ritual, a rhythmic self-purification and self-refinement which allows him to become conscious of a larger pattern. Because Jupiter seeks to expand experience so that its meaning shines through its form, Jupiter in Virgo will seek greater means to develop himself through his work, so that he can make something "big" of it and feel that it holds significance of a kind larger than satisfying the demands of necessity. This planet symbolises the myth-making principle, in the most positive sense of the word "myth".

Jupiter is thus connected with the urge within the psyche to create symbols, and this takes us into profound depths when we consider the creative power that has shaped the great myths, legends, and religions of the world. It is no less a creative power that shapes the symbolism of our dreams, so that each dream is a masterpiece of meaning and could not be altered in any way for improvement. In this way Jupiter is truly a god of the gateway, for he forms a link between conscious and unconscious through the creation and intuitive understanding of symbols. As we have seen, symbols are the primordial language of life; and Jupiter symbolises the function which both creates them within man and intuits their meaning.

The Outer Planets
Once we have passed the boundaries of Saturn, we are in the realm of the collective unconscious — the repository of the archetypal images — and of urges which not only have little

to do with personality drives, but in fact are often inimical to them. One could almost consider the inner, personal planets and the outer, transpersonal planets as yet another pair of opposites, symbolising respectively the life of the ego and the life of the larger matrix from which the ego, with its illusion of separateness, springs.

The urges which the three known outer planets symbolise are rarely available to the consciousness of the individual; for they all mark the transition from one phase of consciousness to another, and consciousness cannot apprehend such transitions. It can only apprehend the phase in which it is functioning at a given moment. Saturn is the great Lord of Boundaries and the Master of Illusion, playing the part of Lucifer and whispering to us that the personal world we experience is the perimeter of reality, to penetrate beyond which is at best foolish and at worst mad. Often we believe the whisper, and identify with what we call "objective" reality, failing to see that it is completely subjective and that we are only creating our own interpretations of life. And like Lucifer, who — as Goethe points out — is secretly the right hand of God, Saturn urges us to identify more and more with our interpretations, so that eventually we isolate ourselves so completely that we are indeed in Hell — a hell of dissociation from the deepest underlying currents of life. In this way Saturn is the great teacher, disguised as the bringer of pain and limitation, for it is only at the point of darkness and decay — which the alchemists called the *nigredo* or the Caput Mortuum, The Dead Head, the first stage of the alchemical work — that we become aware of the Other within us, the true creative power of the Self. This may sound more and more like the mystic's vision; yet it is a psychological process empirically observable in any individual's life — although the ways in which people actualise it are very different.

Uranus and Neptune form another male-female dyad, Uranus being the masculine pole and Neptune the feminine; and we can learn much about these planets, or "gods", when we look at their personifications in mythology. Uranus is the ancient god of the heavens, husband to his mother Gaia, the earth, and grandson of Chaos, the primordial night out of which manifest reality — or consciousness — emerged. Uranus is a symbol of the world of archetypal ideas, the underlying patterns of what in certain theological thought is called the Mind of God and what in Platonic doctrine is the scaffolding of divine Ideas which support the fabric of the universe. It is no wonder that we have a difficult time coming to terms with what this planet means in the individual psyche.

In the individual chart, Uranus, the first god of the heavens and the spirit, seems to personify the need within the psyche to break free of identification with material reality and to experience the world of archetypal mind. So in traditional astrology Uranus is said to symbolise the urge for change, for freedom, for invention and liberation, and for development of the mind beyond the realm of concrete thought bound by facts and empirical knowledge. Uranus has been called the Awakener, because the urge he symbolises, like all unconscious contents, is projected. It appears to come back to the individual as a sudden event emanating from "without" which rips away the fabric of what he has previously identified as his reality, often in a highly painful way. At the same time, it allows him to glimpse the underlying collective idea upon which his small personal experience has been built. That the individual himself attracts this kind of experience usually escapes his realisation; it looks more like the hand of "fate". But one must recognise that his own psyche is his fate, if he is to understand the meaning of what has happened to him and utilise the experience as it needs to be utilised — as an awakening into larger consciousness.

It is less "coincidental" than synchronous that Uranus, a symbol connected with liberation, freedom and invention, was "discovered" in 1781. That year falls between two great political revolutions — both of which involved ideas of liberty, equality and freedom of the individual from the limitations of hereditary privilege or penalty — and at the dawn of what we call the industrial age, which, through the power of the mind to discover, master and apply technologically the laws of the physical universe, sought to free man

from his bondage to matter. It may seem inconceivable that
the discovery of a planet could have any connection with the
Age of Technology and with the American and French
Revolutions; but we must remember that the discovery of the
planet did not "cause" these events to take place. It simply
mirrored their occurrence. The same alterations in consciousness which produced both the revolutions and the urge for
scientific discovery and application also produced the
technical means by which the physical planet became visible
to the conscious sight of man; and the planet's symbolic
meaning, in turn, pertains to that spirit of adventure and
exploration and liberation which made all these physical
events possible. The planet and the state of the world at the
time of its discovery reflect each other: they are synchronous.

Freedom from identification with a particular experience,
or aspect of an experience, may apply to anything. One may
experience Uranus in the urge to change one's understanding
of oneself, one's work, one's beliefs, or one's relationships.
Relationships are experiences which each individual inter-
prets in his own way — and there is within the psyche of each
individual an urge to constantly change his interpretations,
so that they may become more inclusive and more
conscious.

In Greek and Roman mythology, Uranus — or Ouranos —
is the father of Saturn (Cronos), and Saturn, an earth god
goaded on by his earthy mother, castrated his father and
seized the latter's throne. It is said that these events
transpired because Uranus was horrified at his progeny; he
was a god of the upper regions, and recoiled from the dark,
earthbound creatures which he created. One may intuit
many things from this fragment of the myth. Saturn's act of
violence against his father brought to an end the rule of
heaven, and began the rule of the earthy Titans; and we may
have seen the same pattern enacted in human civilisation
throughout our thousands of years of history.

But if we read further, we find that from the drops of blood
spilled from the terrible wound upon the earth, the Erinyes,
the Furies or goddesses of justice and retribution (karma)

arose; and from the severed genitals, cast into the ocean, rose Aphrodite-Venus, goddess of love and beauty and, astrologically, symbol of the urge for relationship. It would seem that through relating, we may find a path through which to bring alive again — or make conscious — the world of the heavens. One cannot comprehend the language of mythology with the intellect alone; it must be heard with the intuition, and with the heart, and only then will it yield its secrets. When one considers this trinity of planets — Uranus, Saturn and Venus — on the birth chart, in the light of the myth, something is implied about a process, a cycle, which exists within each individual psyche. We may also look at the well-known fairy tale of Beauty and the Beast, where the Beast steals Beauty from her father and keeps her imprisoned until she learns to love him for his own sake; for this too tells us about the same process. Something within us disowns something else, and that which is disowned wreaks vengeance. It is a question of painful, often violent, confrontation with ourselves — with our origins and birthright, with what we are and what we engender or create. But from this discordant clash, the possibility for a new harmony and integration arises.

In contrast to the god of the heavenly regions, Neptune is a water deity, and although he is a male figure in mythology, the energy he personifies is feminine. God of the oceans and the depths — and, as Poseidon-Hippios, lord of earthquakes and of the underground waterways of the earth — Neptune is a symbol of the sea of collective feeling which moves us from below to immerse ourselves in the mass, offering up our hard-won and precarious individuality so that we may purify ourselves through dissolution. One may see glimpses of this energy at work in any mob, motivated by a single emotional focus: there are no longer any individuals in a mob, only a single seething organism motivated by one dominant emotion which must release itself — often violently — before individuality can be reclaimed. It would seem that the urge for this kind of disintegration of individual consciousness exists in all of us, and it is a highly infectious thing — one need only go to a football match to see a relatively harmless manifestation of it, or to consider Germany forty years ago to find a manifestation rather more sinister.

Neptune is also connected with Dionysius, god of ecstasy, and the holy ecstasy of immersion in the depths was once a part of most ancient mystery rituals. In some way the individual who experienced this "blessing of the god" was purified, born anew, and cleansed of his past; he could offer all that he had accumulated of himself to the god and would be washed ashore naked, ready to begin a new stage of his journey. Although one face of Neptune is unquestionably destructive to what we call civilisation, another face is deeply necessary to the psyche, for the experience of cleansing through immersion in the sea of the unconscious is truly a religious experience, in the profoundest sense of that term — which, from the Latin root, means to reconnect. On a very small scale, we perform this ritual each night, when we offer up consciousness and descend into the unconscious to "sleep".

One may also see Neptune at work in all symbols of the collective feeling life which we call fashion. Whether it is a fashion of music, of dress, of ideas, or of art, the irresistible urge to do what everybody else is doing is present in all of us — much as some of us fight it, at times quite justifiably, because it reduces the supremacy of the individual ego. In these transient fashions which sweep cultures — and often religious beliefs have the quality of a fashion as well — we may see symbols of the currents of underground feeling life, perpetually shifting and changing as do the currents of the ocean. In many ways it is a healing experience to be swept away by these currents for a time, because through it one discovers respect for the power of the unconscious and develops a more balanced perspective on the role of the ego.

On the individual birth chart, Neptune symbolises the urge towards sacrifice of the personal "I", and sacrifice of personal feeling to the collective feeling life. There are archetypal ideas, and there are archetypal feelings — and Neptune personifies the latter, which we all at some time experience. Fantasy, romance, glamour, ecstasy, the mystical vision — all these are Neptune, and while a steady diet of any one thing is in the end destructive, these aspects of reality are necessary to the psyche and need room for expression in the personal life.

Neptune, like Uranus, is usually unconscious in the majority of individuals. How could the ego be conscious of that which seeks to undermine its supremacy, indeed its very foundations? This would be an admission that other forces exist within the psyche besides the personal will, which is a most uncomfortable admission for the ego. So Neptune, like Uranus, is usually projected and is experienced as an event which the individual has unconsciously attracted into his life and which again assumes the appearance of "fate". Neptunian "events" are generally those that entangle the individual in a situation to whose implications he is in some way blind. In consequence, he finds himself powerless at a certain point to do anything except sacrifice some long-cherished desire. He is subjected to a level of collective feeling which changes him, purifies him, and holds him in bondage for a time, gently releasing him afterward and leaving him the same, yet different, for he has been touched by the power of the god and cannot, ever again, honestly say to himself that his feelings are wholly under his own control.

Neptune was discovered in 1846, with an ambiguity which is so characteristic of the quality of the symbol: there were two discoverers, and a considerable amount of confusion about who was responsible for what. Coincident with the discovery was the emergence of widespread interest in spiritualism and psychic phenomena, hypnosis, suggestion and free association, and the real beginnings of that exploration which was gradually refined, tested, checked and rechecked, until it eventually emerged as psychoanalysis, the study of the unconscious psyche of man. Also coincident was a wave of traumatic revolutions that swept like a sea across the whole of Europe, that irreparably undermined the established order, yet were less coherent, more inchoate than those of the previous century. With the discovery of Neptune, revolution — often for its own sake — itself became a "fashion".

It is fitting that we should give to the outermost planet now known in our solar system the name of the ancient Lord of the Underworld, and it is also fitting that astronomers are not even certain whether Pluto is truly a planet, or a lost moon from some other heavenly body. There is also much ambiguity about Pluto because his density is far out of proportion to his small size, which may suggest that he is actually much larger than we have so far been able to ascertain with our telescopes. Pluto keeps this character in mythology, residing under the earth, presiding over the dead and over the riches of the earth, never venturing above ground except when he is wearing his magical helmet, which renders him invisible to the eyes of man.

In the myths of every nation, as well as in many fairy tales, there is a Lord of the Dead, and this symbol appears to be connected with the archetypal experience of beginnings and endings, death and rebirth. Joseph Campbell, in his book *Creative Mythology*, states:

> ... This ground of being, which is both giver and taker of the forms that appear and disappear in space and time, though dark indeed, cannot be termed evil unless the world itself is to be so termed. The lesson of Hades-Pluto ... is not that our mortal part is ignoble, but that within it — or at one with it — is that immortal Person whom the Christians split into God and the Devil and think of as "out there".[1]

The "giver and taker of the forms that appear and disappear in space and time" is that archetype of ceaselessly cycling death and rebirth personified by the planet Pluto, and the process of endless journey and return exists in every aspect of life. The life inherent in all forms is always life; but life, because it is ceaselessly changing, inevitably outgrows every form, which in turn must die so that life can be released into a new birth, and into a new form. Nature can tell us about this archetypal process in a myriad ways, and if one looks at one's own life, one can see that every experience, every

1 *Creative Mythology*, Joseph Campbell, Souvenir Press, 1974, London.

attitude, every relationship, every feeling, every idea — everything, in fact — has a beginning, a middle, an end, and a new beginning in some other form. We instinctively shy away from this cycle, because, like Faust, we want certain moments to last forever. Change is acceptable if it is pleasant but when that inevitable phase of the cycle of change comes which necessitates passage into the darkness, we draw back: we have no trust in the Lord of the Dead. In many ways the Christian era has robbed us of our understanding of him, because Christianity, shrinking from the prospect of perpetual renewal, has fixed our attention on a single fixed afterlife comprising either punishment or reward — has substituted a state of ultimately stagnant stasis for the vital and dynamic process. The ego, in characteristic fashion, wishes to believe that life is consistent. Fortunately or unfortunately, however, the only consistent thing in it is change. Pluto, in consequence, symbolises an urge within the psyche which is usually unconscious, and like Uranus and Neptune, the planet appears to operate through experiences which "happen" to the individual and which in some way force him to undergo a death within himself. There is always rebirth after death, and the new form is always greater than the old; but when put to the test, the majority of individuals do not believe this, and feel they have irretrievably lost something. Usually it is some *thing* (or someone) to whom there is an intense emotional bond, and through which, in some way, the individual is living a part of his life — a part that should be retrieved so that he can live it out for himself. In some way the bond is lost, the relationship changed, and there is the experience of a death. And if one seeks, among these ashes he will find a new perspective and a new birth.

Pluto is especially significant in the sphere of relationships, for it is in this sphere that so many people undergo emotional deaths and rebirths. Pluto is also connected with sexuality, in the sense that the sexual act signifies — or symbolises, in potential — the death of the sense of individual separateness in the experience of "the other" and of the new creative life force flowing through both. The creation of new life always involves a death of some kind, a change in one's

psychological attitude; the procreation of children will
inevitably produce this kind of change in the psyche, for one
has changed from the child to the parent who has given birth
to a child, and a new phase of life has begun. Death also, in
its most literal form, is the domain of Pluto, for death, while
being the end of one cycle, marks the beginning of a new
one. Although the West as a whole is slow to consider the
principle of reincarnation, many great individual minds —
and Eastern thought in general — have found it acceptable
for many centuries, either as a literal experience or as a
symbol of the eternal livingness of being, "Is-ness", shining
through the transience of individual cycles of life and death.

Pluto is a symbol of the urge for self-transformation. In
other words, there exists within the psyche an impulse
towards growth, which necessitates the constant changing of
the forms through which growth is accomplished. The
individual must grow, whether he wishes to or not, and the
cycle of growth requires a period of death, decay, new
germination, gestation, and new birth. The whole of nature
upholds this principle. That man should reject it, and attempt
to deny it, is characteristic of the loss of contact with the
roots of life which is so typical of the time in which we live.

Like Wolfram von Eschenbach's *Parzival*, alchemy describes the process which astrology calls Pluto in a very beautiful
mythologem. There is a king, says the alchemical symbolism,
who is old, barren, and can no longer rule effectively because
he has lost the power to create new life. His lands are fruitless
and his people dying of starvation and thirst. He must first
perform a sacred marriage — to his mother, or sister, or
daughter, the incest theme suggesting that it is a marriage of
two energies or principles which issue from the same source.
He must then descend into the depths of the sea, or beneath
the earth, to consummate the union. At the moment of the
ecstasy of consummation, he dies, and is torn to pieces and
devoured by the dark woman with whom he has united. The
queen becomes pregnant, and after her period of gestation,
brings forth a new life — who is the king, but the king reborn,
his youth and virility restored, a new life flowing through him

and all that he rules.[1]

   Only that which can destroy itself is truly alive.[2]

                    *   *   *

The planets, as we have seen, are symbols of the powers of the unconscious; they symbolise archetypal experiences or energies, which exist in all of life and exist also within man, who is part of life. Once we have learned the vocabulary of the planets, and their meaning on the individual birth chart, we can look at the chart and get some intimation of how each of these energies will express itself individually. The sign in which a planet is placed is like the adjective on a noun, the garment worn on the body: it manifests the mode or quality of the planet's expression. We can now begin to learn something of the zodiacal signs themselves, and their division into a polarity of male and female, further amplified into a quaternity of four elements. This basic structure of four is, as we will see, also archetypal, and we must return to our exploration of the psyche through the eye of the psychologist to gain greater insight into the realms of air, water, earth and fire.

1 *Psychology and Alchemy*, C.G. Jung, Routledge & Kegan Paul, London, 1953.
2 *Ibid.*

III
Air, Water, Earth, Fire — The Psychological Types

> One sees what one can best see oneself.
> — C.G. Jung

Long before psychology developed its endlessly entertaining pastime of dividing human beings into types, Renaissance philosophy posited four basic temperaments based on the theory of the "humours" in the blood. These were the melancholic (earthy), the phlegmatic (watery), the sanguine (airy) and the choleric (fiery). George Herbert, in one of his lighter moods, wrote in 1640:

> The Choleric drinks, the Melancholic eats, the Phlegmatic sleeps.

What the Sanguine does is left to the imagination, but as he is "ethereal" or airy, we may assume that he probably philosophises.

Nowadays a man would be horrified if his psychotherapist announced to him in sonorous tones, "I am virtually certain that your problem lies in the fact that you have a choleric temperament", and there would undoubtedly be an instant demand for remittance of the hourly fee. But we still find these terms in use in our everyday speech, if only in the form of insulting adjectives, and they still retain their original connotations. In spite of the current vogue for "doing your own thing", the idea of types dies hard.

As Jung has shown in *Psychological Types*,[1] the apparently extraordinary fact that people do tend to fall into certain groupings by temperament has long been a preoccupation of medicine, philosophy, and the arts. Before that, it was the preoccupation of astrology, which offers what is perhaps our earliest description of typology. It is consequently not surprising — except to certain schools of psychology which insist that we are wholly creatures of heredity and environment — that Jung's four function types fit hand-in-glove with astrology's ancient division of the four elements. It is not a case of one being explained away by, or derived from, the other; rather, each is a distinct way of describing the empiric observation of the same phenomenon.

This phenomenon is the simple fact that although all people are unique, they also gravitate towards rough categories based on a fundamental way of seeing, evaluating, apprehending and interpreting life. Aside from being an amusing means of pegging one's friends and relatives, understanding something of this basic typology is an excellent way of learning that most difficult of lessons: that not everybody is the same as I am.

> Everyone thinks that psychology is what he himself knows best — psychology is always *his* psychology, which he alone knows, and at the same time his psychology is everybody else's psychology. Instinctively he supposes that his own psychic constitution is the general one, and that everyone is essentially like everyone else, that is to say, like himself ... as though his own psyche were a kind of master-psyche which suited all and sundry, and entitled him to suppose that his own situation was the general rule. People are profoundly astonished, or even horrified, when this rule quite obviously does not fit — when they discover that another person really is different from themselves. Generally speaking, they do not feel these psychic differences as in any way curious, let alone attractive,

but as disagreeable failings that are hard to bear, or as unendurable faults that have to be condemned.[1]

It will be immediately obvious what this typical human attitude can do to even the most promising of relationships. In more volatile relationships, like that of parent and child, its effects can be positively tragic. A married couple, or a pair of friends, may be able to fight the issue out and come to a greater recognition of each other's individual viewpoint, but a child cannot defend himself. He is at the mercy of the expectations and assumptions which his parents project onto him, and may pay for these for the remainder of his life.

The problem with any study of typology is that it appears to be a system, albeit a natural one; and although we can swallow classifications by species in the animal and plant kingdoms, we have an instinctive horror of being reminded of our own lack of individuality. It is an unwelcome truth. Few of us can really claim to be fully conscious human beings, expressing all that is potential within ourselves; most of the time we prefer to pretend that we are, while slipping with perfect ease into one or another of the typical behavioural patterns. We seem to imagine that individuality, like fulfilment, is not only our potential but our automatic right, and that it requires no effort; and we will do virtually anything to avoid facing the reality that we must work for it. Consequently, anything which implies that we can be grouped, like Jung's typology or any other piece of empiric psychological observation, is maligned as being a rigid structure which does not allow for any individual differences. This is not at all the case; the very fact that we share common ground with another segment of humanity, based on certain similarities in psychological constitution, allows us that much more scope for the creative expression of our own unique potential as individuals. Moreover, no map is the country. Jung's typology, like any other, is merely a pointer which affords us a glimpse of those basic patterns of perception, evaluation and response which we draw from the same collective source.

1 *Ibid.*

Because astrology is a symbolic system, it attempts to express through its imagery and its structure the energy patterns which underlie life and the human psyche as an aspect of life. The first statement that astrology has to make about life is at the same time childishly simple and unutterably profound: everything stems from the relationship of two polar opposites, whether we call these male and female, active and passive, yin and yang.

The zodiac, which symbolises in its division of twelve signs the entire spectrum of potential of human experience, is therefore divided into two groups of six signs each: six masculine or positive signs, portraying different facets of the archetype of male, and six feminine or negative signs, portraying different facets of the archetype of female. Masculine and feminine in astrology do not of course refer to our current social definitions of the terms, but rather to qualities of energy, as exemplified by the initial hexagrams of the Creative and the Receptive in the *I Ching*. Positive signs are associated with the qualities of extraversion, outgoingness, light, mind, activity, orientation towards ideas, the objective world and the future. Negative signs are associated with introversion, indrawnness, darkness, feeling, sensuality, stability, orientation towards the subjective world and the past. That does not really tell us much, for this great symbolic polarisation of life and of ourselves into male and female only hints at what each person must directly experience within himself — the endlessly struggling yet secretly identical opposites of his own nature.

Astrology makes a further statement, which we have already encountered: each man contains within him the seeds of wholeness, symbolised by the zodiacal wheel. But though this is his inheritance and his potential, he is likely to manifest only a part of it, and specialise according to his inherent disposition.

We know that a man can never be anything at once, never complete — he always develops certain qualities

at the expense of others, and wholeness is never
attained.[1]

We have already seen that the inherent disposition, as
viewed by both astrology and analytical psychology, exists
from the very beginning of life. This disposition is mirrored in
those parts of the totality of the zodiac which are picked out,
highlighted, and made available to consciousness on the
birth chart by either a planet being placed in a certain sign, or
that sign appearing on one of the four angles of the chart.[2]
The interplay of ten planets and four angles gives the broad
outline of what areas of experience, and what facets of
consciousness, are most likely to be developed by the
individual. Whether he can go further is a moot point, since
most people never even get close to expressing the psychic
potential of which the chart is a symbol, let alone surpass it.
To these statements astrology adds another. Male and
female can be subdivided, so that there are two groups of
male signs and two groups of female signs. This basic
structure of four is the cornerstone of astrology, in which it is
reflected by the four elements: air, water, earth and fire. That
this structure is archetypal and inherent in all human beings
we know from the work of depth psychology during the last
fifty years.
We all possess those functions of consciousness which
Jung calls thinking, feeling, sensation and intuition.

> (An object) ... is perceived as something that exists
> (sensation); it is recognised as this and distinguished
> from that (thinking) — it is evaluated as pleasant or
> unpleasant, etc. (feeling); and finally, intuition tells us
> where it came from and where it is going.[3]

That we do not fulfil the totality of this structure we also
know. Instead, we develop first one function, then another.
Perhaps we will partially develop a third, but never really

1 *Modern Man in Search of a Soul.*
2 See Chapter VIII for a description of the angles.
3 *The Boundaries of the Soul*, June Singer, Anchor Books, N.Y., 1973.

come to terms with the fourth, which remains largely unconscious. And we often seek in relationships a person who will embody, or enact for us, those aspects of the totality which we are unable, or unwilling, to express ourselves.

In their apparently naive fashion, fairy tales also tell us about this basic quaternity of functions of consciousness. In tales originating from every part of the world and from every period of history we find again and again the same motif. There once was a king who had three sons. The two eldest were wise and handsome and strong, but the third was an idiot, at whom everyone else laughed. This is a splendid symbol of the way in which the human psyche works, for the leading function of consciousness is the king — who inevitably, in these tales, has some kind of problem which usually involves illness, sterility, or approaching death, or the attack of a foe beyond his power to outmanoeuvre. The two eldest sons always attempt to solve the problem, and fail; and it resides with the idiot, the Holy Fool, the least valued, humblest, and apparently most inadequate aspect of ourselves, to find the solution and save the kingdom.

Now it is great fun to decide that I am a thinking type and you are a feeling type, and that is why I am clever, observant, articulate and reasonable while you are always so emotional, bloody-minded and irrational. This is a game we all play when introduced to the study of typology, in much the same way as the uninitiated play the zodiac game. Of course I am always charming, courteous and considerate because I am a Libra, while you are obviously nitpicking, overcritical, self-centred and narrow-minded because you are a Virgo. Whether astrological or psychological, typology can be used as a wonderful catch-all for other people's shortcomings, and it is more often than not misused in just this way. In the first place, we are afraid to take it seriously; in the second, we usually learn from it only what is comfortable while ignoring its deeper implications; and in the third, everyone is really secretly convinced that those things he values — according to his type — are in reality the best of all, and everything else is actually a little inferior.

However, there is an automatic penalty in this game of typecasting. The problem of understanding which functions of consciousness have been emphasised to the possible exclusion of others, and the lifelong struggle of coming to terms with and knowing the Other who exists within oneself, lead into much deeper waters than a superficial interpretation of function types would suggest. And suddenly, one finds one is no longer playing a game; or, if one is, the stakes are much higher than one imagined. The human psyche strives towards wholeness. This underlying truth of psychology is a terribly simplistic yet overwhelmingly important statement, which must be experienced to be fully understood.

Wholeness does not mean perfection. The man who has spent many years cultivating a fineness of intellectual perception and expression, yet who can neither express nor understand his feeling nature, is not whole. Nor is the man who has developed a rich and full feeling life and many meaningful personal relationships, if he cannot understand how to reason or how to see the "objective" and fair viewpoint which can uphold principles and allow for individual differences. Nor is the practical realist with the world of facts at his disposal, who has expressed the full flowering of his organisational abilities, yet cannot see where they are leading, and cannot find any meaning or inner spiritual sense to his life. Nor yet is the visionary or the artist, who lives in a world of endless possibilities yet who cannot cope with the simple mechanics of earthy life, and cannot actualise his myriad dreams. How many of us can claim to function freely and happily with all the possibilities inherent within the psyche? Why are we so compellingly attracted to, or repelled by, those who seem to embody lifestyles and values the importance and workings of which somehow elude us?

Although the zodiac is a symbol of wholeness, such wholeness is not contained in any chart, because there are only ten planets to contend with, only seven of them in any way "personal" in the sense that they refer to the personality or ego structure of the individual; and there are twelve possible signs, and twelve possible houses or sectors of the birth chart, in which they can be placed. There are also innumerable combinations possible in the angular relationships between the planets. Every chart contains an over-emphasis and an underemphasis, and so does every human psyche; it is the nature of the animal. An understanding of typology, therefore, is not a classification system. It is a road map which can tell you where you start, and where your first turning is likely to be; where your car is liable to break down, and what you can do to repair it; and where, hopefully, you will arrive in the fullness of time.

Inherent in the pleasant recognition of those functions of consciousness which are "superior" — that is, well-developed, reliable, and under the control of the individual's will — is the much less pleasant recognition that there is a problem with the opposite functions, which are "inferior". These functions are often unmanageable, erratic, unpredict-able, excessive, rather childish or primitive, and coloured by a peculiar quality of autonomy which, when they erupt, cause people to say things like, "Oh, I'm sorry, I just wasn't myself," or, "Something must have come over me." Such apologies are meant to conceal the fact that we are even more mortified than others when the unconscious asserts itself on its own and moves us to behaviour we cannot explain and do not desire.

Opposite functions are called opposite because they cannot work together. Feeling and thinking, for example, are two totally distinct modes of evaluating or recognising experience; one of them, feeling, is wholly subjective and is performed without logic, based on personal response, while the other, thinking, is wholly "objective" and is dependent on logic, at the expense of personal response. We possess both these functions in potential, but we will use primarily one and not the other; and they cannot both be used at once. The values inherent in each are totally different, and do not mesh. It is possible to back one up with the other, but not to use them simultaneously. Many people base their values wholly on one and pretend the other does not exist.

Intuition and sensation are likewise opposite functions,

because they represent two totally distinct modes of perception. Intuition is often called perception via the unconscious, and it involves a disregard for the physical reality of an experience or object so that the meaning, the connections, the past, and the future possibilities of the object may be seen in one unified vision. Sensation, on the other hand, is precisely what the word implies: it means perceiving through the senses, and the senses will register only that which is tangible and possesses form. Therefore sensation looks at the surface of things in great detail, examining precisely what something is by its form, while intuition looks behind, through, around and away from the surface, so that the purpose and implications may be discerned.

If feeling is the primary mode of evaluating experience, the thinking function will have an "inferior" quality, which is usually expressed as opinionatedness. If thinking is the primary mode of evaluating experience, the feeling function will have an "inferior" quality, which is usually expressed either as coldness or as sentimentality. If intuition is the primary mode of perception, the sensation function will have an "inferior" quality, often expressed as carelessness or impracticality; and if sensation is the primary mode of perception, intuition will have an "inferior" quality, often shown as gullibility or fanaticism.

The "inferior" functions, besides being somewhat primitive, have another interesting characteristic: they are habitually projected and appear to us in the guise of other people or situations who torment us with that very aspect of life we can least capably handle. Then, of course, the inferiority (or what sometimes looks like sterling superiority) appears to belong to somebody else, which is always more comfortable than when it is in oneself.

The unconscious of one person is projected upon another person, so that the first accuses the second of what he overlooks in himself. This principle is of such alarming general validity that everyone would do well, before railing at others, to sit down and consider very carefully whether the brick should not be thrown at his own head.[1]

Whatever the function of consciousness with which we identify, we must acknowledge the existence of its opposite within us. This is almost always extremely difficult because — unlike those "faults" of which we are comfortably aware, not really feeling them as faults — the awkwardness of the inferior functions is a genuine source of pain and inadequacy if it is even partially conscious. Consequently we find many people creating an artificial set of responses which they may call feeling, thinking, sensation or intuition, yet which are poor mockeries of these things, which fool no one except the individual himself, and which have a flagrant ring of insincerity.

Recognition of one's identification with a single aspect of consciousness does not mean that one is doomed for a lifetime to only express this one facet of himself. People are not static, and the psyche always works towards a balance. One grows towards one's opposite. This is at the same time one of the greatest struggles, one of the greatest joys and one of the most meaningful aspects of living experience.

The Element of Air: the Thinking Type

> The intellect in every one of us is God.
> — Menander

The element of air is another way of expressing, in language more typically a product of an age when man was closer to the imagery of the unconscious, what Jung means by the function of thinking. Air, considered astrologically, is a positive, masculine element, and the airy signs — Gemini, Libra and Aquarius — are usually described in astrological textbooks as being detached, communicative, interested in the world of ideas, and favouring rationality. They are, in

1 *Civilisation in Transition*, C.G. Jung, Routledge & Kegan Paul, London 1964.

The Four Elements and
the Functions of Consciousness

short, civilised. Air is the only element in the zodiacal wheel which does not contain any animal symbolism; Gemini and Aquarius are both represented by human figures, the Twins and the Waterbearer respectively, while Libra is portrayed as an inanimate object, the Scales. Air is the element which is most typically human, the furthest removed from instinctual nature; and it is the human kingdom which has developed — or perhaps overdeveloped in the last two hundred years — the function of thinking as its great gift.

All three airy signs, although different in their modes of expression, share the need to relate life experiences to a preconceived framework of ideas. This framework may come from outside, culled from the books, teachings and conversations of others, or it may come from within, painstakingly created by one's own laborious mental processes; but the existence of the framework is all-important and there is a tendency to take all experiences and seek in them the underlying pattern of logic which will make them conform to this preconceived structure.

Thinking primarily differentiates, through logic, between "this" and "that", and it will be apparent why the air signs are associated with a temperament which collects and categorises information, weighing one thing against another, and forming a philosophical framework out of the bits and pieces.

The airy type — and this does not necessarily mean an individual born under an air sign, so much as it does one whose chart as a whole contains a predominance of airy factors — will usually resemble, in general and in particulars, the qualities of the thinking type as Jung describes him. He has all the blessings of that type — the highly developed mind, the sense of fairness and capacity for impersonal assessment of situations, the love of culture, the appreciation of structure and system, the courageous adherence to principles, the refinement. He also has all the failings of the type — in terms of the "inferior" function — and these are euphemistically expressed in the typical characteristics ascribed to the three airy signs: Gemini has a horror of being pinned down in personal relationships, Libra is notorious for sitting on the fence and refusing to commit himself, and

Aquarius is known for his cool detachment and distaste for the emotional displays which so often form a part of personal relating.

In other words, the airy type has a problem with feeling. Implicit in the preponderance of air on a chart is the likelihood that the world of personal feeling exchange will be the biggest problem of the individual's life — although he may not know it until his wife leaves him — because feelings, unlike everything else which comes under his microscopic eye, cannot be classified, structured, analysed, or fitted into the framework.

There are many Aquarians, women as well as men, who pride themselves on the fact that they never cry, because they see displays of emotion as weakness. This is a rather questionable virtue considering what is inevitably building up in the unconscious through such unwarranted underestimation of the feeling function. Ask a typical Geminian what he feels about something, and he will begin, "Well, I think ..." When you tell him you want his feelings, not his thoughts, he often simply does not know what he feels and must go off for half an hour to find out. Gemini being Gemini, he will probably not come back again; and you have lost him because you have been too "possessive" and "demanding". Then there is the characteristic Libran's habit of simply avoiding anything to do with the dark emotional undercurrents of relationships because they aren't "nice"; he prefers to dwell in the ivory tower of his romantic ideals, working out precisely how he would like his relationships to be, and wondering why things never come out that way. And we should not forget that classic Aquarian quote, made to the woman who complains that in forty years of marriage she has never received either flowers or any overt display of affection: "But I told you I loved you when we married. Isn't that enough?"

Is it really everyone else's problem? Or could it be that the airy type, whose cool objectivity and sociability have earned him the reputation of appearing to be the most "normal" of the types, has a rather infantile approach to the world of feeling? Could it be that he *must* appear detached, controlled and reasonable because he is really terrified of what might be boiling away down in the depths? Some airy people are only too aware of the uncomfortable autonomy of their feeling function, and treat it as though it were some kind of dark beast which occasionally escapes through oversight, but on good days remains behind bars so as not to disturb the smooth order of rational life. Other airy people are completely unconscious of their feeling, and mistake for what they cannot genuinely express a variety of superficial substitutes: displays of sentiment, monetary donations of a well-publicised kind to charities, and a kind of saccharine moist-eyed response to "dogs and children".

One might, of course, ask why it should be necessary to stir up the beast; surely life would be better if it remained tame, and one did not have to be bothered with such messy stuff as emotions? When one considers the great gift of consistent and harmonious behaviour which the airy type usually expresses, why complicate matters? Fine, if you are prepared to live in a cave like the Yogi Milarepa, concentrating your energies upon melting snow — but not when you live in a world with other people. It is not that there is something "wrong" with the airy type, or that he is "abnormal"; he is himself, and as such is right for himself. But unless he learns something about the world of feeling, and develops some capacity to relate on a feeling level with others, he remains hopelessly blind to feeling values, and is capable of much unintentional cruelty. One not very pleasant example of a repressed feeling function and its subsequent eruption is the Weimar Republic and the development of the Third Reich, prior to the last war — a problem on which Jung has written extensively in *Civilisation in Transition*. In the present decade science, which is built upon thinking principles, runs the perpetual risk of seeing its discoveries utilised for mass destruction if it cannot retain some awareness of feeling reality and the fact that knowledge by itself, without the wisdom of the heart, is not only incomplete but downright dangerous. If one can excuse inferiority of feeling in his personal life because "it doesn't hurt anybody", he should consider the broader social implications. Usually, however, somebody is hurt on a personal level, and more often than not it is the airy type himself.

One of the more tragic aspects of all this on a personal level is that the air sign personality, because he is rarely in touch with his deeper feelings, is also generally oblivious to everyone else's. Thus it comes as a rude jolt when someone close to him begins to express dissatisfaction with a relationship, or departs with a loud slam of the door and a parting shot about his coldness and insensitivity. If he is the one to terminate the relationship, he usually believes that by still "being friends" everything is made all right, and is rarely aware of the pain he may cause. If he is the one rejected, he is usually forced to learn what he fears most about himself: that underneath the cool mind lies a dependency of feeling which, although often unrecognised and unexpressed, is so potent that the departure of a partner or child can completely shatter the foundations of his life.

Another pitfall which often awaits the airy type is the kind of fatal fascination which Professor Rath, the stiff, pedantic pedagogue incurs for Lola Lola, the cabaret singer in the film *The Blue Angel*. No personality type is quite as prone to this sort of emotional excess as air, because when the airy individual's feelings take him over, they do so with a vengeance. His thoughts, once so crystalline and clear, are then dominated by his feelings and by the individual who has received the projection of this unconscious side of himself; and as long as he remains ignorant of the deeper levels of his own nature the other will appear proportionately more loving, warm, forgiving and sympathetic — one aspect of feeling — or fickle, capricious, unpredictable and a true embodiment of elemental nature in all her moods. The maternal aspect of feeling, and its fascination for the airy person, is also portrayed in many fairy tales where the beloved is long-suffering and can redeem through her patient acceptance, like Patient Griselda; the more volatile aspect of feeling is portrayed by those tales where the hero falls desperately in love with an ondine, a mermaid, a mysterious creature of the depths with a woman's body and a fish's tail, who in the end either leaves him or destroys him.

Some of the objects of the airy person's fantasies can lead him on a merry dance straight to hell — the hell of his own vulnerable and childlike feeling nature. But we create our own fates through the creative power of the unconscious, and when an individual finds himself in this kind of situation it is very likely because this is precisely the situation he needs to help him become conscious of his feeling function. Air has a magnetic attraction to water, which symbolises the opposite function: feeling. Even if the partner is not really a suitable hook — that is, if the other's chart does not show a strong emphasis of planets in water signs — somehow he or she will appear ideally watery when clothed with the unconscious projection. Air is notorious for being a poor judge of partner, because he chooses everything according to reason until Eros chooses him. Then he has no choice at all, but is under the domination of the unconscious. His insistence on logic and consistency in all things will inevitably provoke such stress in the unconscious that he dooms himself to an eruption of the inferior function when the pressure becomes too great to bear.

Even in less dramatic relationships between the thinking and the feeling type than heroes and mermaids, we may hear the following traditional dialogue:

> "Why are you in such a bad mood, dear? You've been cold to me all evening."
> "What are you talking about? What mood? I feel fine."
> "But I know you're in a bad mood. I can feel it. Tell me what's wrong."
> "I tell you I'm perfectly all right. Why do you always have to demand my constant attention?"
> "But I'm not being demanding, it's just that you're being very bad-tempered with me ..."
> "If I'm bad-tempered it's because you make me that way, always demanding and invading my privacy ..."

Those who recognise this parody may well ask what can be done about it. It seems as though one finds someone who truly understands, and then turns out to be a stranger. The

airy man or woman will always find his greatest challenges
and his greatest potential for growth in those situations where
another's feeling, or his own, blocks his path and presents an
obstacle with which his intellect simply cannot cope. His
richest relationships will be with feeling types, for they are
both his greatest fascination and the reflection of his own
inner self.

> To the constantly reiterated question "What can I do?" I
> know no other answer except "Become what you have
> always been," namely, the wholeness that we have lost
> in the midst of our civilised, conscious existence, a
> wholeness which we always were without realising it.[1]

The Element of Water: The Feeling Type

> Where does reality lie? In the greatest
> enchantment you have ever experienced.
> — Hugo von Hofmannsthal

And so we come to the element of water and the watery
signs: Cancer, Scorpio and Pisces. The true watery type —
and once again, this is not necessarily an individual born with
the sun in a water sign, but rather someone whose chart
suggests as a whole the preponderance of this element —
resembles very closely Jung's description of the feeling type.
Nothing is quite so important to the water signs as personal
relationships and human values, and without them the world
is barren, devoid of hope or joy. Anything will be sacrificed
in order to preserve relationships, and it is typical of water to
create any kind of crisis necessary, even at his own expense,
to evoke a feeling response from his partner. The breath of
life to the water signs is the world of feeling, and this includes
the entire spectrum, shading from very light to very dark. In
feeling there are no fine lines of distinction based on
principle — "this" is not distinct from "that". Everything,

1 *Ibid.*

rather, is an aspect of a constantly flowing and ever-changing sea in which everything is one and all differences are merged. The only differentiation water makes is whether a feeling feels right to him; but it is neither "good" nor "bad".

The symbolism of the water signs contains three cold-blooded creatures: the crab, the scorpion, and the fish. In dreams these images are usually connected with instinctual, unconscious energies which are close to the archaic natural roots of man and very remote from the world of rational, differentiated human thought. Most of the water's evaluation of life is done at an unconscious level; and of these signs it may truly be said that the right hand doesn't know what the left is doing. Water simply responds, and his responses to any personal situation are almost unerringly accurate and appropriate. In contrast, air's responses are contrived, based on principles, usually appropriate in theory, but completely wrong for the particular human situation in which the individual finds himself. While air is busy forcing himself into behaviour consistent to a preconceived framework, water is unpredictable and will respond to each situation as though it had never happened before.

The watery type is usually well-acquainted with the darker side of human nature, which earns these signs their reputation for compassion and empathy. There is the inherent capacity to feel what another feels, and to assess things in what appears to be a totally irrational way which can be infuriating to the airy type, who must reason everything out. "Why don't you like him?" says air, and water replies, "I don't know, I just don't feel good about him." "But you must have a reason." "I don't need a reason, I just know." "But surely you don't expect me to accept your judgment without a reason!" In this situation, water, who usually feels intimidated by air's superior capacity for logic, will usually make up a reason so full of half-baked opinions, generalities and pretensions to intellectual acumen that it is no wonder air views water as being a not particularly intelligent type. Intelligence, however, is not the problem; water is in fact usually more intelligent than air, in terms of wisdom and insight into people. When he is put on the spot, however, he will show his own inferior thinking; and since our age places great value on intellectual dexterity, water tends to be underestimated. In our modern educational institutions it is the gifts of the mind which are nurtured and encouraged, not the gifts of the heart.

Water has all the blessings of the feeling type — sensitivity to atmosphere, subtlety, charm and insight, a strong sense of values in human relationships, and the capacity to bring individuals together and instinctually understand their needs. Even Scorpio, much maligned because of his impenetrable facade of cold ruthlessness and his usually unjustified reputation for sexual excess — emotional excess would be a better description — is a true feeling sign with a soft heart underneath a tough carapace. At the same time, of course, water also has the failings of the type, and these, too, are expressed in the classic sign descriptions we have inherited from ancient astrology. Cancer tends traditionally to be clingy, possessive, clannish and fearful of the future; Scorpio has a reputation for emotional fanaticism and a kind of dark, heavy, brooding atmosphere which makes every relationship resemble a scene from *Othello*; and Pisces is notorious for his gushing sentimentality, his romantic escapism, his vacillation, his unpunctuality, vagueness and lack of principles.

Water, in short, has a problem with reason, and is usually completely unaware of the steady flow of irresponsible second-hand opinions, judgments, negative criticism — both of self and others — and *idées fixe* which constantly issue from his mouth and intrude secretly on his feeling relationships. Water can be rather infantile about the world of ideas. It may seem charming to many men to have a woman who knows "absolutely nothing about all that political stuff," because "it's way beyond" her, yet who can "cook a good meal"; but this unconscious inferiority of thinking has a particularly ugly face when it surfaces as malicious gossip, backbiting, and a kind of ideological fanaticism. In their milder form such characteristics make for someone who consistently tells others how they should live; in their more extreme form they are splendid ingredients for the creation of a good terrorist.

There is a typical story concerning a woman who had a close, although innocent, association with an IRA terrorist wanted for several killings and bombings. When asked why she did not turn this man in to the police, she replied, "But he's really a very nice man when you talk to him, and he never did anything to hurt *me*." This little example says a good deal about the less pleasant repercussions of inferior thinking. Water lacks objectivity, and nothing which does not come into the watery type's personal field of vision, nothing which cannot be related to through feeling, has any real significance. The mind boggles when one considers what a world would be like populated wholly by feeling types. There would probably be no world, for any objective concern for humanity would be secondary to what is good for me and mine. Just as the thinking type must develop an awareness of personal values in order to avoid unconscious brutality, the feeling type must develop an awareness of objective values to avoid a differently motivated but similar brutality.

One of the greatest problems water encounters is that, through his overemphasis on feeling, he can easily alienate those whom he cares for most — because he simply cannot understand that there is a world outside which requires energy and attention. Although he is always responsive to pain in others, he is often incapable of understanding objectively that people think differently and have different needs and values, and tries to smooth the overwhelming blanket of his solicitude over everything which disturbs his sense of harmony in the same way. In doing so, he may not realise that some people find it not harmonious, but simply suffocating. In personal relationships water may often be the one who exits due to a feeling of being injured or emotionally rejected; in such situations he will usually have found someone else who is more "responsive", only to discover with horror that the new lover has a different face but is in fact the same person as the old. Water tries to mother everyone — and this is true of men who are true watery types as well as of women — without seeing that some children want to be allowed to grow up. And the watery type may unleash the destructive criticism of his undigested thinking on his own children, under the guise of what is "best" for them — unconsciously fearing the day when they will draw away and sever the feeling link which is his sustenance.

The watery type is more often the one who is rejected in relationships, largely because if his little personal world feels good to him, he does not bother to wonder whether his partner might need more stimulating intellectual pastures in order to grow. Water has a tendency to live through others, which is always a highly dangerous pursuit; its effect on the other is like that of the mistletoe on the oak. The parasite suffocates his host.

Water is magnetically attracted to air, and if these two types could cease their endless skirmishing they could learn much from each other about their own unconscious lives. Water's greatest challenge lies in those individuals who cannot readily respond through the language of feeling; for the thinking individual will inevitably provide an opportunity for his feeling partner to awaken, open his eyes and take a long, refreshing breath of the clear air of the heights.

The Element of Earth: The Sensation Type

> The trouble with always keeping both
> feet firmly on the ground is that you
> can never take your pants off.
>
> — J.D. Smith

The element of earth correlates with the function of sensation; and since one purpose of this function is to determine that something exists, earth gives the impression of being a fairly accessible, even simple type. We relate to the world of objects through the senses, and it is difficult to discount or repress our response to objects in the way that many people discount or repress thoughts, feelings or intuitions — particularly in an age when most of the empiric sciences have given their stamp of approval only to that which has concrete form. In consequence, most people find the element of earth fairly easy to understand — except the earthy person himself.

The earthy type is usually described in the astrological textbooks as practical, efficient, full of common sense, sensual, "realistic", well-organised and fond of money, security and status. This description applies to all three earth signs: Taurus, Virgo and Capricorn. The function of sensation is the "reality function", and in this sphere the earthy type excels, managing somehow to make order out of the random array of stimuli which assault the senses by relating to each one individually, savouring it, learning its nature, and moving on to the next. In this way, he builds up a body of facts which allows him to deal with each successive situation in the most efficient manner.

The earthy type has all the virtues of Jung's sensation type. He is at home with his body, frequently identifying himself with it, and is usually healthy because he can express his physical desires directly. He is at home with things, and can usually manage money and responsibilities in an effortless way which is mystifying to those who are more intuitive by temperament. He has a gift for actualising his desires, and this capacity for "earthing" shows at its best when combined either with thinking, to produce the careful empiric thinker, the impeccable researcher and statistician, or with feeling, to produce the happy sensualist, the affectionate lover and father, the patron of nature and of all beautiful things.

The earthy type also has all the potential failings of over-emphasised sensation coupled with inferior intuition, and these are once again aptly summarised in the traditional descriptions of the earthy signs. Taurus is notorious for his dogmatic narrow-mindedness, his overpossessiveness of what he considers to be his property, and his tendency to reduce the subtlest and most complex of life's experiences to a philosophy of "Either I see it or it doesn't exist." Virgo proverbially cannot "see the forest for the trees", and becomes lost in a maze of detail and irrelevant trivia without ever seeing the point of his unceasing labours or realising that some people appreciate a little chaos in their lives. And Capricorn has a rather unpleasant reputation for justifying the means by the end and moulding his behaviour to the appropriate social expectations; this enables him to enjoy the

status he seeks without sacrificing anything of himself to get
it.

In other words, while earth excels at the accumulation of
facts, he misses the significance of the connections between
the facts, the relationships that link them with common
meaning; and while he manages with ease the complexities
of the world of objects, he is liable to miss the inner
significance of his own life. The earthy type, being sensation-
oriented, possesses as his inferior function a rather primitive
intuitive sense. In some cases, this stunted intuition
beleaguers him with irrational fears and vague apprehensions
of a negative kind which perpetually interfere with his simple
black-and-white world. In other cases, he represses intuition
entirely and lives in an endless grey twilight of labours and
routines that gradually increase the pile of objects around
him while doing nothing to ease the hollow space within him
— which cries out for some sense of purpose, some feeling of
being part of a larger life, and some hope for the future which
can allow him to rest from his labours and enjoy the present
in a creative way. Another way of describing the earthy type's
problem is that he does not know how to be a child, nor how
to play. He is old when he is young; and unless he can break
loose from the treadmill of his bondage to what he calls
reality, he is especially liable to fear death as the final
reckoning — a definitive summation of his own life, whose
underlying significance has somehow eluded him.

Earth has a longing for what he calls the spiritual, although
this is frequently expressed as a secret fascination or "belief"
in ghosts, psychism, and other parapsychological phenomena
without any understanding of the implications inherent in the
existence of this sort of "supernatural" world. He will often
be found pursuing a love-object who personifies his idea of
the medium, the inspiratrice, the guide who can in some way
share with him the secrets of the cosmos and alleviate the
dull ache within. Unfortunately those who are in touch with
the inner mysteries cannot parcel them out like bread and
cheese, because such intuitive experience is wholly individual, intensely personal and cannot be explained in the
concrete form which earth likes his explanations to assume.

The earthy type can accept nothing unless it is backed up by the testimony of his senses. There are earthy types who are like dogs bound by a long lead to a post; they run round and round, yet can never get beyond the circumscribed length of chain, which is forged by their insistence that the senses are the only means of apprehending reality.

The earthy type may be a wonderful builder, provider, homemaker, and conscientious servant of the needs of those he loves. His worst sin in this case is his lack of vision, which can stifle those close to him and crush his own, as well as others', nascent creativity through his over-insistence on the practical. "Why are you wasting your time on that rubbish?" says the earthbound father to his son who is learning how to paint/play piano/ study philosophy/master the architecture of smoke-rings. "You should be out learning how to make money."

The truly serious damage that such attitudes can do to children is well known; we have an entire generation of dropouts and runaways who have rebelled violently against earthy values consistently forced upon them by well-meaning parents — parents who, having lived through two world wars and a severe economic depression, have forgotten that the future always contains new possibilities. Sensation values only that which it can perceive, and it is bound to miss a lot as a result. The fact that one might want to "waste" one's last shilling on hyacinths for the soul is an outrage and an insult to the hours of labour the earthy type has spent to provide others with the things he believes they want, because he wants them himself.

Earth, if he is reasonably satisfied sexually and has a situation gratifying to his need for material stability, will generally stay in relationships which would drive the other types wild. Because he bases his reality on what is in front of him, the fact that his partner is physically present means to him that a relationship exists. At the same time, the subtler nuances escape him, and often his partner does as well. On the other hand, the unconscious intuitive side will sometimes erupt as a fascination for someone who embodies life, vitality and chaos, which of course brings chaos into his own

carefully ordered world. Often the fascination will be for a
religious or spiritual movement of some kind, and this is one
of the stranger expressions of inferior intuition: an intense
and sincere but gullible religious fervour.

Here the unconscious intuitive search for meaning in life is
structured and crystallised by the senses into dogma, which
attempts to define God, put spiritual reality into concrete
form, and translate the numinous into sacrosanct objects —
an adherence to the letter of the law, in other words, and
obliviousness to its spirit. The Spanish Inquisition is perhaps
a good example of inferior intuition breaking out through a
heavily sensation-oriented culture: the rigorous and fanatical
coercion of belief into one structure, outside which any
individual is a heretic who must be physically destroyed,
admirably exemplifies the ugliest face of inferior intuition.
Most witch hunts — whether conducted by a band of
seventeenth-century Puritans, a band of twentieth-century
Puritans wearing the mask of excessive "realism", or a band
of old ladies of both sexes impelled to shove the Christian
message down the throats of poor benighted heathens,
neighbours and friends — smack of inferior intuition
projected upon an appropriate scapegoat.

More commonly, inferior intuition in the better-balanced
earthy type communicates itself as vague negative hunches.
The earthy type tries to see the future and it comes back to
him blackened by the soot of his own unconscious
projections, so that others are invariably "out to get" him,
nothing will "ever work out", and nobody is to be trusted.
Taurus is famous for his horror of losing what he owns; Virgo
becomes terror-stricken if anything in his carefully ordered
world gets slightly out of order by the intrusion of some
irrational, unexpected element; and Capricorn is well known
for his suspicions of others who might attempt to take his
position away from him. These are, of course, extreme
examples. But one might consider Richard Nixon, who, with
the sun in Capricorn and Virgo on the ascendant, has a
strongly developed sensation function; and one might
plausibly suggest that the unreasonable paranoia and
suspicions of an inferior intuition led him to use those

methods which inevitably brought about his political downfall. Most earthy types do not lead such dramatic lives, nor are they so extreme; but the dark world of fantasy is always a terror and a fascination for this deceptively simply type. The search for some kind of inner spiritual reality is absolutely necessary for the earthy type if he is to find his own wholeness, for his deepest unconscious need is a craving for meaning which, if it is not given room to live, will injure the concrete foundations upon which he has built his life.

Earth has a magnetic attraction to fire, and it is common to find those with a preponderance of earth in the horoscope seeking inspiration and drama from a fiery partner. Earth-fire relationships are often less difficult than air-water relationships because sensation and intuition are what Jung calls irrational functions — that is, they are not irrational in the colloquial sense, but rather, they are unconcerned with judgment, either by principles or by feeling, but simply take experience and experience it. They are therefore less likely to try to change each other, and although there are some typical dialogues common to these relationships which generally hinge around accusations of one partner being too woolly-minded and impractical (fire) and the other being too narrow-minded and bound to habit (earth), the pairing seems to be easier — although not necessarily better — than air-water pairings. Earth tends to feel that he is always cleaning up after fire, and fire tends to feel that he is being nagged at and criticised for things he considers petty and unimportant. Earth wants guarantees that the future will be secure, and fire sees life as a gamble where nothing is secure and the real joy of living is to ride the changes creatively. Earth generally feels he is the giver in any relationship, because he expresses his affection in tangible forms; fire, on the other hand, is generally more self-centred and feels that he is his own best gift. But there is an unending fascination between these two opposite types, for fire seeks the stability and form of earth while earth yearns for the drama and spontanaeity of fire's great vision.

The Element of Fire: the Intuitive Type

> Man's perceptions are not bounded by organs
> of perception: he perceives more than sense
> (tho' ever so acute) can discover.
> — William Blake

We come at last to the element of fire, which in fact begins
the zodiacal cycle with Aries, and which is probably the most
confusing element when an attempt is made to correlate its
traditional attributes with those of Jung's intuitive type. This
is partially because many astrological textbooks seem to
accept at face value the traditional statements that fire is
"warm", "outgoing", "self-centred" and "lucky" without
questioning why he is like this and what truly motivates this
curious temperament. There is also a considerable amount of
confusion about what Jung means by intuition. It is
commonly associated with mediums, seance parlours, and
other assorted oddities which belong more to the realm of
feeling.

> Because intuition is in the main an unconscious
> process, its nature is very difficult to grasp. The intuitive
> function is represented in consciousness by an attitude
> of expectancy, by vision and penetration ... intuition is
> not mere perception or vision, but an active, creative
> process that puts into the object just as much as it takes
> out.[1]

June Singer describes intuition as

> ... a process which extracts the perception uncon-
> sciously ... Just as ... sensation strives to reach the most
> accurate perception of actuality, so intuition tries to
> encompass the greatest possibilities.[2]

1 *Psychological Types.*
2 *Boundaries of the Soul.*

If this is confusing to the reader, it is often more so to many intuitive types, who because they are given no insight into their own psychic constitutions by science and orthodox education — who generally claim that such a function does not exist — are often unsure and mistrustful of the very aspect of themselves which is most highly developed. Intuition is generally permitted to women, with a certain patronising attitude — for it is never taken quite seriously by those who are not aware of possessing it — but there are as many intuitive men as there are women, and they suffer for this lack of understanding.

The fiery signs — Aries, Leo and Sagittarius — share a vitality and spontaneity which is often envied and sometimes resented by more peaceable types. They are children at heart, and are inclined to live in a world of fantasy where people are really knights on white horses, or princesses imprisoned in castles, or dragons which must be challenged and slain. The fiery type has a strong need to mythologise his experiences and relate them to an inner world which belongs more to the world of fairy tales than to "reality". It is no wonder that so many fiery types are drawn to the world of the theatre. The fiery type's behaviour is often exaggerated, but it is unfair to accuse him of doing this purely to get a show; he is generally perfectly acquainted with his propensity for exaggeration, dramatisation and love of colour, but he does it for himself rather than for others, and it is more important to him to experience life dramatically than to accept the apparently drab and sometimes threatening world that more pragmatic types insist he recognise as the real one. "We can accept the unpleasant more readily than we can the inconsequential," as Goethe says.

Fire is considered in traditional astrology to be somewhat insensitive and egocentric, which he undoubtedly appears to be when it comes to the practical details of life. He possesses an inferior sensation function and tends to repress his awareness of objects in order to draw closer to the essence of a situation, its possibilities and its meaning in a larger context. It is not that he cannot be bothered with details; they are actually threatening to his way of perceiving the

world. Fire is interested in the future, and in its endless
potential. The past is to him like a novel someone else wrote,
and the present is a series of doorways which can lead
anywhere and which must be unlocked one by one. When
confronted with the unpleasant demands of the material
world, the fiery type may often drop a situation and move
elsewhere, thereby earning himself a reputation for irresponsibility or callousness. He is neither of these; he simply
cannot bear to be imprisoned.

The fiery type has a knack of perceiving the undercurrents
in a situation and reaching a conclusion at a completely
unconscious level, so that he suddenly has a "hunch" which
often flies in the face of the evidence of the senses yet is
unerringly accurate. What this involves is an appreciation of
the components in a given situation simultaneously and as a
whole, rather than the sequential process involved in
thinking. He appears to have an inordinate amount of
confidence in "luck", but it is rather an innate conviction
that "something" — the unconscious — will eventually
produce a solution which will get him out of his difficulties
and pave the way to a rosy future. This is infuriating to other
types, because fire's successful peering round the corner of
the future is disconcerting to them and his failures even more
disconcerting — because he is not in the least embarrassed
by them. It will "all come right" later. The fiery signs all share
a kind of *joi de vivre*, an irrepressible childlike trust in the
bounty of fate; and one who is deficient in this element may
well stare in amazement at the way in which fire gambles
with money, time, emotion, energy, and sometimes people.
It is all a great game to him, and the object is not the
winning, but the style of play.

Fire will often avoid more conventional paths of religious
aspiration because he cannot bear to see life imprisoned in
form, and he is also instinctively closer to the centre because
of his openness to the unconscious. He is often found in the
world of business and finance, where he can satisfy his
instinct for play by juggling with companies and fortunes. He
will often come out on top in these fields, because he is not
very seriously concerned about the results. The more

introverted fiery type is likely to express his perception of the unseen currents of life through devotion to his own unique spiritual path, or through the arts, where the inner world of images and symbols captures his attention. Through art, he can create a reality which extracts the essence out of daily living experience and forms a myth which transcends the limitations of the historical time in which he lives.

Along with these unusual virtues, the fiery type also possesses some rather dramatic vices, and these are well expressed in the traditional attributes of the fiery signs: Aries has a reputation for an ill-tempered individualism and a Don Quixote-like tendency to tilt at windmills when everyone else wants a little peace and quiet; Leo is known for his sometimes overpowering selfcentredness and his tacit assumption that because he is a child of the gods, no one else could possibly be as well; and Sagittarius is notorious for his irresponsibility with promises, his horror of routine, and his tendency towards exaggeration and "trendiness".

In other words, fire has a problem coping with the world, which is, unfortunately for him, full of objects and the presence of other people; and he must either conquer the world in grand style, or withdraw from it into his visions. The world may seem to thwart him at every turn. These frustrations may take the form of government structures, traffic laws, taxes, bills, the necessity of earning an income, and the problem of remembering to feed, clothe and take care of his body. The world of sensation is often a real stumbling block to the fiery type. This is not only true of dealing with objects, but also of dealing with society — which is generally conservative, at least twenty to fifty years behind the leaping intuition of fire, and consequently insensitive to the promise of his ideas and visions.

The fiery type may be wonderfully successful in business — if he is allowed to speculate rather than being chained to details — or he may have a clear perception of the deepest wellsprings of spiritual life within him; yet he often cannot leave the house without forgetting his car keys or his wallet, or drive down a street without incurring a traffic violation — if he can get his car to start at all. It is this kind of behaviour which often gives him the feeling that society is against him, or denigrating his offerings. But it is really his unconscious senses which are against him. There are also many fiery types who can function well enough in society, yet who find their greatest enemy within their own bodies. There it appears as apprehension of physical illness or hypochondria which must be compensated by strenuous athletic or dietary disciplines, or as an underlying and often deeply unconscious feeling of sexual failure which creates much difficulty in relationships.

The fiery type is most prone to what we are pleased to call sexual problems, although these are not so much problems as a mark of his own and others' failure to understand his needs. Sex often means something different to him than merely a physical act; it is a symbol, as is everything which affects his senses, and the element of fantasy in his relationships is usually very strong. This often seems somehow "perverted" to more literal types. In fact, the elements of expectation, anticipation and romantic and erotic fantasy are often far more important to the fiery type than the actual physical act. This becomes a problem when he is extreme and can no longer relate except through fantasy.

As he often chooses a sensation-oriented partner, upon whom he projects his inferior function, fire is likely to be resentful because he feels as though he is expected to perform — a situation which can produce disastrous consequences. Impotence and frigidity, which are terms we tend to think of as physical problems, are common with extreme fiery types, but the difficulty is not really a physical one; fire simply cannot perform unless his imagination is with him, and if he cannot learn to appreciate sensual experience as a pleasure in itself, he may blame his partner for his failure. He must learn to relate to the body for its own sake; otherwise he may be driven to search from one relationship to another, always seeking the ideal image which in the end exists within his own psyche; and he will become dissatisfied with every partner because the experience is always less than the expectation.

Fire often overcompensates for his feelings of sexual inferiority by "proving" himself; thus we have the Don Juan of both sexes, seeking confidence through conquest. Because romantic situations may, for the extreme fiery type, begin as a fairy tale and end as a cage, he is sometimes unreliable in relationships. And because he also has a problem articulating his needs — often being unable to objectify them — his partner may be in the dark about why he has begun to stray. The usual response is, "I don't know, it's just that something is missing in this relationship." What is missing is his belief that there are no further possibilities to explore.

It is also the fiery type who fears being controlled through his sexuality, and who often gets involved in power struggles in relationships because he must keep the upper hand in order to protect himself. Or he may be highly inhibited in expressing physical affection, which may be acceptable to an understanding partner but can be highly destructive to a child.

The fiery type is more liable than anyone else to sudden physical passions — which he calls love — that cause him to sever existing relationships rather brutally in order to pursue the desired object. This unfortunate scenario often ends with his sad discovery that "all cats are grey at night", and the new love-object is no more satisfactory than the old. Anyone familiar with the life of Henry VIII will recognise this pattern, which appears to correlate well with his Sagittarian ascendant and his extraverted intuitive temperament.

There is also an ascetic fiery type, who is intensely spiritually motivated and may forcibly repress his sensuality because he believes it to be evil. Lewis' classic story of *The Monk* is an excellent example of this pattern, as well as of the typical revenge of a violated unconscious.

One can see easily enough from this description the typical problems of earth-fire relationships, which have already been touched on. These relationships often have a highly magical or compulsive quality about them, but once settled, a familiar pattern emerges. The heart of the fiery type is true, but it is true to an ideal rather than to an individual; and unless he can make some contact with the reality of the senses, he stands to lose his childlike trust in the happily ever after. The result will be a trail of broken relationships and a sense of having produced nothing of permanence with his life. Fire, if his experiences are not to be "like a tale told by an idiot, full of sound and fury, signifying nothing", must learn to understand his dark side so that he can anchor his visions and build something of worth in the world. His dreams are necessary to the world, but they must be communicated with some adjustment to the world's terms.

*   *   *

One can see more clearly now the inherent problem with all four temperaments: each of them sees, and values, a different aspect of reality, and each of them tends to assume that his reality is the only one. The descriptions given here of the four types are meant to be caricatures, and have been deliberately exaggerated; they will rarely be met with in the real world because no one individual is wholly composed of one element alone, or one psychological function. It must be remembered that we all possess all four; but there will inevitably be an overbalance and an underbalance, and one function will be much more highly developed while one will remain relatively unreliable. It should also be remembered that by the age of thirty, most of us have at least two of these functions of consciousness developed to a reasonable degree, one "superior" function and one "auxiliary" function; the second backs up and enriches the first, so that our vision is more extensive. This "auxiliary" function will never be the opposite to the dominant one; if thinking, for example, is the main mode of relationship to life, either sensation or intuition will back it up, but never feeling. The birth chart will often give a clear inference of this pattern of development through the relative prominence of a second element. We may therefore speak of air-fire charts, suggesting an intuitive thinker; air-earth charts, describing an empiric thinker; fire-water charts, expressing intuitive feeling; and earth-water charts, portraying sensory feeling.

Sometimes a birth chart will show a dominance of two elements which imply equal balance of two opposite functions, such as air-water, or fire-earth. This almost always suggests great tension within the individual, for one end of this pair of opposites is likely to be expressed as the dominant function and the other end as the inferior function. The psychological drives symbolised by the planets in the "losing" element will then operate unconsciously, but because they are powerful on the birth chart they cannot be avoided and the problem of integrating the inferior function becomes critical. When an element is weak or missing from the chart, the function it symbolises will usually be weak; but the individual may succeed in avoiding the problem for a long time. When the opposites are present on the chart, the problem is usually recognised early in life and continues to create a lifelong and often highly creative dilemma.

We are always unconsciously drawn to that which we lack, and these four temperaments are inexorably drawn to their opposites because relationships of this kind provide an opportunity to develop greater inner integration. There is almost always a great deal of projection in this sort of relationship, and the problems begin when each individual tries to remodel his partner. He is really trying to remodel himself, which is entirely possible if only he could realise the significance of his perpetual criticism. If we could stand on our little mountain peaks and survey the landscape while realising that others stand on different peaks and see a different landscape, we might appreciate that the richness of life only becomes available when there is a sharing of different realities, and when one recognises the worth of another's values. And we cannot do this until we have ceased to scorn, reject, and fear our own inner "inferiority". Fire can learn to live with, and learn from, his earthy partner only when he is willing to experience his senses at their fullest, and acknowledge their importance; earth can accept and learn from his fiery partner only when he has confronted his own deep longing for freedom from bondage and has recognised that vision is as important as the form in which it is housed. Water can learn to relate to and appreciate air when he understands that not everything in life can be evaluated by his own personal feeling responses; and air can begin to understand and learn from water when he acknowledges his inner feeling needs and recognises that human relationships are as valid a field of human experience as the world of ideas.

The Birth Chart and the Psychological Types

It is always difficult to "type" a chart, and it usually cannot be done without some personal knowledge of the individual. In fact, if we are to use astrology in a productive way to aid the process of self-understanding, we must be able to relate to the individual first, and directly experience something of his identity, before considering the birth chart to see how this reality will be expressed. The person comes before the chart, a fact which many astrologers are prone to forget. It should be remembered that the chart may as easily be that of a chicken, a horse, a building, or an opera society; it is the reflection of a moment in time. The chart is not human; the individual is. The horoscope maps out a set of potentials, but one cannot say what the individual has done with that potential; and there are many important factors which are not reflected on the chart, the most important being the sex of the individual.

Men and women tend to respond to different aspects of the birth chart, and will make a very different living reality out of this map of possibilities. It is not as simple as counting up the number of planets which occupy a particular element, for the specific planets will affect this tally and so will the sex of the individual. For a man, the masculine planets such as the sun and Mars seem to be more "accessible" — that is, the energies which these planets symbolise are more readily available to masculine consciousness. The feminine planets such as the moon and Venus seem to be more accessible to feminine consciousness. As we have seen, the planets group themselves into male and female in the same way that the signs do, and the principle of femininity may be said to be symbolised both by the six feminine signs — Taurus, Cancer, Virgo, Scorpio, Capricorn and Pisces — and by the four feminine planets — moon, Venus, Neptune and Pluto. The principle of masculinity may be said to be symbolised by the six masculine signs — Aries, Gemini, Leo, Libra, Sagittarius and Aquarius — and by the four masculine planets, sun, Mars, Jupiter and Uranus. Mercury is an androgynous planet and appears to deal with synthesis; and Saturn, most mysterious of the planets, may be considered feminine but appears to shift from one side to the other and is also rather androgynous.

Many other factors will affect the balance of elements on the birth chart. One cannot evolve a formula to extract the psychological type of the individual from the horoscope; one must first experience it in the individual, and this knowledge should then be applied to the chart. Otherwise Jung's typology becomes an inanimate structure, rather than the living reality upon which he based his work. A good deal of intuition is necessary to see which parts of the chart have been "highlighted" by being developed in consciousness. People also overcompensate at times when they are aware of a lack in themselves, and this tendency is peculiar to human nature but is not reflected within the chart itself.

For this reason a horoscope done by post, based on birth data but with no direct knowledge of the individual, is likely to be a dismal failure from the point of view of psychological exploration. Astrology used in this way is an interesting characterological map, but can do little as a tool to help the individual on his journey towards self-unfolding. But once there is some feeling for the individual's orientation, which must come from personal contact rather than from the chart, it is easy to see how planets in the "unconscious" elements are likely to function and what may be done to help integrate them. Certainly a dominance of a particular element will suggest that this function of consciousness needs to be developed; but it may not lend itself to such development without conscious effort, particularly if it is an "undifferentiated" function.

There is another problem to "typing" a chart, a phenomenon which June Singer in *The Boundaries of the Soul* calls the "turntype". This is an individual who by natural temperament should have developed a particular function but who because of the influence of a particularly powerful parent, or

the pressures of social or educational demands, has been
forced to violate his natural inclination and develops another
function instead, often the "inferior" one, in order to
psychologically survive. This always causes great damage
and a strong inner feeling of inferiority, for if one identifies
with what one does least well, a price is bound to be exacted.
The process of breaking through the layers which mask the
real identity is not an easy one, and the individual often
cannot accomplish it alone. Here the chart will offer
significant clues; for where there is a predominance of a
particular element, unchallenged by a concurrent emphasis
of the opposite element, yet where the individual is not using
the former, there is a strong suggestion that something has
interfered with the natural line of development. For example,
an individual whose chart shows a bias towards the element
of water and no emphasis in air, yet who is disconnected
from his feeling nature and finds it difficult to cope with his
emotions, may be suspected of being a "turntype".

Sometimes the "turntype" is produced by something more
complex than one insensitive parent. In our society we tend
to assume — possibly not without historical and biological
reason, but perhaps with unreasonably rigid expectations —
that the world of thinking and sensation belongs to men and
the world of feeling and intuition to women. This may be true
in general, and on an archetypal level; it may have been true
for most of our past history. But it is possible that the division
is less sharply demarcated than before, and it may not apply
to the individual, who always contains all potentialities
within his own nature. There is reason to suppose that the
more dominated we are by our biological and historical
heritage, the less we are able to use the individual blueprint
of the birth chart; and there is also reason to suppose that
part of what the contemporary *Zeitgeist* involves is the
capacity to balance this heritage with an increasing
awareness of the potential for individual development. There
are as many men born with a bias towards the feeling
function as there are women, and as many women with a bias
towards the thinking function as men; and while it may
previously have been difficult for a person to transcend his

circumstantial factors and avail himself of this bias for his own unfolding, such transcendence seems to be increasingly possible as we enter a new era in the development of human consciousness.

The pull of the past creates its own pain. The feeling-oriented man, for example, with a preponderance of water on the birth chart, or the intuitive man, with a preponderance of fire, often learns early in life that others will consider him weak, effeminate, cowardly, irrational, or latently homosexual if his natural predisposition is given free rein. Such men sometimes learn to be very different from their natural temperaments in order to "make it" as a man "should". The feeling type's own negative thinking will help him along to this conclusion, since he is terribly prone to swallow social values whole, without thinking them through and questioning their applicability to his own situation. And the intuitive type's sense of inadequacy about being "capable" will often cause him to question the value of his visions. There is then an enormous split between the real identity and the mask, and a very uncomfortable need for which one must overcompensate.

This also applies to the thinking woman and the sensation woman, who are often described as "butch", cold, ambitious, heartless, unfeminine, brittle and neurotic if they follow their natural inclinations into the world of ideas and mundane achievement. Inferior feeling will conspire to help the thinking woman along with her lack of self-acceptance because she feels inadequate in personal relationships; and inferior intuition will often convince the sensation woman that she is dull, boring, unimaginative and only equipped to be the servant of those with greater gifts. Such women may either become armoured Amazons, or attempt to develop the "inferior" function by playing the role of the overbearing, ambitious mother and wife, who wears a mask of sentiment and effusive emotional display over a cold and steely determination to make something of her children, her husband, and anyone else who happens to be her property. Somehow one must find the delicate balance between the physical sex, with its accompanying psychological bias, and the inherent disposition suggested by the horoscope at birth. This is no mean task, particularly if those factors oppose each other. Yet such oppositions, if they are handled gently, with understanding and without doing violence to one pole or the other, can lead to a truly rounded and enriched individual.

The world is full of "turntypes", and they damage themselves and others without realising that the true self lies imprisoned and suffering beneath an impenetrable armour of other people's expectations. Jung's advice is to "be what you have always been", and this is the real path to inner integration and to relating with others. One of the greatest assets of the chart with its interwoven patterns, especially if taken in conjunction with typology, is that it can provide a richer, more comprehensive picture of what one has always been — which is also what one can potentially be.

IV
Beauty and the Beast

It is in vaine to goe about to make the shadowe
straite, if the bodie which giveth the shadowe
bee crooked.

— Stefano Guazzo

Some understanding of the nature of the psychological types
facilitates our approach to the ambiguous domain of the
destructive side of human nature, which Jung calls the
shadow and which in astrology is connected with Saturn, the
"Dweller on the Threshold".

"He sees enough who doth his darkness see,"

says Lord Herbert of Cherbury, yet although this sounds a
relatively simple task, most of us will do anything to avoid it.
Many people very understandably wish to let sleeping dogs
lie, and as long as things do not become too unbearable there
is a certain wisdom in this attitude — up to a point. It is much
more pleasant to think that one is a decent, "okay" sort of
fellow — maybe with a few flaws, but basically alright —
and much easier also to assume that it is the government,
the blacks, the hippies, the Communists, or the foreign
immigrants who have created all the evil in the world. For
some people it is easier to assume that the Devil has created
all the evil in the world, thereby removing human
responsibility from the issue altogether.

Unfortunately, the repercussions of this kind of apathy and
blindness may, although not touching the individual for
many years and sometimes not even in one lifetime, ripple

out to become an important and even devastating social problem. We are all acquainted with the attitude that if it does not happen on my doorstep, it cannot possibly be my responsibility; and it is only when his own darkness catches up with him and engulfs him that a man will begin to question himself.

Edward Whitmont describes the phenomenon of "shadow projection", as it is known in analytical psychology, very aptly in his book *The Symbolic Quest*:

> This type of situation is so classical that one could almost play a parlour game with it — if one wished to court social ruin. Ask someone to give a description of the personality type which he finds most impossible to get along with, and he will produce a description of his own repressed characteristics — a self-description which is utterly unconscious and which therefore always and everywhere tortures him as he receives its effect from the other person.[1]

Unfortunately, although this shadowy side of the personality is usually "utterly" unconscious in the individual, it is not so hidden from everyone else; and the more repressed and unconscious it is, the more obvious it will become to others. Often we may hear a man declare, "I simply hate dictatorial people, they make everybody's lives miserable," and then, on another occasion, the wife or friend says, "Well, he really behaves like a tyrant sometimes, but whenever I try to tell him this he flies into a rage and I can't make myself understood at all." It may be people who are dictatorial, lazy, stupid, selfish, prejudiced, bad-tempered, manipulative, or unfeeling who drive us mad, but blindness to one's own dark side — and projection of it upon others — is incredibly common and few of us are exempt from expressing it. What we generally do not do, with occasional exceptions, is understand what it means.

It is important to comprehend something of the

1 *The Symbolic Quest*, Edward Whitmont, G.P. Putnam's Sons, N.Y. 1969.

implications of the shadow before we can look at the astrological chart to see what inferences may be drawn from it. Ideally we should perhaps not need such things as horoscopes to help us to see our own shadows; but the shadow is, as its name implies, almost always unconscious, and it is not a question of will or intellectual acumen, nor even good intentions, when one is trying to deal with this extremely unpleasant aspect of the human personality. The road to hell is of course paved with good intentions, and certainly with intellectual acumen as well.

> The shadow is a moral problem that challenges the whole ego-personality, for no one can become conscious of the shadow without considerable moral effort. To become conscious of it involves recognising the dark aspects of the personality as present and real. This act is the essential condition for any kind of self-knowledge, and it therefore, as a rule, meets with considerable resistance.[1]

Recognising one's own darkness appears to be a necessary prerequisite not only for self-knowledge, but also for knowledge and acceptance of others. Like everything else in the unconscious, the shadow, if it is not brought into the light, will be projected. The problem of the shadow is not only significant in an individual's own development and in his capacity to form personal relationships; it is also extremely important in a collective sense. Were we more cognisant of this darkness in ourselves, it is entirely possible that collective phenomena which exhibit the projection of a group shadow — such as persecutions, inquisitions, purges, racial intolerance and prejudice, and other phenomena which involve the sacrifice of the scapegoat — would never occur. Even among children we find this ugliness manifesting: there is inevitably one child in any group who, for reasons which may be inherent in his own psychology but which are scarcely his fault, attracts the shadow projection of

1 *Aion*, C.G. Jung, Routledge & Kegan Paul, London, 1959.

the group and becomes the scapegoat, the outcast who is mocked and ridiculed. He is made to bear the brunt of that childish savagery and brutality which, if unchecked in childhood, will eventually express its least destructive side in bigotry, and can attain its most horrific flowering in such examples of appalling bestiality as Auschwitz and Belsen. We have a mercifully dim awareness of the extent of our potential cruelty to each other in even the smallest things; and although many people would prefer to forget about Auschwitz and its ilk because "somebody else" was responsible (certainly not decent people like you and I), we can see the pale reflection of this mechanism in the time-hallowed practise of the social snub.

The shadow consists of all those qualities which are inherent in the potential consciousness of the individual yet, because of their apparent darkness or destructiveness, are excluded from consciousness during the course of development. The individual then remains comfortably unaware that these qualities belong to him. We have seen how each psychological type has his "inferior" side, and the components of the inferior function of consciousness colour heavily the nature of the shadow. To this are added other factors, which the individual would find intolerable as components of his own makeup, repressed because of such sources as parents and religious training. The shadow generally appears to human consciousness first as a human figure, an image most commonly traceable in those dreams where the dreamer is hunted or attacked by a mysterious and malevolent enemy of his own sex.

As a rule the projection of the shadow falls on one's own sex, and one can gain great insight here by an honest consideration of those qualities which we find abhorrent in others of our sex. One has only to hear a woman saying, "I hate that dull, instinctual sort of housewife who thinks of nothing except diapers and recipes, and who has no independence or mind of her own," to get a clear picture of her shadowy side; and there is her polar opposite, who may be heard to declare, "What a dreadful person she is; she is only concerned about herself and her own pleasures. She is so unfeminine, and doesn't understand the meaning of sacrifice." If these two extreme ladies could see whom they were truly describing by these thoughtless remarks, they would probably shrivel up with embarrassment. They are clichés, but amazingly prevalent. There is the man who abhors those of his sex who are weak, sissyish, effeminate and dominated by their women; and there is his opposite, the man who condemns those brutal, aggressive and ruthless types who love war for the glory and have nothing to do except gather together in pubs at night to discuss the merits of their secretaries' bodies. The pacifist contains within him a bully, and the hero a coward; as Mick Jagger sings in *Sympathy for the Devil,*

> Every cop is a criminal,
> And every sinner a saint.

Like the old Roman god Janus, we are all double-faced, and the individual must acknowledge this if he is to have any conscious voice in the matter of whether his dark side or his light is expressed to his fellow men.

Sometimes the shadow projection falls on an institution, or a religion, rather than an individual. This phenomenon is readily observable in fanatical ideological hatreds of all kinds. Shadow and ego put together make a whole, and wholeness, as we have seen already, is not merely or necessarily perfect; it is, however, complete.

All of our opinions, when they carry a high emotional charge, are suspect.

> When we find ourselves the victim of an emotional reaction that is out of proportion to the situation, or where we have such a reaction in regard to some situation that is not really within the range of our concern but is strictly someone else's business, we should suspect that we are reacting to something of our own that we have not recognised as ours ...[1]

1 *The I and the Not I,* M. Esther Harding, Princeton/Bollingen, N.J. 1965.

We have seen how each type, and consequently each
astrological element, carries a weakness in the opposite
function. When we see these qualities as evil, judge them,
and force them into the unconscious, they fester and become
precisely as evil as we believe them to be. It is our viewpoint
towards the unconscious which produces its apparent
enmity.

> The unconscious has an inimical or ruthless bearing
> towards the conscious only when the latter adopts a
> false or pretentious attitude.[1]

And one of the most pretentious attitudes of which human
beings are capable is the belief that it is always someone
else's fault.

Children instinctively know about the autonomy of the
shadow, and many imaginary playmates are personifications
of it. These creatures of "mere" fantasy are often made
responsible for the messier, more unacceptable aspects of
the child's behaviour; it is the playmate who smashed all the
dishes, painted patterns on the wall, pulled the cat's tail, or
stole Daddy's cufflinks, but certainly not the child himself.
When accused of lying, he will become defensive and
upset; and yet he is, in his fashion, telling the truth and is
correct in calling this figure "somebody else", for certainly he
had no conscious control over it. This kind of destructive
double often appears when a child is coerced into being
"good" too much of the time. Adults react in a similar way
when accused of behaviour which is a manifestation of their
own dark side, for the shadow, when confronted, is a sore
point in proportion to one's lack of insight regarding it. To
tell someone he is expressing his most hated unconscious
qualities is to threaten his entire self-image, and this will
usually evoke extreme anger and an outburst of enraged
justice grossly disproportionate to the observation — which
may be a true one and constructively offered. Were we as

1 *Two Essays in Analytical Psychology*, C.G. Jung, Princeton/Bollingen,
  N.J. 1953.

honest as children, we could say, quite justifiably, "No, it wasn't me, it was my shadow again." And more importantly, we could say: "I wonder what he wants?" Like all unconscious contents, the shadow seeks consciousness, and it would perhaps be more helpful to stop judging this aspect of the psyche so harshly, to stop attempting to fight it in others, and to take an objective look at it to find out what it has to offer. For many people, the shadow is a shameful secret that must at all costs be kept from view; and we have the extraordinary idea that we must not show our common humanity, which is after all half an animal, to each other for fear of moral condemnation. In consequence we attempt to show each other only perfection, and the strain of the effort is both an intolerable burden and a guarantee that we will always fail in our expectations.

The shadow is an archetype; that it, it is an inner experience common to all mankind, in every century and in every civilisation. Art and fairy tale offer their wisdom here and tell us of the hero attended by a peculiar and often primitive, ugly, or slightly malicious companion, sometimes an animal, who creates endless problems because of his bestiality and stupidity. At the same time, this figure is always the one who, through his instinctual, natural wisdom, saves the hero when he is caught in a dilemma which his own prowess or high birth cannot help him overcome. A classic example is that of Don Quixote and Sancho Panza. On other occasions, the shadow figure is an enemy, a sorcerer or savage warrior who attempts to destroy the hero. Yet always, in some curious way, the shadow's intentioned evil makes it possible for the hero to achieve his goal, albeit sometimes by a circuitous route. Fairy tales tell us a most important fact about the shadow: secretly, behind his clumsiness and darkness, he conceals many qualities which, far from being "evil", are qualities which in embryonic form are necessary to the ego in order to become an integrated whole. The shadow cannot be removed by trying to make conscious behaviour "better", and if we do not integrate its qualities, they may wreak vengeance by forming their own autonomous "alter ego" or *"Döppelgänger"* — the sinister figure who haunts the works of Poe, Dostoevsky, and R.L. Stevenson. One cannot change one's shadow, still less dispel or exorcise it, by criticism or condemnation; what is required is a change in the conscious attitude. The more balanced a man is in permitting some inferiority to express itself in his personality, the more balanced his shadow will be; but the more strenuously righteous he is, the blacker and more destructive the shadow.

*   *   *

Because the shadow is an archetypal experience, we may expect it to be represented among the planetary hierarchy, and there seems to be a close connection between it and the symbol of the planet Saturn. In mythology, Saturn has a particularly unsavoury reputation, having castrated his father Uranus to seize the throne of the gods and devoured his children to protect his power. In traditional astrology, Saturn also has a rather unpleasant reputation, being considered a "malefic" planet — that is, a bringer of woe and misfortune. Traditional astrology probably has had less insight into this mysterious planet than medieval alchemy, which considered Saturn to be the base material from which, after transmutation, spiritual gold could be extracted; and here we have a reflection of what art and fairy tales tell us, that within the dark side of human nature lies the seed of true inner integration. We may also see echoes of this theme in the figure of Lucifer, Satan or Mephistopheles. At face value, he is the enemy of God, reigning over the legions of hell. Secretly, however, and despite himself, he is the right hand of God, carrying out the divine plan by offering humanity a choice whereby it may come to its own understanding of the problem of good and evil and the opposites they comprise. It is Lucifer, Satan or Mephistopheles who allows man to be free, because he learns through the pain of his choices. As Geothe writes in *Faust*,

> Say at last — who art thou?
> That Power I serve

Which wills forever evil
Yet does forever good.

   The position of Saturn on the birth chart suggests a sphere
of the individual's life in which he has been somehow
stunted, or arrested in growth, in which he may well feel
inadequate, oversensitive or clumsy, and in which he will be
prone to overcompensate by attempting to show a brave and
sometimes callous face. No point on the chart can be
interpreted literally, and Saturn is no exception; but we must
also remember that the unconscious side of personality is
built up partially of those qualities which belong to us but
which we cannot, or dare not, express. We may thus infer
from the placement of Saturn that area where the shadow will
express itself most readily, where one is perhaps most
defensive and critical of others, and where one is most liable
to attract the hostility and opposition of the environment
because of one's own unconscious attitude of inferiority. The
position of Saturn suggests where one is most likely to be
mean, and petty, and narrow; and as long as one is ready to
blame the world for one's misfortunes, the birth position of
the planet certainly suggests the direction from which
misfortune most probably will issue. However, if one is
prepared to work with the shadow, and examine what lies
within oneself that serves as the attraction for this
misfortune, one may discover that — like the peculiar
companion in the fairy tale — Saturn becomes a source of
strength and a beacon illumining the path to the goal.
   Saturn tends to bring out the worst qualities of the sign in
which he is placed at birth, because he intensifies fears
associated with the particular attributes of that sign. This
engenders a concurrent sense of inadequacy, and the
reaction to it is usually one of two extremes. Either the
individual will withdraw, intimidated by his apparent shortcomings, and torment himself with them, or he will seek to
overcompensate for them by exaggerating the attributes of
the sign in which Saturn is placed. Sometimes both reactions
will occur in one individual, and sometimes he will be
unconscious of them. For example, an individual with Saturn

placed in Aries may find that his greatest fear is of being second, or losing; he will find it difficult to express the natural Arien love of challenge and confidence in his ability to meet life and conquer it. He may become passive, allowing himself to be easily dominated; and in this case he will harbour a secret resentment and anger, which may surface as waspish sniping at those who can express their drives more honestly. Or he may become a bully, and overassert himself because he is so unsure of his own prowess. At the risk of oversimplification, one might say that in Taurus, Saturn brings out the fear of losing what one possesses, or of material failure, or of the instinctual nature and its integrity; in Gemini, he brings out the fear of becoming committed, or of losing the freedom to explore the world of ideas; in Cancer, he brings out the fear of emotional isolation and rejection; in Leo, he brings out the fear of being mediocre and unnoticed and unloved; in Virgo, he fosters the fear of chaos and of the unknown; in Libra, he stimulates the fear of darkness and of the destructive power of intense emotional involvement; in Scorpio, he accentuates the fear of others' domination or control through emotional vulnerability; in Sagittarius he aggravates the fear of meaninglessness and bondage to fixed routines; in Capricorn he exacerbates the fear of control by the material environment and by the authority of others; in Aquarius he emphasises the fear of being different and of being excluded from the group; and in Pisces he intensifies the fear of dissociation from a greater emotional whole, and of emotional solitude.

It is very common for a person to dislike intensely those born under the sign in which Saturn is placed at his birth; it is equally common for a person to find them attractive and fascinating. Probably the latter is a healthier response, because it can be productive of a relationship which fosters growth in a positive way. The former will also foster growth, but much more painfully. Saturn is a planet frequently involved in the comparison of charts between people enmeshed in close relationships. In fact, it might be said that a relationship which does not contain at least one strong Saturn tie may be a pleasant one, but is unlikely to affect the deeper emotional life of the individuals concerned.

One may perform a very useful exercise by examining the position of Saturn on the birth horoscope, and then examining the charts of partners, relatives or associates to see whether any of their planets falls within about eight or ten degrees of one's own Saturn, in the same sign. Also significant are planets which are directly opposite one's own Saturn, one hundred and eighty degrees away. The angle of ninety degrees is likewise significant. These three aspects, or angular relationships — respectively called the conjunction, opposition and square in astrology — are the commonest of all aspects in chart comparisons; and they inevitably occur in relationships which somehow force the individual whose Saturn is involved to examine himself and his own responses, so that he may discover something about the workings of his shadow. In any relationship involving these Saturnian aspects between charts, we can anticipate a good deal of shadow projection. The important thing is for the individual to recognise that he is the source of the problem, through his defensive or over-critical reactions, rather than to blame his partner for whatever discord develops. One must also learn to live out the meaning of the Saturn sign, even if it is awkward and embarrassing, rather than run away from it and then resent it when it is expressed by others. Here at least the shadow can be recognised and given room to breathe, which is an excellent remedy for many of his less attractive qualities.

The ambiguities and paradoxes of Saturn deserve a separate work, which they have in fact been accorded,[1] and it is really a gross oversimplification to merely consider the sign in which the planet is placed. The mundane house in which he is placed must also be considered, the angular relationships he forms to other planets within the birth chart, and the birth chart as a whole with its inevitable bias towards a particular direction of conscious development. But if some care is accorded the interpretation of this planet one can

1 *Saturn: A New Look at an Old Devil*, Liz Greene, Samuel Weiser, Inc., New York, 1976.

obtain a good idea of the greatest obstacles in one's life; because Saturn is indeed the base material out of which — by attracting experiences conducive to greater understanding through struggle — the psyche seeks to attain greater integration.

The chart shown on the next page illustrates to a very marked degree the autonomous workings of the shadow, as well as the paths by which the individual can become conscious of his problem and extract some meaning from it for his own growth and the fulfilment of his most valued ideals.

Paul is an extraverted intuitive type, whose vision of the future, like that of so many intuitives, led him to embark on an enterprise that would externalise it: he wanted to help those individuals he thought were under-privileged and suffering at the hands of a society he deemed was suffocating the creativity of the individual. He set up an informal school in New York, the city of his birth, which was intended to help develop creative skills among the poorer minority groups. The fees for this training were nominal; Paul poured his own extensive savings into it, paying the salaries of those who helped him out of his own pocket. There were classes in speaking and writing English; there was a place where children could be looked after while the parent pursued his own studies; there were classes in painting, sculpting, modelling, weaving, dress-making, and other creative expressions which might help these people bring some beauty and light into the dreary struggle for survival which was so often their existence. The idea behind all this reflected Paul's characterisically intuitive longing for the fulfilment of his opposite function: a return to the valuing of individual craftsmanship in a society which reduced the individual to a nameless, faceless component of a city without any appreciation of the dignity of his own creative efforts.

Paul's co-workers, as well as the people who came to his school to develop themselves, soon learned to trust him, for he was completely devoid of condescension and did not exhibit the psychic distance which so often exists between the well-meaning idealist and the people he seeks to help. Paul's well-developed feeling function helped him to see the need

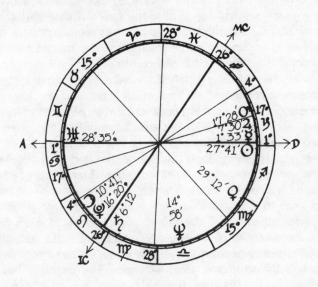

Paul

for this personal contact, particularly since many of the people who came to take his classes had a background of violence and hatred of those who came from the stratum of society which Paul represented.

The sun in Sagittarius, and the moon and Pluto together in Leo, both fiery signs, reflect the prominent intuitive side of Paul's temperament; and the Cancer ascendant, which is a watery sign, seems to symbolise the sensitivity of feeling and personal response which marked his dealings with people. The placement of the sun in the seventh house, that of personal relationships, suggests that self-fulfilment for Paul must come from his serving as a catalyst for others, bringing together opposites between which he himself is the bridge. There is a tremendous amount of energy and creativity indicated by this chart, and Uranus, the planet which symbolises the need for freedom and perception of a larger world of ideas, is placed directly on the ascendant; this implies the strongly unconventional and visionary attitude towards life which is one of Paul's dominant characteristics. The grouping of Mercury, Jupiter and Mars in Capricorn, an earthy sign, points to a potential for extraordinary self-discipline, the capacity to work long and hard towards a chosen goal, and the practical commonsense necessary to earth one's vision. Potentially, this is a dynamic and creative chart. The problem lies in integrating it, because fire and earth are psychological opposites yet here are evenly matched and bound to bring about a battle within the psyche sooner or later.

Paul's background was an extremely conventional one. He came from a monied family and went to the appropriate school; and he was expected to conform. This is asking too much of a fiery intuitive with Uranus on the ascendant. The first obstacle lies in the lack of understanding of his temperament shown by his parents, but like so many parents of their generation Paul's had no idea that a child could possess an individual disposition and have a unique and individual path in life; he was to them an empty vessel which could be filled with their values and would grow up to live out the unlived side of their own psyches. Like others of his temperament, Paul sensed too much wrong with the environment in which he found himself. His parents' marriage was a wonderful piece of well-disciplined hypocrisy, and there seemed to him too much stagnation, self-deception and resistance to change; and these things are anathema to the intuitive.

The grouping of earthy planets in Paul's chart forms a balance to the self-expressive vision of fire, but they are not functioning as consciously available qualities in his nature. This is perhaps connected with the fact that Saturn, who rules Capricorn and thus presides over these planets, is also placed in an earthy sign, Virgo, and is located in the fourth house — which relates to the early home life and the relationship with the father.

One's shadow projections are usually expressed in the sphere of life symbolised by the sign and house in which Saturn is placed at birth. It is in this sphere of life that the enemy is objectified and externalised. Thus Paul's inferior sensation function, which coloured heavily the dark side of his nature, was naturally projected upon his father. Paul's shadow expressed itself as a powerful unconscious material- ism, a rigid conventionality, oversensitivity to the opinions of those in authority, crude sensuality and a propensity for physical violence. Most of these qualities Paul denied vehemently; the only one he would acknowledge was the sensuality, because that harmonised with his self-image. These less pleasant qualities seemed, naturally, to belong to his father, who appeared to him as Saturn: authoritative, conventional, grasping and concerned only with money and material values. The projection extended beyond his father into society, which also appeared to him as Saturn; and he hated both. Admittedly, Paul's father provided a hook on which to hang the shadow projection; but he was no better and no worse than many other men of his generation, and had many outstanding qualities.

Through his father and the society which his father upheld, Saturn in Virgo also symbolised to Paul a suffocating inhibition and an adherence to meaningless rules. This was abhorrent to his characteristic Sagittarian love of personal freedom. The world seemed full of deadly order, which threatened to petrify the life out of him. It never occurred to

him that the positive side of these dreaded earth qualities was
the practical wisdom necessary to actualise his dreams.

Like many other intuitives, Paul felt he was a law unto
himself, but he did not take into account the shadowy side of
his nature. Consciously he was full of bright ideals and was
truly concerned for the improvement of his fellow men.
Unconsciously, at the roots of his psyche, the dark side
symbolised by Saturn worked to make use of his natural
abilities for the purpose of controlling others; and it alienated
him first from himself and then from his associates through
eruptions of tyrannical behaviour, violent temper, physical
assaults, and a certain ambiguity in his dealings with money
— all behaviour patterns he frequently ascribed to authority
figures such as the police, the government, and in particular
his father. These outbursts, which he always rationalised in
the classic way — "Something suddenly came over me!" —
of course began to drive away the people he needed most to
help him. The organisation began to founder because he had
gained the reputation of being a little Hitler who could not
live the ideals he preached so glibly to everyone else. He was
deeply hurt by these accusations, and believed them to be
totally unjustified.

Conspiring to exaggerate Paul's difficulties is the absence,
on the birth chart, of any personal planets in air. This
suggests that he is lacking in the objective and impersonal
assessment and analysis of his own motives and behaviour
which might have permitted him to realise what he was
doing. As a tool of consciousness, Paul's thinking function is
no more reliable than his sensation.

It would be unfair to accuse Paul of deliberate hypocrisy.
He could no more control the thing within him than a child
can his destructive side; he did his best not to look at it,
thereby committing no worse sin than most of the rest of us.
But one cannot force the shadow into the unconscious
without incurring consequences. By repressing almost every
aspect of his sensation function, and by denying the validity
of sensation values, he doomed the shadow to a life in the
underworld; and because he viewed any appreciation of
material things as evil, the shadow began to behave in an evil

way. Paul's dealings in male-female relationships were crude and unsatisfactory. By maintaining a veritable harem of women, and by publicly flaunting his conquests, he sought desperately to compensate for the vague feelings of sexual inadequacy which plague so many intuitives. Yet he never really succeeded in gaining any confidence in his manhood, nor could he sustain a valid relationship for more than a few months. When he became interested in having his birth chart explored, he was being disturbed by a peculiar series of dreams which are highly characteristic of a shadow gone wild: he was hunted and tortured by dark figures in the guise of brutal policemen or Gestapo officers, all of whom he immediately associated with his father. That these figures represented his own unconscious was a fact he could not accept.

If an element is dominant on the birth chart, one cannot deny expression to the side of the psyche it symbolises. But because of Paul's extreme reluctance to accept his dark side, the four earthy planets on his chart, all channelled through Saturn, remained unintegrated, and behaved as though they were a separate entity intent on destroying him. And the shadow in this instance was indeed intent on destruction, but not wantonly; for the unconscious always attempts to compensate for the one-sidedness of the conscious attitude and will at times resort to the necessity of breaking down the ego in order to achieve the balance it seeks. Thus, in fairy tales, there must be an enemy who attempts to destroy the hero, for only in this way can the hero attain his goal.

We have in Paul's case a classic example of someone involved in a violent struggle with an aspect of his own psyche. Saturn placed in the house connected with childhood suggests an intense feeling of inadequacy and a desperate need to recreate the childhood that was never properly experienced — a childhood which his temperament, being strongly feeling-biased, required, yet which his family failed to allow. In consequence, the small and vulnerable child constantly alternated with the tyrant. And the feelings of inferiority found compensation through the unconscious as an enormous inflation which began to assume archetypal,

Homeric proportions: Paul secretly felt himself to be a kind of martyred messiah, a misunderstood and maligned prophet whom everyone else persecuted, the king offered up for ritual sacrifice that his subjects might partake of his power. He made the rounds from one therapist to another and always interrupted his therapy — or became ambiguous about payment of fees — whenever the problem of his shadow came under scrutiny. Like a child, he wanted someone else to make all the bad things go away. But as the fairy tale tells us, you must love the beast for his own sake before he can become the handsome price.

As a result of Paul's problem, his organisation, which meant more to him than anything else in his life, finally ejected him. It even continued to operate successfully without him, which was an even worse blow to his ego. Although it might have been integrated into a wonderfully productive tool, the terrible split in his nature between dark and light eventually produced the worst possible situation for an individual so strongly in need of others: complete isolation. It is through this kind of experience that Saturn, disguised as Lucifer, brings us to our knees. Yet it is only through this kind of experience that we can be made aware of the psyche's full potential.

The experience of the shadow might have been a springboard for a real step in psychological growth, had Paul been willing to undertake the moral task of accepting his own darkness. There is no easy solution to this kind of problem, for as Jung says, it requires an enormous and often daunting effort to become conscious of the shadow. This psychic figure epitomises everything we most despise in ourselves; and in order to recognise that he personifies the missing half of us, the centre of consciousness must shift from the typical ego perspective to one somewhere in the centre, between the pull of the opposites. This is an arduous enterprise, because the ego feels it will be destroyed by such a shift. What will in fact be destroyed is not one's ability, nor one's identity, but rather the belief that the ego is master in the house. It is a lesson in humility very different to that which we are taught in our Christian ethic, for the god within to whom we owe allegiance has, like Janus, a double face.

As this is being written, Paul is still foundering, feeling persecuted, disillusioned and betrayed. He cannot comprehend why he has been rejected, and prefers to believe that someone else in the organisation wanted his place of power. It is entirely possible that the real meaning of this important and potentially valuable experience will not emerge for Paul until the time of his Saturn return, when the planet has transited back to Virgo, the sign in which it was placed at his birth. At the critical age when this occurs, as Marc Roberton has shown in *The Transit of Saturn*,[1] all that is false within the ego structure begins to break down and the unconscious makes a concerted push towards integration. For Paul, that time is a full two years away, and he has the opportunity between now and then to learn the lesson Saturn has to teach: nothing dies that is not lived out, and while one may see what one can see best oneself, it will be a poor and narrow viewpoint compared with the wisdom of the integrated psyche. And that which one cannot see will remain the true master.

Saturn, as an astrological symbol, is both our greatest enemy and our greatest friend, for through our pain and frustration we learn the essence of his meaning: the shadow is an enemy because we make him one. We cannot wholly rid ourselves of our inferior and primitive side; but perhaps it is only our human ideal of perfection that makes us defy nature and deny her the right to include what we call inferiority in the work of creation. A careful look at Saturn on the birth chart should remind us that there must be baseness for there to be gold; and an astrological analysis of the planet can help to place in perspective a psychic energy which is elusive and difficult, sometimes destructive, but always striving towards integration.

1 *The Transit of Saturn*, Marc Roberton, The Astrology Centre of the Northwest, Seattle, 1973.

V
The Inner Partner

Work of sight is achieved,
now for some heart work
on all those images prisoned within you; for you
overcame them, but do not know them as yet.
Behold, O man within, the maiden within you!—
creature wrung from a thousand natures,
creature only outwrung, but never,
as yet, belov'd.

— Rainer Maria Rilke

It does not much signify whom one marries,
as one is sure to find next morning that
it is someone else.

— Samuel Rogers

When Rider Haggard wrote his description of Ayesha in the
novel *She*, he obviously had in mind a clear and well-defined
image of the ideal woman, a personification of all that is
mysterious, fascinating and powerful about the feminine.
Ayesha is hardly a portrait of a flesh-and-blood woman; she is
a symbol of all women, containing — as all symbols do — the
apparently irreconcilable opposites of the feminine principle
within her. She possesses the lucid wisdom of centuries, yet
behaves in an incredibly stupid and bloodthirsty fashion; she
loves with intense passion and abandon, yet is capable of
extreme coldness and aloof withdrawal; she embodies all
kindness and healing, yet is able to perform savage acts of
great cruelty with appalling disregard for human life. She is
both superhuman and subhuman, and, on the whole, does

not bear much resemblance to the girl next door. The same may be said of the portrayals of any artist or writer who has succeeded in putting into form his innermost fantasies of the feminine; one could cite an endless number of examples (from Leonardo's Mona Lisa through Dostoevski's Nastasya Ivanovna in *The Idiot* to Fowles' *The French Lieutenant's Woman* and Durrell's *Justine*). The complementary image of man portrayed by women writers and artists is not so well-represented, but one might consider as examples Heathcliffe, that extraordinary creature of Emily Brontë's fantasy, the heroes of Anne Radcliffe's Gothic novels, *The Scarlet Pimpernel*, and more recently, Francis Crawford of Lymond, portrayed in Dorothy Dunnett's best-selling historical novels — which may not be "great literature" but do serve admirably to demonstrate the phenomenon. These artistic creations may be based upon a living man or woman, but they are not lifelike portraits of any individual; they all have the curiously archaic, superhuman and subhuman quality of the arche-type, a mythic, larger-than-life stature. They are portraits of that unconscious ideal image which the living man or woman has the capacity to activate within the artist. And this image may, in fact, be powerful enough to demand expression, whether or not there is an actual individual to serve as catalyst or not.

Those of us who are not artists may still carry this inner image, and many men and women can describe a type of individual who embodies all they seek from the opposite sex. These inner images have a curious fascination and auto-nomy; they are contents of the unconscious psyche, and like all other contents in the unconscious, they will be projected upon actual people who in some way serve as suitable "hooks". We have, therefore, the typical situation of the man who has a clearly defined — although often unconscious — inner image and interpretation of woman, which he continually projects upon those women he meets; he believes himself to have found this perfect woman when he falls in love; and when the projection wears a little thin, and the real woman peeps out from behind it, he is forced to acknowledge that he must make adjustments in his attitude towards the relationship. Often he may react by feeling severely disappointed, as though he had been deceived or cheated — in which case he fails to realise that it is his own projection which has deluded him. It is astonishing how many people say accusingly to their partners after the honeymoon, "But you have changed!" when in fact the partner has not changed at all, only the projection. Alternatively, a man may accept the challenge, and attempt to relate to his woman as she is, as a whole person, while still acknowledging the inner image as his own and attempting to make conscious within himself those qualities which it symbolises. The image, after all, belongs to his own psyche. This classic fork is what is colloquially known as falling out of love, and it is a crisis point which inevitably strikes any couple after a certain amount of time has passed. Here in a nutshell is the course so many relationships follow; and here, most of all, is where we bungle things, because we fail to see the meaning of what has happened.

Every man contains a woman within him, and every woman a man; and this basic truth is not only biological — for we all contain in a recessive form the hereditary vestiges of the opposite sex without our own bodies — but psychological as well. Jung has defined these transsexual unconscious images as *animus* and *anima*, and astrology infers the same inter-relationship of male and female within the individual from the presence of both masculine and feminine signs and planets in his birth chart. Not much perspicacity is required to see the developing awareness of this inherent duality in many modern movements geared towards the modification of traditional sexual roles; and while it may be a little embarrassing for some people to recognise, the truth underlying such movements is apparent within one's own psyche. But to live out the sexual duality in a creative and constructive way, without doing violence either to one's biological inheritance or one's unconscious, requires a considerable effort.

The anima and animus are two of the most mysterious figures explored by analytical psychology; and although Jung's terms are highly descriptive — *anima*, the feminine, means soul, while *animus*, the masculine, means wind, breath or spirit — they have been known by other names throughout the history of man, have been portrayed in the myths, fairy tales, religious themes, and arts of all cultures down the centuries. Even with the multitude of descriptions offered by Jung's work, these unconscious images remain abstract concepts except to those who have consciously and directly experienced their power. Yet abstract as they may at first seem, it is worth making an effort to understand something abut them, and, even more, to achieve some meaningful relationship with them; for around these symbols hinges the entire world of male and female interaction in all its complexity.

> The animus is a psychopomp, a mediator between the conscious and the unconscious and a personification of the latter ... The animus gives to woman's consciousness a capacity for reflection, deliberation and self-knowledge.[1]

The woman who is able, however slightly, to recognise the attributes of the animus, and to distinguish her feminine ego-consciousness from him, can begin to work cooperatively with the unconscious transsexual side of her own nature; she can thus begin to free herself from the usual habit of projecting him onto a living man. Consequently she is in a position to relate more meaningfully to the masculine values of her partner, instead of being bewildered by them and him; and she also gains an increased awareness not only of her own womanhood, but of the creative potential of her mind and spirit as well. Woman's psychology is rooted in instinct, and in instinctual response to the flow of life. The great gift of the consciously developed animus is the gift of meaning, which allows her to reflect, discriminate, and discover the meaning of her own life and actions.

Just as each woman contains within her this masculine energy, each man contains within him a feminine aspect.

1 *Aion.*

It belongs to him, this perilous image of Woman; she stands for the loyalty which in the interests of life he must sometimes forego; she is the much needed compensation for the risks, struggles, sacrifices that all end in disappointment; she is the solace for all the bitterness of life. And, at the same time, she is the great illusionist, the seductress, who draws him into life with her Maya — and not only into life's reasonable and useful aspects, but into its frightful paradoxes and ambivalences where good and evil, success and ruin, hope and despair, counterbalance one another.[1]

The man who has some understanding of the anima, and recognises her autonomy, can begin to cooperate with this unconscious feminine side of himself; and in doing so, he will be far more capable of perceiving the identity of his partner, thereby allowing her to be herself. He will also gain greater acceptance of his own manhood as he becomes conscious of the hidden and secret source of his feelings and his capacity for love, while opening new possibilities for the expression of creative imagination and sensitivity.

One obstacle to understanding these inner partners to whom we are wedded all our lives is that we are fettered to social definitions of masculinity and femininity, which make it difficult for the anima and animus to find room for more constructive expression. To many people, masculinity and femininity are defined as a set of actions, or behaviour patterns, rather than as archetypal energies which permeate the entirety of life. According to this limited and two-dimensional view, a man is someone who is successful, aggressive, and dominating, while a woman is someone who is domesticated, passive and submissive. The problem of attempting to define the indefinable is further aggravated by our current violent rebellion against sexual "roles". While this is perhaps necessary and inevitable at the moment, it nevertheless obscures and complicates any attempt to fathom and appreciate the workings of the male and female within oneself.

1 *Aion.*

If one is willing to listen to people and experience them, it is clear that there is a basic difference between masculine and feminine psychology. As Swinburne says, man embodies the love of truth, while woman embodies the truth of love. This basic difference, which Jung describes as the polarity of Logos (mind) and Eros (love), exists in all of life and is a reflection of the archetypes. To many people, however, it seems to constitute a threat — particularly to that extreme end of the Women's Liberation Movement which feels that such a distinction is a denigration of women's rights. Analytical psychology has never postulated that men are only capable of thinking, and women of feeling; the existence of the anima and animus within each person is testimony to each individual's wholeness. But the values and the deepest springs of motive are different in male and female psychology. It is a pity that so many contemporary misunderstandings have occurred, and it is also a pity that Freud's concept of "latent homosexuality" should still be an old bogeyman for many individuals who feel that expressing the transsexual side of their natures will somehow make them homosexual. If anything, the opposite is more likely to be true; for what we call homosexuality is often the result of a complete repression of unconscious figures which — like any other component of the unconscious — will become antagonistic and overwhelm consciousness if they are treated with arrogance or contempt by the ego.

It is useless to postulate as a theory that women, however gifted on the intellectual side, tend to place more value on human relationships, and that men, however creative and sensitive, tend to place more value on achievement, structure and the world of ideas. One must experience these things oneself. For many individuals the anima and animus remain wholly unconscious and are projected; or they may rebel against the ego's repression and subtly take possession of consciousness to such a degree that they damage the individual's natural relatedness to his own sexuality. The individual may then unwittingly identify with this unconscious element in himself, thinking that it is his best side; and this is not a pretty spectacle, because anything unconscious has a rather primitive and "inferior" quality, being unindividual. For this phenomenon we may aptly adopt the word "animosity", which is the characteristic result of unconscious identification with the anima or animus.

The animus-dominated woman is often oblivious to the fact that the arguments which come out of her mouth, and the apparently knowledgeable but often dogmatic opinions which govern her mind, have not been earned by her own reflection, but in fact are borrowed; and they are usually promulgated not for the sake of truth, but simply in order that she may know better. She will walk about with a gigantic chip on her shoulder and a secret conviction that all men are out to dominate her, never realising that she is in reality held in domination by the unconscious man within herself; therefore she feels she must prove her superiority to men first. This is in no way the same as the woman who is truly seeking understanding and development of the mind; there is an immense difference in the aura that each emanates, and the former can usually be recognised not only by the curiously clichéd quality of her arguments but by the fact that every man in the room bristles at her approach. The anima-possessed man, unconscious of his unpleasant moodiness, compulsiveness, personal vanity and touchiness, will walk about spreading a cloud of poisonous atmosphere; he displays a peculiar waspishness and pettiness, an indirectness, a weakness in the face of conflict, and a manipulativeness which is downright slippery and immediately inspires mistrust in women. He is secretly convinced that he must wheedle what he wants from others, and loses his natural honesty as a result. Or he may spread a delicate patina of glamour over everything he says and does so that one is left with the distinct impression that he is always on stage, performing a part, rather than relating to individuals.

As the animus is partial to argument, he can best be seen at work in disputes where both parties know they are right. Men can argue in a very womanish way, too, when they are anima-possessed and have thus been transformed into the animus of their own anima. With them the question becomes one of personal vanity and touchiness (as if they were females); with women it is a question of *power*, whether of truth or justice or some other "ism" — for the dressmaker and hairdresser have already taken care of their vanity.[1]

It is not only a denial of the human psyche's movement towards wholeness to refuse conscious acknowledgment of the anima and animus; it is also usually highly destructive to personal relationships.

… When animus and anima meet, the animus draws his sword of power and the anima ejects her poison of illusion and seduction.[2]

Whereas the cloud of "animosity" surrounding the man is composed chiefly of sentimentality and resentment, in woman it expresses itself in the form of opinionated views, interpretations, insinuations, and misconstructions, which all have the purpose (sometimes attained) of severing the relationship between two human beings.[3]

In every human relationship, as many writers have pointed out, there are not merely two people; there are four. The conscious ego of the man, and the conscious ego of the woman, appear to be the participants; and there are the two inner partners as well. One cannot make too much effort to be observant of the subtle change which occurs when these archetypes invade consciousness, which almost always occurs in the throes of powerful emotion. Were it not so embarrassing, one would do well to carry about a small tape recorder so that one could listen to oneself during an argument and hear the voice of the unconscious. Anima and animus would scarcely remain abstract concepts after a few minutes' replay. Rather than assume that these archetypes

1 *Aion.*
2 *Ibid.*
3 *Ibid.*

are mere theory and that one is always in control of one's words and actions, it is probably wise to treat these unconscious figures with the respect they deserve, as autonomous entities co-existent with us and living inside the same skin; for they certainly behave that way.

Like the shadow, the anima and animus are frequently first perceived as images in dreams and fantasies. They remain free, autonomous, and outside the individual's control, for they are part of the natural life of the unconscious psyche and can never wholly be subordinated to the ego's wishes. In fact, the reverse is closer to the truth, for the ego is the object and the unconscious, personified by animus or anima, the subject. Like living physical partners, these two archetypes cannot be dominated without incurring severe consequences of unconscious sabotage; and they require our cooperation in their demand for conscious recognition as well as some humility on the part of the ego.

> Both of them are unconscious powers, "gods", in fact, as the ancient world quite rightly conceived them to be. To call them by this name is to give them that central position in the scale of psychological values which has always been theirs whether consciously acknowledged or not; for their power grows in proportion to the degree that they remain unconscious. Those who do not see them are in their hands ... [1]

Only by the effort of recognising these figures can a real inner union within the individual take place, so that he can express both sides of his psyche in a creative way.

> ... the integration of the shadow, or the realisation of the personal unconscious, marks the first stage of the analytical process, and ... without it a recognition of anima and animus is impossible. The shadow can be realised only through a relation to a partner, and anima and animus only through a relation to a partner of the

1 *Aion.*

opposite sex, because only in such a relation do their
projections become operative.[1]

Relationships which contain any element of "falling in
love" inevitably contain anima and animus projections; and
the curious feeling of familiarity one has about the loved one
is only too explicable by the fact that one has, in actuality,
fallen in love with oneself. What distinguishes it from
narcissism is that the "beloved" is not one's conscious ego,
but an aspect of the unconscious self. The sense of familiarity
has often been explained by reincarnation. Such relationships, it is suggested, are a continuation of some encounter
begun in another life, from which the recognition of the
loved one derives. This argument is not necessarily
irreconcilable with what we have said about the anima and
animus; for we do not really know the true nature of those
images, nor from what primordial roots they spring.
Reincarnation notwithstanding, however, projection is most
certainly involved in "love at first sight", though this does not
mean that such projections are harmful or negative. On the
contrary, they are a necessary catalyst for relationship, just as
relationship is a necessary catalyst for self-awareness; the
quest for the inner partner is responsible for our embrace of
life. The anima and animus are, accordingly, guides in the
deepest sense, for they connect the individual with the great
heritage of collective images and experiences which stands
behind his personal life; and they are indeed the instruments
of fate, directing us into situations which we would otherwise
undoubtedly avoid — and thereby avoid any struggle, and
any consciousness. Although we seek these inner partners
outside ourselves, they live within us and propel us into
precisely those experiences which are opposed to our
conscious desires. The anima continually seduces man into
the dark world of feeling and emotional entanglement, which
is as uncomfortable to his natural psychology as underwater
submergence is to a cat; and woman is continually being
driven by the animus into isolation, independence, and self-

1 *Aion.*

realisation, which are antithetical to her instinctual propensity to live life through personal relationships and unconscious identification with others. We may well feel at times like cursing our treacherous guides, who instead of bringing us happiness bring us instead to the edge of the precipice, and often plunge us headlong into it; yet without them there would be no growth, no joy, no understanding and nothing that warrants the word life. In the figures of animus and anima lie the deepest mystery, and it is through them that one can truly see how relationships are a path of inner development and the living embodiment of a journey to the deepest centre of one's own being.

Like other archetypal figures, the anima has a double face. This is often a real problem for a man's conscious acceptance of her value, for while the "light" side — creative, inspiring, magical — may be digestible for him, the darker and more savage side often is not. It is much easier to project the latter onto actual living women, and see them as destructive and devouring. Yet light cannot exist without darkness. The anima embodies all man's collective experience of woman, and is therefore a symbol of the archetypal feminine principle; she is connected with relatedness and with feeling, and personifies that aspect of a man's unconscious which strives towards union with others. In some respects the figure of the anima is the same for all men; one might say there is only one Woman, one essence of the feminine which can never really be articulated in words, but which possesses the same attributes for all men. It is this sameness, this collective unity, which gives anima figures like Ayesha, or even anima-type women like Marilyn Monroe, their great power and fascination.

But along with this collective face of the anima there is also a personal side. For one man the inner image may be dark, sensuous and languid; for another, it may be blonde, effervescent and innocent. The anima as a collective embodiment is also highly coloured by the individual man's experience of women, particularly his mother. So while the essence of the feminine remains the same, the inner image is different for different men. The full-bodied nymphs and goddesses portrayed by Rubens may have pleased Rubens, but for another man the slender and boyish figure of an actress like Mia Farrow is far more magnetic. One may also see physical types coming into fashion during different periods of history; the ideal image of the beautiful woman in Elizabethan, or even Victorian, times was very different from what is considered beautiful today. The Romans expressed a philosophy about this problem: *de gustibus non disputandum est*, one should not quibble about tastes. The physical qualities of the image are symbolic, and embody inner qualities which are much more difficult to articulate. If one allows physical features to speak to the heart and the intuition, they reveal the essence of the person.

In *The Symbolic Quest,* Edward Whitmont elaborates a "tentative typolological classification of 'the Feminine'", described by Toni Wolff.[1] It is an archetypal classification, and cannot be interpreted too literally; but women tend unconsciously to identify with, or embody, one of these four basic aspects of the feminine principle. And the same four images are also applicable to the anima. They are called the Mother, the Hetaira, the Amazon and the Medium. Usually one of these faces of the anima is turned upward towards the light of a man's consciousness, which draws him to that type of woman as a representative of the feminine.

The Mother is a figure full of protective, nurturing, caring qualities. Her bright face is that of home and security, comfort and forgiveness; it embodies all compassion and instinctual wisdom. Her dark face is that of the possessor, devourer and destroyer, the dark womb which draws man away from life into death. The man who has got himself fettered to this image, who cannot understand the many facets of the feminine but is bound only to this one, will usually find himself drawn to women who can indeed mother him; and he will usually struggle against the dependency, helplessness and paralysis which too much of such a relationship entails. The Hetaira is a very different kind of figure, and ancient courtesans were apt symbols of this

1 *The Symbolic Quest.*

anima image: intellectually gifted, cultured, aesthetic, devoted to the personal aspects of love and courtship, capricious, unstable, promiscuous and butterfly-like. The bright face of this image is that of feeling refined to embrace culture and love of beauty. The dark face is cold, merciless, unpredictable, deceptive and fickle, incapable of maintaining loyalty in any relationship. For a man bound to the image of the Hetaira, woman may seem like a bright butterfly, bringer of beauty and brightness and colour, but untrustworthy, changeable as the wind, unable to offer any sense of security or rootedness.

The Amazon — named after the warrior women of Greek mythology who worshipped the virgin goddess — is a strong, capable, earthy figure, efficient, supportive, practical and full of earthy wisdom. Her bright face is the capacity to cope with reality, to deal with the material world and its complexities, to offer safety and stability. Her dark face is domineering, managing, self-assertive, imprisoning, structured, dogmatic, bound to tradition and law. The man bound to the anima as Amazon may seek relationships in which his life is efficiently managed and organised for him, leaving him free to pursue his creative vision. Perceived negatively, this may amount to unobtrusive imprisonment in a state of perpetual boyhood, which permits him to do nothing for himself. The Medium, antithesis of the Amazon, is the visionary and seeress, the prophetess who can unlock the secrets of the universe. She communes with the gods, and brings spontaneity, joy, ecstasy and abandonment to the flow of the moment. Her bright face is that of the intuitive, the inspiratrice, the vessel of creative spirit; her dark face is hysteria, madness, chaos, frenzied surrender to the forces of the collective and the daemonic powers of vision and delirium. The man bound to the anima as Medium may find that he has found a muse, a catalyst to the expression of creativity and meaning in his life. Alternatively, he may find he has been sacrificed on the altar of chaos, his will and structure and need to achieve something of worth in the world distintegrating in a swirl of phantasmagoria, or in a dream-world which leads him to believe he has become the hero without having done the deed.

The qualities embodied by these four figures are aspects of the unconscious psyche of the man himself. In their totality, these figures cannot be identified with a living woman, for they are symbols; but some women are better hooks than others upon whom to project one symbol or another. The problem lies in bringing the wisdom and life inherent in these symbols to consciousness; for they are one's own, and cannot be lived out through a partner if a man is to make the real inner marriage by which he establishes a relationship with the anima. If he attempts to remain unconscious, his partner, carrying the burden of the projection, will usually — willingly or unwillingly — continue to play anima for him. Sooner or later, this will bring about some emotional entanglement which pulls him from his sleep and forces him to become conscious of the woman within him who is secretly directing his choices.

Sometimes a man will seek the anima in embodiments of the feminine that are other than human, such as mysticism (Mother Church is a good example) or artistic creation; but whether the anima is clothed in woman's form or any other, her essence remains the same. But whatever the image, a man will never find it *in toto* outside himself because no living woman can embody the mythological spectrum of opposites contained within the anima. The real woman is bound, at some time or other, to catch a cold, leave dirty laundry in the bathroom, or be caught in a bad temper with her face cream on and her hair in pins. No self-respecting anima would be seen in such a state. Many men have a curious distaste for ordinary feminine habits and biological attributes — particularly the menstrual cycle and its accompanying discomforts — because these detract from the image he is projecting upon the woman; they serve to remind him that she is human and requires a human relationship.

Even a minimal understanding of some of the more personal qualities of the anima can help a man to become more conscious of the patterns to which he adheres in relationships. The experience of anger, bitterness, recrimination and hurt when the living woman does not fulfil the unconscious expectations of the anima is so typical that it should hardly require discussion. One encounters it literally everywhere, and the resentment emanating from unconscious assumptions and expectations is like a noxious effluence which makes relationship impossible, yet which a man is apt to deny as he claims that he is *not* in a bad mood, there is *nothing* wrong, and would she please stop pestering him with her emotional demands. Perhaps only women, sensitive to such a feeling atmosphere, know how much emotional suffering comes from this kind of unspoken criticism and unvoiced disappointment. If a man cannot recognise the difference between his woman and his anima, and honour each, then he will always expect his woman to conform to the inner image — and she will inevitably fail him.

One of the attributes of the anima is her earthiness; woman, symbolically, is earth, matter, and many men therefore hold her unconsciously responsible for the care, nurturing and ordering of their material lives. Another component of the anima is feeling, and woman is thus held responsible for creating the atmosphere of loving and caring in the home, for imbuing it with the qualities of compassion, softness, sensitivity and responsiveness. These qualities are certainly aspects of the feminine principle — whether in a man or a woman — and to a greater or lesser degree they are inherent in the psychology of women. The problem, however, is the matter of degree. Archetypally and historically, woman has always served as custodian for certain values in society and for man; but however valid such custody may be in principle each woman has her own individual way of expressing it — which creates much difficulty in individual situations. It is not so much that caring and nurturing and responsiveness should not be attributed to the feminine; it is that man, seduced by the anima, has a tendency to expect them to an inordinate degree, forgetting that woman also have a masculine component which requires its own independent expression. An individual woman may not be so concerned with the material or feeling side of life, if she is an intuitive or a thinking type; although she is still woman, she may wish to have time to develop her own independent interests. This is a question of the inherent disposition of the woman. One of the many problems facing a woman striving for conscious-ness is the dichotomy between her inherent temperament and her instinctual nature. The problem is compounded by a second dichotomy, comprised of that between her resolution of the first and the projection of a man's anima upon her. There is no simple solution to this dilemma for either partner; and it is probably impossible to even approach a solution without several critical blunders. But a man can help enormously by making more conscious the qualities of the anima so that he can meet his partner halfway, and appreciate her struggle, instead of unconsciously expecting her to embody, in one frail body and in one short lifetime, the archetype of Woman in all its totality.

The animus is the archetypal image of man existent within every woman. He is the hunter, the warrior, the statesman and the intellectual, the builder on both the material and mental planes. He is powerful and full of purpose; he possesses the keys to the laws by which life functions, and the meaning behind the plan of its unfolding. He is related to mind and spirit, and personifies objectivity, will, knowledge, direction and impersonal perspective. Like the anima, he has a light and dark face; his bright side is like the sun, and brings illumination and clarity, purpose and strength, while his dark side is the destroyer, who severs relationship and brings the death of feeling and the coldness of eternal isolation. Like the anima, the animus contains both a collective and a personal component; the relationship with the father particularly will colour the latter, while the former embodies all of woman's collective experience of man throughout the ages. The animus for some women may be a powerful force of nature, like Heathcliffe; he may be brutal, virile, aggressive, lustful and omnipotent — something like a cross between Jehovah and Tarzan. Or perhaps one might cite Mary Shelley's *Frankenstein*, in which the baron and the "creature" epitomise the dual face of the animus. For other women, the intellectual or spiritual component of the animus is paramount, and she will project upon her men the qualities of vision, logic, brilliance, capacity for planning and organisation, or even spiritual wisdom and insight. The animus may even appear in plural form for many women, as a council of elders or a group of wise men. In this capacity, he also embodies the authority of society, of structure, of law.

Whitmont suggests that the animus, like the anima, may assume one of four basic forms. Each is an embodiment of the masculine principle, and he calls them the Father, the *Puer Aeternus* (Eternal Youth), the Hero and the Wise Man. While men may identify unconsciously with one of these four figures as a symbol of their particular masculine expression, women too will usually be attached to one or another as the most conscious face of the animus.

The Father is a supportive, sheltering, caring figure; because he is a man, he embodies the hierarchical social order, custom, tradition, the sanctity of the past, and the values of the family. His bright face is protective, strengthening and reassuring, and offers a woman a sense of security in the larger world in which she lives; his dark face is stifling to growth, for he keeps her a perpetual little girl by denying her right to discover her own values. A woman bound to such an animus figure will often find herself in a relationship with a man who plays father to her, shelters her, takes care of her, patronises her and expects her to obey his word as law, thus imprisoning her in constant childhood. The *Puer* is antithetical to the Father, and like his feminine counterpart, the Hetaira, he is flighty, airy, aesthetic, spirited, youthful, brilliant, and incapable of establishing loyalty or permanence in relationship. "Both Son (*puer*) and Hetaira types 'love them and leave them', but with the Eros-motivated Hetaira the greater emphasis is on the former; the *puer* is better at leaving."[1] The *puer*'s bright face is like quicksilver; he symbolises the glittering, shifting, butterfly play of the differentiated mind, and is like a spirit of the wind, bringing change and the exhilaration of flight. His dark face is cold and devoid of feeling, cruel, callous, prone to destructive criticism and the poisonous word. A woman

1 *Ibid.*

bound to this animus figure may fetter herself to just such a man — magnetic, irresponsible, childlike, scintillating, and much better at slipping out of the relationship than he is at sustaining it.

The Hero is a warrior, a creature of earth, and like his feminine counterpart, the Amazon, he strives to battle and win in the objective world. He may be the successful businessman, the influential, charismatic politician, the soldier, the statesman; his bright face offers drive, assertiveness, courage, common sense, tenacity, endurance and a powerful will. His dark face is sensuous, materialistic, insensitive, brutal, domineering, possessive, and destructive to all creative gifts and things of the spirit. A woman bound to this animus figure, if she is unable to express or recognise any other facet, may find herself involved with, and projecting upon, a man whose prime consideration in life is his position; and he, seeking power and material gain, will drag her along with him (or rather, she will allow herself to be dragged along, under the sway of the animus) because all things, including relationship, must be sacrificed to conquest. In contrast, the Wise Man, antithetical to the Hero and corresponding to the feminine Medium, is a symbol of creativity, wisdom, vision, spiritual insight and a bridge to the Mind of God. His bright face is that of the magician, the prophet who unfolds the mysteries of the larger meaning of life; his dark face is the abyss, the searing, fanatical and totally impersonal power of chaos. Bound to such an animus, a woman may allow her man to act as spiritual guru and guide, fount of wisdom and all-seeing prophet; she may expect him to live out her unborn creativity and devote her life to the service of his mundane needs so that he can proceed with his noble vision. And she may never realise that she possesses inspiration and wisdom of her own. One may cite, as a negative example of such an animus, the unconscious power within them that hypnotised Charles Manson's female followers into seeing him as a Messiah.

Through the animus, woman is plagued by the same problem that man is by the anima — the problem of unconscious assumptions and expectations, and of ensuing resentment when unspoken demands are not answered. If she lacks conscious cooperation with the unconscious man in her own psyche, a woman will expect her partner to live out her own potential, making it intolerable for him ever to fail. Obviously no living man is capable of being perpetually steadfast, courageous, decisive, successful, logical, and ready with all the answers to life's uncertainties. Occasionally he may tell a bad joke, display ignorance about something, make a bad business move, show feeling or pain, express fear or indecision, or display other annoyingly human qualities which mar the perfect animus image his partner has bestowed upon him. And while she may accept him when he lives out the bright side of her animus, she may not like it at all when he expresses the darker side of masculinity; then he becomes a bully with a crowbar, a tyrant, a cold, unfeeling beast. Alternatively a woman may feel bitter and resentful because the figure she thought was all-wise and all-powerful turns out to need her help, at which point he appears to be an abject failure. For a woman bound to the animus in this way, no relationship can be satisfactory, for he will always whisper the destructive word in her ear which severs the relationship. By doing so, he will doom her to a sterile, empty and isolated life, while one man after another confirms her secret suspicion that they are all failures.

Individuals blind to the sexual opposite within them, be they men or women, never realise that the partner they choose is chosen because he or she bears some resemblance to the anima or animus. The anger and hurt felt at the "true discovery" of the partner's failings is really anger and hurt directed at oneself; and this would become apparent, were one to see the dark figure within one's own unconscious impelling one into a particular relationship. Like always attracts like; rather than railing at the partner, one should take a long, close look at one's own psychic makeup. But it is easier to complain bitterly — to analysts, marriage counsellors, and also astrologers — that yet another relationship has collapsed and yet another partner has proved to be a bad choice. It is also fashionable to blame this on the failures of the parent of the opposite sex; but the past continues to live within a person not only because in some way it is part of his own substance, but also because he permits it to do so. When a disastrous relationship occurs once, we may fool ourselves into believing it is chance; when it occurs twice, it has become a pattern, and a pattern is an unmistakable indication that the anima or animus is at work in the unconscious, propelling the helpless ego into relationships or situations which are baffling, painful, and frighteningly repetitive. Again, it is much wiser to look within oneself for the source of the pattern, rather than at the inherent failure of the opposite sex. For these destructive patterns are the psyche's way of making itself known, although great effort is often required to fulfil its demand for transformation. And great sacrifices also are required — of such precious commodities as one's pride, one's self-image, one's self-righteousness.

* * *

Like the shadow, the anima and the animus are archetypes, "gods", and we may therefore expect to find them among the planetary pantheon. When one examines the birth horoscope for some glimpse of their signature, it is important to remember that there is no formula, no set of rules which the intellect may apply to produce a neat and tidy package. Symbols cannot be apprehended by the intellect alone. When comparing two charts, one may find that individuals are suited to each other by mutual interests, common goals, and similarity of temperament; but the two invisible partners of the quaternity, the anima and animus, still control the outcome of the relationship. Everything here depends upon how conscious one is of these inner partners, for if they work wholly in the dark, the result becomes predetermined, regardless of the individual's choice. We must always bear this in mind when we assess compatibility based on horoscopes; for though a particular planetary combination, or sign combination, between two charts may show harmony or friction, that is only a potential. It is the anima and animus which determine whether potentiality becomes actuality.

The traditional techniques of synastry are a useful lens through which to perceive the moving energies at work in a relationship. If one employs these techniques too literally, however, with too much of a structured framework, they can be worse than useless — they can be utterly misleading. One can never base one's decision to enter a relationship, or to sever one, on chart comparison alone. There is no such thing as a pair of divinely suited birth charts. Nor, probably, is there such a thing as two divinely suited human beings, except as a symbol of the inner marriage. And there is, moreover, that inexplicable X-factor, the Self, which is not mapped on the birth chart and which contains the mystery of the individual's purposeful development over his lifetime. This mysterious process may entail relationships which are not "compatible", or which involve obstacles, because of the opportunities the resulting stress provides. One should never take a difficult chart pairing as an indication that the relationship is a "bad" one, any more than harmony between charts will make it a "good" one. All the charts will show is the kind of mutual exchange which may be expected if the individual chooses to become involved. And often he does not choose at all, but is compelled through his projections and his state of "in-loveness" to jettison the best intentions in the world. Or the feeling, abruptly or slowly, may drain out of a perfectly "suitable" relationship, however nicely matched the charts happen to be; and one must then ask what the inner partner is up to, for the animus and anima are inevitably behind such inexplicable vicissitudes.

In traditional synastry, the harmonious link between the sun on one person's birth chart and the moon on the other's (usually the man's sun and the woman's moon) is considered the best indication for a happy and enduring relationship. Jung found in his analysis of married couples'charts[1] that the sextile aspect, an angle of sixty degrees, appeared most frequently between the sun of one partner and the moon of the other. Other planetary contacts, such as one person's

1 *Synchronicity: An Acausal Connecting Principle*, C.G. Jung, Routledge & Kegan Paul, London 1972.

moon to another's Venus, or one's Mars to another's moon (all, again, traditional indications of attraction and harmony) also occurred with frequency. Before we ask what this means in psychological terms, we should consider first whether the image of the inner partner, that controlling factor in all relationship choices, may be inferred from the birth chart. There are certain traditional synastry contacts: sun-moon, Venus-moon, Mars-moon, moon-moon, sun-Venus, Mars-Venus, sun-ascendant, moon-ascendant, and so on. There are also other important but inexplicable contacts which occur no less frequently in chart comparisons: sun-Saturn, moon-Saturn, Venus-Saturn, Mars-Saturn, and the sun, moon, ascendant, Venus or Mars of one person to Uranus, Neptune or Pluto on the other's chart. Each of these must first be examined in the light of the individual needs implicit in the two birth charts.

We have already seen that the unconscious compensates for consciousness. We have also seen that the anima and animus — as symbols of the unconscious forces at work within the individual and as gatekeepers between the personal and collective spheres — perform just such a compensatory function. Thus an intuitive, with a chart full of fire, will not only be likely to express his inferior sensation through the shadow, but the anima or animus may also embody some of the attributes of earth. Once freed from the shadow, they will offer these attributes as keys to the numinous experience of the Self. The sensation type, earthy and reality-oriented, may bear within him a fantastic fiery creature of vision and prophecy; the thinker, structuring his reality according to his conceptual framework, may be bound to an inner partner who embodies the fluid, shifting, magical, unpredictable and irrational depths of water; and the feeling type, living through personal relationships and evaluating experience through subjective human values, may house a clear, cold, impersonal, objective winged spirit of air. This is an oversimplification — as every attempt at describing the anima and animus must be — but the inherent temperament bias of the individual chart will often provide an intimation of the invisible creature which embodies one's unconscious life. One may in fact take the fourfold images of anima and animus and suggest that they bear some relation to the four elements, although one must be careful not to be too literal. The Mother, as anima figure, is a watery creature; she is most often the image haunting the airy, thinking man. The Hetaira, an airy creature, is most often the unconscious feminine image of the watery, feeling-oriented man. The Amazon, a creature of earth, may dominate the fantasies of the intuitive man; and the Medium, an embodiment of intuitive fire, is the typical Muse of the earthbound sensation-oriented man. Likewise the Father, who is watery, belongs to the airy woman; the *Puer*, who is airy, belongs to the maternal, watery type of woman; the Hero, who is earthy, belongs to the intuitive woman, and the Wise Man, who is fiery, belongs to the hard-working sensation woman. Again, these are oversimplifications; but they should provide some food for thought and individual investigation.

The feminine planets on a man's chart, and the masculine planets on a woman's, also point to the image of the inner partner. One cannot be bound by rules here, for there are always exceptions, but transsexual planets often provide a basis for further insight. This is particularly true of the moon and Venus in a man's chart, and of the sun and Mars in a woman's. Perhaps that is why the traditional combinations of sun-moon and Venus-Mars are considered "good" auguries in a relationship; for in these cases the unconscious inner image of one partner is matched by some quality in the other. If a man has the moon in Scorpio, and if other components in his chart conspire to suggest that his anima image is one of deep feeling, passion, mystery and darkness, he will find a much more suitable hook in a woman with Scorpio — and to a lesser extent, the other two water signs, Cancer and Pisces — dominant in her horoscope than he will in an airy, fiery or earthy woman. Whether this is really "good" or "bad" is a moot point; it can be either, for the woman who happily and unthinkingly carries her man's projection for a lifetime will certainly contribute to a more stable marriage. At the same time, however, that stability may stifle the possibility of his cultivating in himself the qualities of his anima; and it will also retard his wife's own maturation. On the other hand, for people who are creatively *working with* their relationship as a means for self-discovery, such a woman may be a catalyst, because she can understand her man's inner partner seeking release through conscious development. Once again, everything depends not on the charts, but on the individuals and what they do with the resources at their disposal. Marriages involving congenial combinations tend to last because they are easier. A struggle for consciousness, on the other hand, is never easy, and may be facilitated by a little conflict between charts and a little healthy resistance from an angry partner.

Uranus, and to a lesser extent Jupiter, must also be considered as symbols of masculine energy, while Neptune and Pluto must be considered as symbols of feminine energy. These planets are also implicated in chart comparisons, but because Uranus, Neptune and Pluto are transpersonal planets they are all more difficult to deal with even though they often promote greater growth. Some people are especially "prone" to combinations involving these planets. Uranus is the dynamic wind, the numinous power which rends the veil of apparent mundane reality and exposes the world of Divine Mind. Jupiter is the prophet, the intuitive seer, the spiritual guide who vouchsafes a glimpse of meaning and wholeness. On the feminine side, Neptune is the mermaid, the melusine, who draws a man down into the depths of the ocean of collective feeling; and Pluto is the inexorable, dark, devouring mother who gives the gift of life and then draws a man into the womb of sleep, death and rebirth. These planets are connected with the collective side of the anima and animus, while the personal planets — sun, moon, Venus and Mars — are more connected with the personal side, coloured by personal experience.

Saturn and Mercury have not yet been mentioned. This is not because they are insignificant but because they are often overlooked or underestimated in the area of chart comparison, and also because they both seem to possess an androgynous quality. In consequence they are not so much anima or animus figures as they are symbols of synthesis and integration. In alchemy, Saturn is the old king, the ancient

Mercurius (Mercurius Senex) who must be reborn as the youthful Mercurius through the transmutation process of the alchemical work. Through darkness, struggle and pain come understanding and light. Saturn, particularly, is important, both in chart comparisons, and on the individual chart (when one is seeking some indication of the anima or animus image). He implies that, through relationship, an awareness of all that is base and shadowy in the personality may be brought into the light and have its wisdom made available. In this way the door to the inner partner is opened.

Certain combinations of planets within the individual chart will suggest certain aspects of the anima or animus image. The moon in conjunction with Pluto, for example, brings together the personal image of the mother — caring, nurturing, responsive — with the collective archetype of the Dark Mother — possessive, destructive, devouring, transforming. When this conjunction is found on a man's chart, it suggests that, as he brings the personal elements of the anima into consciousness, he will bring up the collective as well; and he may be attracted to women who embody the dark, archaic, primitive and potentially destructive qualities of Scorpio and its ruler, Pluto. Such a man may find that his associations with women — beginning with his mother — strike to the very roots of his being. They will always threaten to submerge him yet always serve as means through which his own feeling nature can die and be reborn into a greater awareness of relationship values. He may be terrified of women because of the dark figure lurking within his own psyche, yet he will inevitably be drawn to women who embody that very archetype. Venus and Pluto found together on a man's chart is a similar configuration; the image of woman as ideal companion is linked with the archetype of the Dark Mother, and the powerfully erotic qualities of the figure may permeate his fantasies. The moon and Neptune together, as another example, will suggest a very different quality: the image of the personal mother is coupled with that of the martyr, the mystic, the seeress, the redeemer. A man with this combination on his chart may seek, through a woman who embodies Neptune-Pisces qualities, to lose and dissolve himself in the sea of his feeling. He may even be attracted to women who, because of their helplessness or suffering, allow him to make a sacrifice of himself. The moon or Venus in connection with Saturn suggests that the image of woman is heavily contaminated by the man's own shadow, so that he may project power, control and imprisonment upon the opposite sex. Here is the true "marriage" of anima and shadow. It may engender in a man a need to protect himself and control those whom he feels threaten him, and this will interfere with his creative gifts, making him use them and his feeling responses to further his will to power. Because he will not permit himself to be vulnerable enough to relate, such a man will inevitably suffer disappointment through relationships, until he learns to take back his projections.

A woman possessing the sun or Mars in combination with Uranus on the birth chart may have her personal experience of man linked with the archetype of the magician, the spiritual wind; and her inner image of man will then be coloured by the image of the destroyer, the shatterer of illusions, the awakener. She may find herself in relationships which perform the function of this dual figure — the man, and the fashion in which she interacts with him, serves (often unwittingly) to shake her, wake her up, open her eyes, and shatter identification with her feeling values, frequently through the shattering of the relationship itself.

The transpersonal planets, when they are connected with the moon and Venus on a man's chart or the sun and Mars on a woman's, suggest that the individual needs to bring personal relationships into a broader, more transpersonal sphere — a sphere in which the less individualised archetypes have more room to express themselves. In such a sphere, they can perform their integrating function; but if confined to the circumscribed perimeter of the personal, they will be suffocated, and by their demand for air, constitute a disruptive influence. Relationships for people with such planetary contacts need to be almost mythological; they must contain turbulence and crises and deaths and rebirths, and they must always serve the growth of the total psyche, rather than the contentment of the ego. Such an individual must recognise the drive within him to seek something larger and deeper than mere compatibility and ease in marriage. Union, for him, is often a real inner journey of a dramatic kind, punctuated by dramatic climaxes, disappointments and pain, but always leading to the centre. It is not for everyone to seek this kind of relationship; but if the chart reflects the need, it is better to know about it than to be surprised when the crises erupt and to blame them on the other person.

The signs in which the four "relationship" planets — sun, moon, Venus and Mars — are placed, coupled with the contacts they make to other planets, are important clues to understanding the unconscious drives within the individual that shape his relationship patterns. Such planetary patterns must always be taken together with one's inherent disposition and primary functions of consciousness. Most often these two factors will concur, or complement each other. Sometimes, however, they will conflict. Once again, no definitive formula exists. One must learn something about the person in order to discover how apparent contradictions will be expressed through relationships.

In addition to what we have already discussed, we must also consider the sign which falls at the descendant of the chart, and any planets which fall in the seventh house. These too will suggest some qualities which are linked with the anima or animus image, which are sought in the partner yet which belong to the individual himself. Some explanation of the meaning of the chart's ascendant-descendant axis is necessary here.

The axis of the horizon, which forms the ascendant and descendant of the birth chart, is the division of the night sky from the day sky, and marks the point where the earth meets the heavens; it symbolises the individual himself as he expresses in an earthy body, to an earthy environment. The ascendant (or rising sign) is at the eastern point of the chart. It is that sign which was emerging over the eastern horizon at the moment of birth; and it is like the doorway to the house within, peopled by the various planets in their combinations of patterns. This sign is the key to the relationship between the individual and his environment, just as the sun is the key to his essence, his path in life. The ascendant is the door, the gateway, the window through which the individual looks out at the world and through which the world, in turn, looks at him. All that he sees is coloured by the viewpoint symbolised by the sign at the ascendant. Like attracts like and the inner reflects the outer. Thus, the circumstances in the environment, and confrontations with it which shape an individual's personality, are attracted into his life — or he is attracted to them — by the creative power of his own psyche, synchronising with what is "out there". That psyche, as well as what it attracts, will be embodied by the sign which stands at the gateway. The viewpoint towards life, symbolised by the ascending sign, is shaped by the kind of life the individual experiences; and in turn the kind of life he experiences is attracted by his own substance, his own inner viewpoint, which is once again symbolised by the ascending sign. Outer and inner worlds are thus images of each other.

Anyone familiar with basic astrology will know that the ascendant is usually much more obvious in the individual's behaviour, and in his way of relating to others as a conscious individual, than the sun-sign. But everything in the birth chart has its opposite, and no sign can be evaluated without consideration of the opposite sign which is both its antithesis and its other half. The descendant, which is at the western point of the chart, at the opposite pole of the horizon, is always opposite in sign to the ascendant. In traditional astrology, this point is called the cusp of the house of marriage, and is said to signify those qualities which the individual seeks in a partner, as opposed to the qualities inherent in his own personality expressed by the ascendant. In fact, the descendant, rather than denoting "qualities desired in a partner", suggests those qualities which are unconscious within the individual, obverse of the things with which he identifies, yet necessary to create a whole and balanced perspective through which he can express himself to others. And these qualities symbolised by the descending sign, because they are unconscious, are usually projected. It would be more fitting to say that they belong to the inner partner, rather than to the outer one. The descendant is the unconscious underside of the ascendant; and it is often helpful to remember that the zodiac is really made up of six signs, each containing a pair of opposites unified into one basic experience or axis of energy. Both poles of this axis must be integrated, although one is often inimical to consciousness — which can usually only see one thing at a time.

It is perhaps helpful to review the basic qualities of the six pairs of astrological signs, in order to derive some insight into the meaning of the descendant.

The creative, self-assertive, self-centred individual (Aries) seeks to become aware of others, and to develop a capacity for objective cooperation with them in relationships (Libra); the rational and reasonable individual, adept at compromise and cooperation (Libra) seeks to develop a capacity for initiative, self-assertion, and independence (Aries).

The earthy, realistic individual, accepting the evidence of his senses and building stability through the simplicity of his values (Taurus) seeks to experience the subtle world of feeling which will allow him to penetrate beneath the surface of things and gain an understanding of unconscious motive (Scorpio); the intense and emotional individual, adept at seeing beneath the surface and caught up in the complexities of the under-world of feeling currents (Scorpio) seeks the peace and stability which stems from a realistic relationship with the world and a simplifying of values (Taurus).

The inquisitive, intellectually attuned individual, adept at recognising facts and differentiating information through categorisation (Gemini) seeks to understand the intuitive connections and associations between facts which can weld them into a meaningful whole (Sagittarius); the intuitive and broad-minded individual, with a sense of the overall meaning and pattern of life (Sagittarius) seeks to understand the specific ideas and facts which will enable him to communicate his vision in understandable terms to others (Gemini).

The sensitive, fluid, responsive, instinctual, feeling-oriented individual, easily influenced by others and living through them (Cancer), seeks the structure and self-sustenance and self-motivation which is the fruit of individual effort (Capricorn); the disciplined and self-motivated individual, capable of mastering the environment through harnessing of energy (Capricorn) seeks the warmth and security of human relationships and intimate feeling exchange (Cancer).

The creative individual, intent on developing his own uniqueness and creative power (Leo), seeks to become aware of the larger human family of which he is a part, so that he may offer his creative gifts with an objective understanding of their value to others (Aquarius); the group-conscious man, aware of the importance of the needs of others around him (Aquarius), seeks to develop a sense of his own value and creativity so that he has something of his own to offer (Leo).

The discriminating and refined individual, adept at craftsmanship and motivated by a quest for truth and purity and self-refinement (Virgo) seeks the sympathy and compassion and feeling for the unity of life which will allow him to offer his services through love rather than through duty (Pisces); the compassionate and understanding and imaginative individual, sensitive to the needs of others and gifted with a flow of creative ideas (Pisces) seeks to develop the discipline, skill and discrimination which will allow him to offer service in a practical and truly helpful way (Virgo).

This basic astrological principle may be applied to the sign which falls on the descendant, which provides a clue about the qualities the individual seeks in relationships because he is seeking to develop them within himself. And the descendant must also be considered in combination with the balance of elements in the chart as a whole, as well as with particular combinations of planets which indicate the anima and animus images in the individual psyche.

A planet falling in the seventh house — that area of the chart which follows the descendant moving in a counter-clockwise direction — is also traditionally associated with qualities sought in a partner. Here too it would be more accurate to say that these qualities, symbolised by the planet, belong to the individual, but are unconscious and embodied in the image of the inner partner. One usually attempts to live out a seventh house planet through the partner, or through the kinds of experiences the relationship brings — but this attempt must be made conscious if it is to be utilised in a cooperative and creative way. Seventh house planets are usually most influential when they are transpersonal, because transpersonal planets — Uranus, Neptune and Pluto — are generally unconscious anyway. It is terribly common for a person with one of these strange planets in the "house of marriage" to encounter disruption, crisis, disillusionment, and awakening through union. But he will generally assume it is emanating from "outside" himself, from the external partner, rather than realising that it is the inner partner who attracts certain experiences into his life. If he blames his Uranian partner for being cold, unfeeling and indifferent to the relationship, or his Neptunian partner for being deceptive and conducive to disillusionment, or his Plutonian partner for being power-driven, possessive and inimical to his emotional freedom, he had better look to himself to discover whom he is really talking about. Planets placed in the seventh house do not depict the marriage partner; they depict how the individual sees the partner, because he is projecting his own inner transsexual image and unwittingly precipitating his experiences himself. He may choose a good "hook" — a person who reflects the appropriate planet in his or her own birth chart in a prominent way — but what he incurs through the partner is his own, and his own unconscious choice.

Thou shalt not ask, "Why does this always happen to me?", for deep down thou knowest that thou invitest it, whatever it may be.[1]

There are many volumes published on traditional horoscope comparison, and these are useful in a general way for understanding the effects of particular planets in combination. But no method of chart comparison can tell a person whether he should or should not be in a relationship, or whether it will last. This cannot be overemphasised. A tremendous amount of damage has been done through the popular assumption that decisions can be made by the birth chart — damage to both astrology and to individuals. The charts of two people, analysed through synastry, can only suggest *why* a relationship has come into being, what the energy factors are at work within it, but no more. Once again, the fate of the relationship does not reside with the planets; it resides with the individuals, and in their relationships to their own inner partners. Only when a person has some awareness of the invisible mate can he look with any objectivity at the visible one, and apply any information the charts yield in a constructive way. The inner work must be done first, perhaps with the aid and understanding of the partner but always with a true recognition of where responsibility really lies. Only then is it possible to use the chart to shed light on factors like difference in thinking processes and modes of communication, difference in feeling values, difference in tastes, harmony of temperament or of interest, and other spheres of human interchange.

*   *   *

An example may be helpful here. There are four charts reproduced below, those of a woman and three men with whom she became deeply involved at different times in her life. It may be said that these three relationships were, to a large extent, the work of the animus. Whether this implies

1 *Below the Belt*, Beata Bishop & Pat McNeil, Coventure, London 1977.

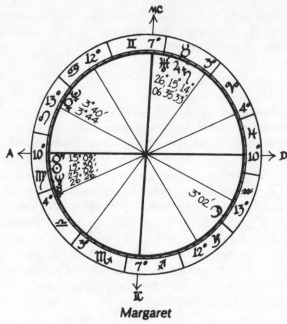

Margaret

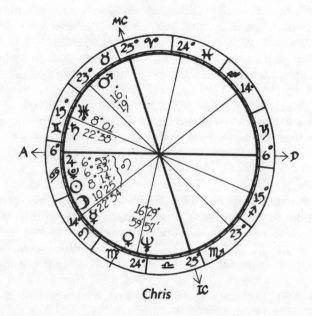

Chris

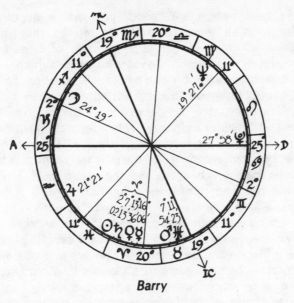

Barry

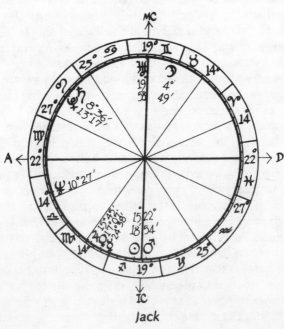

Jack

that the relationships are "good" or "bad" is a pointless question, for all three relationships offered the woman something of value in her understanding of herself and others; and to that extent, they are all valid. Whether they might have lasted or not is also a pointless question, for one simply cannot know; and durability is not necessarily a gauge of anything relevant to our discussion. In the end, the inner partner and the outer are not really two separate realities; for if one pursues things far enough, there is no inside and outside, only the experience of the psyche — which is both. The inner partner changes, and the outer must as well; otherwise the time comes when the inner seeks a different outer reflection. We are so much a part of each other, so much bound up with the psyches of one another, that self-awareness is like trying to interpret a dream; the "other" people in the dream are other, but they are also oneself.

Margaret's chart is predominantly earthy. She is true to her element, a sensation type, with a strong thinking function and a basic approach to life's exigencies which is traditionally characteristic of a Virgo-Aquarius combination: she must dissect, analyse, and understand the logic of things in order to relate to them. This applies to people as well as to her work, her views and her hierarchy of values.

Margaret was an adopted child, and never knew anything about her real parents. She was raised in a devoutly Catholic home, amid an atmosphere virtually devoid of love and understanding; she remembered her foster-mother, who died when she was ten, as an aloof, withdrawn woman whose prolonged illness culminated in death before Margaret had a chance to really know her. Being a very physically oriented child, Margaret craved open demonstration of affection, and was left with only her foster-father to provide it; and he, although basically a kindly man and a powerful influence on her attitudes, was bound by religious scruples and constantly disapproved of her. She deeply needed him, but his attitude towards her was one of anger, rejection, rebuff and criticism. The more she tried to please him, the more she inadvertently did the very things that provoked his wrath. Left with no real understanding or closeness from either parent, yet with the sensuous and affectionate disposition of the typical sensation-oriented child, she developed a deep sense of inadequacy. This was aggravated by her Catholic conscience to the point where she did not believe she deserved anything from life except punishment.

She married twice, and both marriages were failures. The first was contracted when she was seventeen, and resulted in the birth of a daughter. Her husband, however, was violent and subject to psychotic episodes, and eventually she left him, taking the child with her. The second marriage lasted longer, and brought her a son; but here too communication broke down. Margaret's insistent need for attention and affection, directed towards the remote and introverted intuitive temperament of her second husband, made her seem demanding and overbearing. The more affection she craved, the more he withdrew. And although the marriage ended amicably, the cumulative effect of this second failure imposed a heavy burden on Margaret's deeply rooted sense of personal inadequacy. After her first marriage, Margaret had undergone some psychotherapy which she had sought because of sexual inhibitions and an apparent tendency towards both emotional and physical masochism. Although she benefited from it, and was subsequently able to work through many of her anxieties, the more profound sense of failure and lack of self-worth persisted.

When she was twenty-nine, Margaret, together with her two children, moved from Chicago, where she had been born, to New York, determined to begin a new life for herself. She had excellent office skills and a quick and versatile mind, and easily found work as a well-paid secretary. The only problem was that she immediately became emotionally involved with whomever her employer happened to be. This pattern had really been inaugurated by a personal involvement with her psychotherapist — which promptly brought about the termination of the therapy. Subsequently it extended to the various men for whom she worked both in Chicago and New York. She had a fascination for successful men in roles of authority. While involved with a partner of this kind, her work output was excellent and she always managed to attain positions of responsibility. She also, at these times, felt that her life held some meaning. But unless such an involvement existed, she did not enjoy her work, and found it and her life meaningless. In short, her only object seemed to be one of fulfilling a fantasy of a powerful, successful father-lover who could bring the best out of her through his approval and need of her support. Left to her own devices, she had not yet begun to even remotely tap her own creative potential.

Some six months after her move to New York, she met Chris, the creator of a highly original advertising agency. Margaret took a job with him, and immediately fell into her pattern of passionate emotional attachment. Like the other men with whom she had become involved, Chris, whose chart is shown above, was a successful, creative, intuitive man with a highly volatile temperament and neither the interest nor the capacity to become the loving father-figure of Margaret's fantasies. Her relationship with him, which endured for seven years and caused her both considerable pain and considerable growth, was punctuated by a desperate need to be accepted — for which she was willing, over and over again, to submerge her own identity, as well as to accept insults and rejections in exchange for the brief cyclical periods of interest which Chris displayed towards her. She worked faithfully for him, not only as secretary but also as laundry girl, romantic advisor, and personal agent; she took care of all the practical arrangements of both his business and personal life. But he, although he came to rely on her efficiency and loyalty, had no intention of limiting himself to one woman. She suffered his many romantic episodes stoically, telling herself she did not mind, while her self-confidence ebbed lower and lower. Nothing seemed important, vital or alive for her save Chris and Chris' company. To compensate for his defections, she took on more and more responsibility; she began to take drugs as well, which dulled the pain she would have had to face in her wholly one-sided and largely fantasy-dominated liaison. That there was no possibility of a real match with Chris, she knew; he was already married, although estranged from his wife, and had no intention of marrying again. Yet something in her doggedly clung to the daydream, hoping and waiting for some magical transformation to occur. This powerful unconscious expectation drove Chris to periodic displays of overt, albeit unconscious, emotional cruelty, simply to dispel the oppressiveness of her unspoken demands. He can hardly be blamed for this cruelty. Despite emotional problems of his own, he never pretended to be other than he was, and it was the fantasy Margaret projected onto him which kept her from seeing him and accepting him as himself.

During the period of this relationship, Margaret had numerous "crushes" and brief romantic episodes; but she could never manage to pry herself loose from Chris, or break the power he wielded over her by virtue of her own projection. Eventually she became involved with Barry, another highly successful and creative advertising man; but this affair backed her into the same corner. Barry, too, was married, with no intention of leaving his wife; and although he enjoyed her company and his friendship with her, he was not prepared to play full-time the role of devoted and constant father-lover; he merely wanted to have fun with her. She handled this relationship better than the one with Chris, largely because Chris still commanded her real emotional commitment. Thus she was more able to let Barry be himself, and to enjoy him on his terms. However, she was still hurt by what she interpreted as his neglect; he did not offer the perpetual emotional security and reassurance she so desperately needed. Eventually, the associations with both Barry and Chris developed into genuine friendships. But the pain which Margaret endured in learning to allow these men to be themselves without taking their behaviour as a personal affront was, at times, almost unbearable.

Jack, whose chart is the fourth one shown above, was the owner of a highly successful promotion agency which handled touring rock groups. Once again Margaret found herself infatuated by a volatile, creative, dynamic and unstable intuitive type who was not prepared to provide her with the emotional reassurance she wanted. Margaret's relationship with Jack, which occurred when she was thirty-three, proved very explosive and very brief. She destroyed it by reacting violently with highly charged emotional scenes to what she deemed Jack's faithlessness and rejection of her. Like a typical intuitive, he was not able to tell her where he was, and with whom, at all times. Over and over again she found herself attracted to this type of man, frequently falling in love before she even knew the individual, reacting first to his position and the glamour surrounding it. She would then fantasise about the wonderful secure relationship which would ensue, and the compliment to her which being loved by such a man would constitute. And she would never recognise that such a man cannot bear a cage built round him, and will inevitably kick against the pressure of powerful unconscious projections. These three relationships were three among many, and the others, some longer and some shorter in duration, were invariably with the same type of man; they also invariably left Margaret feeling hurt, rejected and betrayed.

Margaret tried to approach these relationships through her main functions of consciousness, sensation and thinking; she placed great emphasis on the sexual side of the relationship, not realising that to an intuitive the sexual act is an adventure rather than a commitment, and inadequate glue to constitute a bond. She also tried to analyse the behaviour and the motives of each man, working out a plan of approach — what to say and how to say it. In doing so, she forgot that her feelings and her intuition — both unconscious and "undiffer-entiated" functions — would have told her the truth a lot more quickly, both about the possibilities of the relationship and about the real character of the man. What her definitive, inflexible schematic idea did was deny each of her partners the right to be unpredictable. And she could not offer adequate recompense for what she demanded. She could provide intellectual stimulation, a quick and biting wit, an attractive aloofness and a flattering sensuality; but without the feeling component, she could not elicit a deeper response, and was left feeling isolated. It was only after she ceased to be in love that she could begin to become a friend. Then men could accept, with respect and affection, her fine

mind and her natural integrity, without the feeling that she
might exact some inexorable commitment in return.
Although commitment was the last word to pass Margaret's
lips, the unconscious and unspoken wish made itself felt.

At thirty-six, Margaret has come to an understanding of
many of these patterns, and is beginning to consciously
develop the masculine side of her nature more fully. She is
interested in her work, has more creative energy to put into
it, and is beginning to live out for herself the creative
potential which first drew her to her lovers. But these three
relationships are a typical pattern of animus projection, and
it will be valuable to explore the chart patterns to see the
process at work in astrological symbolism.

Because of the overwhelming predominance of earth — a
total of seven planets, plus the ascendant and midheaven fall
in earthy signs — the prominence of the sensation function is
to be expected. This chart is an unusually clear example of a
psychological type. The moon in Aquarius, although the only
planet in air, is important because of its significance in
women's charts. Here it reflects the importance of thinking as
the second function of consciousness: Margaret© natural
mode of evaluating life situations is to analyse them and seek
the logical pattern in them. The element of fire, reflected by
the exact Venus-Pluto conjunction, is functioning largely
unconsciously. Inferior intuition first colours the shadow —
which in Margaret has the characteristics of an exhibitionistic
and attention-seeking child — and then to the animus, who
embodies the Leonine qualities of uniqueness, creative
vision, lordliness, self-confidence, grandeur, success and
glamour. Although both feminine planets, Venus and Pluto
pertain in this case to the animus figure, suggesting the
attributes of aestheticism, love of beauty, involvement with
the arts, intensity, power and compulsiveness. Margaret's
animus is aptly figured by the conjunction; and it is not
coincidental that both her husbands, as well as the three men
whose charts are shown here, are all born under fire signs.
Her first husband was an Aries, her second a Sagittarius; Chris
is a Leo with five planets in Leo, Barry an Aries with four
planets in Aries and the moon in Sagittarius, and Jack another

Sagittarius with four planets in fire. These men are all excellent hooks for the projection of the animus figure which Margaret unconsciously hoped would provide her life with meaning, creative vision, life, adventure and excitement. As she gradually discovers that these qualities in fact exist within her, she can overcome the heavy, ponderous feeling of so much earth and learn to simply relax and have fun — a capacity which all these men possess in the extreme, and which she has exhibited hardly at all.

Because there is no water on Margaret's chart, feeling is likely to be an inferior function. Like many people with this deficiency, Margaret was subject to compulsive and over-whelming emotions, which periodically possessed her, hurling her into terrible fits of depression and self-destructiveness. She was never really able to listen to her feelings; instead she decided analytically what she thought she ought to feel, failing to realise that one cannot impose such mandates on the living psyche with impunity. Various psychosomatic illnesses — compulsive eating and drinking and strong attraction to drugs, as well as acute moodiness — stemmed from this violation of the feeling function. Early in life, Margaret had learned to suppress her feelings; the unsympathetic and disapproving atmosphere of her child-hood reinforced her natural inclination to emotional repression (reflected by the Aquarian moon in opposition to Pluto) and dissociated her almost completely from a conscious awareness of her feeling nature. Although capable of deep devotion — primarily expressed towards her children — she could not express her feelings spontaneously to her men; she was always inhibited and calculated in her responses.

Further clues about Margaret's animus figure are provided by the conjunction of the sun with Mars on the one side and Neptune on the other. The former suggests drive, will and self-determination; the latter suggests imaginativeness, creativity and instability. The animus is thus not only a figure endowed with power and prominence; he is also a mystic, an artist and a visionary. Margaret was consistently attracted to highly creative men, while remaining ignorant of her own creative potential reflected by the sun-Neptune contact.

The sign on Margaret's descendant — Pisces — suggests once again the imaginative, sensitive, visionary quality which so attracted her in men. Sometimes her partners displayed distinctly effeminate traits, or obvious bisexuality; sometimes they were deeply involved with drugs of one kind or another. The peculiar aura of Neptune colours her animus image, and sounds the silent note of her own unconscious disposition: efficient, organised, practical and discriminating on the surface but dreamy, helpless, vague, romantic, imaginative, vulnerable underneath, longing for self-immersion in the life of another. This unconscious side of Margaret's personality inevitably expressed itself in her relationships as her complete abnegation of her own wishes and feelings; but the objects of her devotion were unfortunately incapable of appreciating it (and through no fault of theirs). In accordance with the early pattern established by her father-relationship, Margaret tried to make real the fantasy of the strong and loving parent she had never had; she constantly sought approval and affection but found instead only rejection and rebuff. At the same time her Catholicism, although consciously abandoned, had struck roots deep within her, as suggested by Saturn placed in the house of religious attitudes (the ninth). Her animus, therefore, was not only a poet and a successful businessman; he was also the God who punishes and the Christ who suffers. Margaret was deeply attracted to men whom she felt needed salvaging in some manner, despite their success; she hoped to organise their lives in an earthy way so that she would be indispensable to them.

The contacts between Margaret's chart and those of the three men are not what would be considered, in traditional astrology, happy links. Although some of the traditional aspects of harmonious union are shown between her chart and Chris' — her Mars is conjunct his Venus, they have a mutual sun-Venus conjunction, his Mars is in trine to her Venus — the presence of numerous Saturn contacts suggests that this is a relationship of struggle and growth rather than one of ease. Margaret's Saturn falls on Chris' Mars, a contact

which tends to reflect rejection and hurt in the Saturn partner
and anger and frustration in the Mars partner; moreover, her
Saturn is in square to his sun and moon. In short, she felt
threatened and inadequate in the face of so much shining
Leo spontaneity, and became aloof and critical; this made
him feel restricted, incapable of relaxation in her company.
Despite the sexual attraction suggested by the Mars-Venus
exchanges, each irritated the other and both were always on
the defensive. Chris' Saturn is square to Margaret's sun; when
they were together, she could not relax either, because her
need for order, structure and literal explanations —
suggested by the Virgo emphasis — threatened his need
(reflected by his twelfth house Saturn in Gemini) for
evasiveness, solitude and self-concealment. The hook for the
fiery qualities of the animus appears to have been the
stellium (or grouping) of planets in Leo; the impetus for the
father-projection is indicated by Margaret's Saturn, which
implies a desperate need for security and stability yet
functions, in true shadow-fashion, as a drive to control.

The contacts between Margaret's and Barry's charts are not
so difficult, but they are similar. Once again, there is a Mars-
Saturn tie, Barry's Mars on Margaret's Saturn; his Sagittarian
moon is in square to her Virgo planets, and he irritated her
with his need for freedom and his unpredictability. She in
turn annoyed him with her need for precise, methodical
structuring of time and personality. Her sun is trine his
ascendant, a more harmonious tie, suggesting that the inner
man within her shares his ambitions and understands his
drive for success (Capricorn on the ascendant); and once
again the hook here is fire, for her Venus-Pluto conjunction is
closely in trine to his sun-Saturn conjunction in Aries.
Because the Saturn contacts are not so difficult here, the
relationship was not a deeply painful one, and there was a
good deal of mutual affection and enjoyment in it. Yet it was
also less productive in terms of Margaret's quest for self-
understanding.

Between Margaret's and Jack's charts the contacts are
again quite difficult. Again we see the Saturn pattern, where
his Venus-Jupiter conjunction in Scorpio falls opposite her

Saturn. There is another sun-ascendant contact, a conjunction this time, again suggesting that Margaret, through her animus, can share and appreciate (and perhaps live out through him) Jack's desire for material success. The sun in a woman's chart is one of the main contributors to the animus image, and here an effective hook is provided by the meticulous, thorough and expeditious way in which Jack pursued his career. But the dominant note is again fire and the attraction of the intuitive temperament.

All these men possessed an unconscious need for an earthy partner. There is always cross-projection in such relationships; otherwise they would have been wholly fantasy on Margaret's part and no actual relationship could even have existed. But Margaret, although happy to play earthy anima to all three men, found herself angry and frustrated when they would not play father as well as Wise Man to her. The animus in her case is associated strongly with the father, and is the primary reason for the unspoken demands and expectations exercising so much destructive power. A fiery man would be a good match for Margaret, but only when she learns to respond to fire with some fire of her own and, instead of attempting to cage and domesticate it, shares the adventuresome attitude to life inherent in the element. She is an ideal companion for such a fiery man; but as her own image of herself becomes more positive and more realistic, and, as she learns to appreciate her own potential, she will attract and be attracted to a stabler temperament. All three of these former lovers are, in one way or another, emotional cripples; every one has a Venus-Saturn contact, and each has a problem expressing feeling about which he has done nothing. This again reflects Margaret's masochistic pattern, stemming from her father-relationship. She needs a fire-water type, an intuitive feeling man who can appreciate her fine mind, her love of truth, her honesty and clarity while also responding to the depth and power of her emotional needs.

The motivating factor in Margaret's relationships was not her feeling for any of her men — she never really saw them until the relationships were over — but rather, the animus, which made her choices for her until she had fulfilled the old pattern of rejection and failure. As she gradually grows more conscious of this masculine force within her, and disengages it from memories of her unhappy childhood, she becomes more whole; the old wounds will heal, and, as she values herself more, she will in turn be valued more by the men with whom she becomes involved.

The traditional comparison of charts alone cannot paint the whole of Margaret's picture. One must know her, and something of her history, to perceive the workings of the inner partner who has led her to such loneliness, pain, rejection and finally to insight, understanding, and the beginnings of real peace. Her relationship pattern will never be easy because of the kind of man she favours; Venus-Pluto requires far more depth than is implicit in conventional marriage. But her real potential is only beginning. Earthy signs grow slowly, and do not flower until the second half of life. Having failed at so many outer unions, Margaret is learning at last to build the inner union, which for her is the only possible road to a valid relationship with another individual.

VI
The Sex Life of the Psyche

> There is still a great deal unknown about this
> phenomenon capable of transporting an
> ordinarily "civilised" man and woman into a
> state which under other circumstances we would
> associate only with a frothing lunatic.
> — Robert Musil

> A friend of mine says he will never make love
> to a woman who admires his horse. I feel the
> same way about my hat. I never make love to
> my hat, no matter how many women admire it.
> — J.D. Smith

Among the many modern relationship myths we have
evolved to liberate ourselves from almost two thousand years
of repressed instincts, one of the most ambiguous is that of
sexual normality and abnormality. Closely connected with it,
and particularly popular in the present decade, is the myth of
good and bad sexual performance. The ambiguity of both
stems perhaps from the fact that we do not understand fully
the psychological and symbolic implications of sexuality, and
normality and abnormality are, after all, dangerously relative
terms, whose meaning shifts depending upon the individual
and the age in which he lives.

Because there are many current psychologies — a
phenomenon which can only occur when the psyche
attempts to psychologise itself — there are many different
clinical approaches to sex. Freud's theories of infantile
sexuality and the Oedipus complex are reasonably well-

known to the layman, and many people believe them to be psychology *in toto*. This is unfortunate. If one is always certain to arrive at the same formula in the end, there will be a very understandable resistance to exploring sexuality from a psychological point of view. But Freud's thesis is conservative and almost ladylike compared to some of the ideas which have branched off from his original work, and some of the techniques, like massage and "sensitivity training", which are being developed by the current "growth movement".

Organised religion, on the other hand, is as monotonous on the theme as some psychological schools. Thus we have religion on the one hand expressing its condemnation of the fleshly weaknesses in Thirteenth Century terms, psycho-analysis and its offshoots on the other insisting that the human psyche is filled with nothing but these very weaknesses, and that even a longing for God is really a repressed father-complex. In consequence, it is very difficult for a person to know his own mind about the subject. There are no authorities any longer, either through God or through science. And there are, moreover, assorted fascinating viewpoints offered about sex by various esoteric teachings. One may find anything from the argument that orgasm is the key to illumination, to the argument that only abstinence and sublimation can take one to heaven (or clean up one's karma). The traditional western esoteric interpretation of spirit being "higher" and matter (including sexuality) being "lower" carries with it the obvious implication that if we give the instinctual nature full expression, we are not "evolved"; and this can be an even more powerful mode of suppression than the condemnation of the Church, because it appeals to one's spiritual pride. There is also an esoteric viewpoint on "perversion" and its accompanying and devastating karmic consequences. For some reason, gifted seers and clairvoyants like Edgar Cayce, otherwise luminously sane in their cosmological perspective, begin metaphorically to turn red and stammer on the subject of sex; and it is no help to our understanding if we are told by such spiritual authorities that a man who is sexually excessive in one life will be an epileptic in the next. These pronouncements — whether they come from psychology, religion or esotericism — only serve to create more confusion, because they pass judgment. The "new" morality, which is a noble attempt to shake free from the repression of the dying Piscean Age, has swung so far to the opposite extreme that it possesses an equally dogmatic idealogy: if an individual is not able to fully abandon himself to his instincts, he is neurotic and "uptight". For some unfathomable reason we can talk with relative intelligence about everything under the sun, except those two ancient nasties, sex and death. And we do not really understand either one.

One may walk down a London thoroughfare and see, glowing in a shop window, primers on sexual techniques flanked by an assorted array of mechanical erotic devices that suggest the Grand Inquisitor's interrogation chamber; and across the street one may see a kindly old man pacing back and forth, bearing a placard which states that eating less animal matter will decrease lust. It would seem that there is an extraordinary muddle about sexuality, both within different sections of society and within the individual himself. Yet far from being illuminated by our supposedly freer and less inhibited attitudes concerning sexuality, and even with prophets like Reich egging us on, we do not seem to have solved anything; people still suffer from misunderstandings and fears about sex. Nor is the situation improved by advertising, which is constantly intimidating us with innumerable brooding spectres inimical to a happy relationship — bad breath, foot and body odour, yellow teeth, frizzy hair, flying dandruff and a host of other woes that suggest the only sexually healthy people in the world are those who smoke cigarettes. No wonder we are self-conscious.

We are far more mature intellectually (as Musil says) than we are emotionally, and we cannot cope with the resulting gulf. We possess highly advanced ideas and scientific knowledge, grafted onto medieval feeling values — not to mention archaic drives and desires which are no different now than they were a million years ago when we were still chasing woolly mammoths across arctic tundras. In place of the state-sanctioned homosexuality that existed in classical

Greece, we have the Gay Liberation Movement; and instead of suffering wives clenching their teeth and enduring dutifully their husbands' conjugal rights, we now have impotent men retreating in terror before the onslaught of aggressive animus-driven women who light their men's cigarettes, open their own doors, possess black belts in karate, and have the audacity to initiate the sexual act. In our larger cities not many people pay attention to Mrs. Grundy any more, but the new morality is as pitiless to the offender as the old, and with even wilder rationalisations. Once upon a time, the "fallen" woman suffered; now the woman who says no after the second date (especially if the dinner has been expensive) suffers as badly, because she is "sexually hung-up". One may laugh, read the cartoons in *Playboy*, peer secretly through the curtains into neighbours' windows, go to porn films, wife-swap, look suitably jaded at the quaintness of *Lady Chatterley's Lover*, and gossip about who is sleeping with whom. But it is not so funny when an individual must confront within himself an experience of sexual disappointment, whether from incompatibility or "perversion" or failure or guilt, and when he finds he cannot really talk about it with anyone except in a clinical fashion — a fashion that intensifies his self-recrimination by implying that something is indeed grievously "wrong". It is very painful. The depersonalisation of sexuality has let us out of one cage merely to put us into another; it is solely a question of what pattern bars we prefer to have on our windows. The only difference is that now we are attempting to bring sexual problems out into the open, where before we could not. And perhaps Durrell is right when he says that "sex, like dying, should be a private matter."

A good place to begin is probably with the premise that sexuality, like love, intelligence, talent and other intangibles of this kind, varies according to one's experience of it. At least this permits one to have his own particular sexual nature, just as he is entitled to other expressions of individuality. We can no more make a definitive statement about sexuality than we can about God. One may protest, and insist that sex is a purely physical act, and that psychological complexities are irrelevant; but the fact remains that for many people the sexual encounter in fantasy is far more real, satisfying, meaningful and exciting than any physical encounter could ever be. For some people, sexuality is an experience of the creative imagination, a state of mind, rather than a physical pleasure. For some, there is nothing quite so sexually stirring as music, or the creation of a painting, or the exhilaration of dance; and far from being "sublimations" of the sexual drive, these avenues for expression of creative energy are as "sexual" as the act of coitus itself. For some, sex is the prelude to procreation, an aspect of the process of creating new life — a viewpoint promulgated by much organised religion. For some, sex is an intimacy of feeling which allows people to deeply meet each other in an emotional communion, a rapport of such subtlety that the physical act is but a symbol of it. For some, sex is a dirty joke, to be enjoyed over a magazine in the bathroom with the door locked. For some, sex is a fine balance between pleasure and pain, and for others it is a release of violence. Some people experience sex autoerotically; whether they have a partner or not, the experience is essentially their own and the partner merely a vehicle to it, easily replaced by another partner or by their own hands. For other people, the real passion is in the passion of the other, and the experience is only meaningful by virtue of the other's pleasure. Sexuality can be holy, obscene, physical, mental, emotional, spiritual, symbolic, procreative, amusing, transforming, loving, or anything else you wish it to be or care to imagine. None of us is in any position to decide which of these myriad expressions are normal or abnormal. Sexuality is most certainly not one thing only, and if we are to understand why so many problems arise in relationships because of it, we must first abandon the idea that it can be defined in one sentence. Like everything else in life, sex is both a concrete reality and a symbol — and a symbol's meanings are as inexhaustible and as infinite as there are individuals to respond to them.

We must also realise that sexuality is a different experience to masculine and feminine psychology. This is not a blanket statement that all men relate to sexuality wholly in one way, all women wholly in another; we must remember that each individual contains both sexual principles within him. But there is a distinction between male and female sexuality which becomes apparent to anyone who takes the time to talk to men and women about their fantasies. Despite the noble attempts of the more liberated woman, it is apparent that men stubbornly persist in being aroused by visual stimulation; and the familiar modern sight of the strip club and the porn cinema is continuing testimony that men throughout the ages react to a physical display of feminine charms. There is an erotic component to the anima which appears to be absent from the animus, although present in the instinctual psychology of the conscious woman. The connection with the earthy plane of all things feminine suggests that physical impressions produce a greater impact on men than on women. The animus, in contrast, has affinities with mind and spirit, and it seems that qualities like intellect, talent, success, ambition and "personality" are more meaningful to a woman than the shape of a man's body. Women seem forever to be craving something deeper than appearances, and the cosmetic and fashion industries have long recognised this dichotomy. A dress which reveals the beauties of the feminine body is always a success; but it is difficult to imagine a man dressing in an obviously enticing way and succeeding in attracting anyone other than those of his own sex who prefer masculine partners.

There is also a quality of impersonality about masculine sexuality, a quality of greater personal involvement about feminine. This is a frequently heard complaint in long-standing relationships; "he" seems to need sex to obtain any emotional closeness, while "she" cannot respond to sex unless such rapport already exists. "He" will interpret his extra-marital fling as a simple satisfaction of desire, having nothing at all to do with love or with his marriage; "she", on the other hand, knows that such an involvement on her part generally stems from a serious lack within the marriage, and poses a threat to its stability. These are not hard-and-fast rules, and people are flexible and multi-faceted. But as a general tendency, the distinction seems to be valid. It is only a problem, however, when one is saddled with an ideology or a rigid code of behaviour that confines one to an inhuman consistency. The woman who must always be "feminine" in bed is as trapped as the woman who has "evolved" beyond such trivial "roles" and has inadvertently thrown the baby out with the bath water.

In the miasma which obscures our understanding of sexuality, one of the main problems is that we take things much too literally. We judge psychic states by actions, thus drawing a veil over psychic states themselves and their intrinsic meaning. We say that a "feminine" woman is a good cook, while a "masculine" man is successful; we say that a man who feels the compulsion to dress up in his wife's underclothes is "abnormal" while the man who has three or four women in regular revolution around the bachelor bed is "virile". But if one shifts one's focus from behaviour to the symbol behind it, the entire landscape looks different. We act out symbolically what we are; but if we are too rigid about interpreting the structure in which the symbol is embedded, it loses its life, its organic flexibility, and we are trapped in an ossified scaffolding; and then we begin to debate with frightening intensity and violence, how many angels can fit onto the head of a pin. In every action, particularly those which are compulsive and which we "must" do, it is prudent to ask what the action means rather than to name it, classify it, and force ourselves or others into a labelled category because of it. A woman who does not cook may not cook for many reasons. She may be an intuitive who has a problem coming to grips with objects, but this need not preclude her expressing femininity in a free and flowing way through feeling relationships; she may be animus-dominated and feel such things to be "beneath" her, a capitulation to male chauvinism; she may have had a terrible mother-relationship and now rejects anything connected with instinctual life; or she may work at a nine-to-five job and simply be tired when she comes home. No one is in a position to say whether she is feminine or not because she performs, or does not perform, a certain sequence of actions. Femininity is a principle, a life energy, not a set of behavioural patterns. And no one is in a position to judge a sexual situation by such patterns either. If we could put our highly charged epithets — "perverted", "abnormal", "hung-up", "sick" and their ilk — aside for a time, we might be able to see the person who is expressing the action, and why.

Orthodox psychiatry, too, has a problem with sexuality; a man can still be given hormone pills for his impotence. Yet the body cannot be separated from the whole person, and sexual behaviour is one of the many possible expressions through which a person reveals himself. An apparently physical problem cannot be dissociated from the psyche which experiences it. Sexual propensities, habits and difficulties are not merely organic. They *mean* something to the person and say something about him, on levels which may be too deep for him to understand.

Unfortunately, astrology too carries its arsenal of preconceptions and misconceptions about sexuality. There are many astrological textbooks published on the sexual proclivities of each sign; and even the more serious astrological student can fall into the trap of believing the birth chart will disclose such patterns as homosexuality, impotence, sadism and other social no-no's in a clearly defined way. Very frequently, for example, charts of notorious offenders like Oscar Wilde and the Marquis de Sade are trundled out to demonstrate how one can diagnose aberrations from the planetary map. Hindsight of this kind, of course, is easy — but it fails to explain why other individuals, whose maps exhibit similar aspects, do not express their sexuality in a similar way. Behind the chart stands the individual, and behind all sexual expressions — whether of performance, preference, or moral values — also stands the individual. As a well-known humanistic psychologist was once heard to remark to a man who expressed concern about the "tendencies" he might be repressing: "I would say that you are a latent human being."

Let us begin by considering the exhaustively explored issue of what we call homosexuality. *The Concise Oxford Dictionary* defines the word as "having a sexual propensity for persons of one's own sex." For the moment, we will leave aside the ambiguous question of precisely what constitutes a sexual propensity. There follows a random sampling of opinions about homosexuality, drawn from literature, psychology, and personal interviews.

Homosexuals are made, not born, and the bias stems from a psychological problem with the parent of the opposite sex.

Homosexuals are born, not made, and the bias stems from a hormone imbalance.

Homosexuality (or bisexuality) is the natural state of humanity, which is moving gradually towards androgyny as a spiritual ideal.

Homosexuality is nature's way of offsetting the population problem.

A homosexual is a person who has spent several past incarnations in a body of the opposite sex, and is having trouble adjusting to the new one.

Homosexuals should not be hired in the diplomatic service.

All interior decorators are homosexual.

And lastly, a piece of graffiti scrawled on the wall of the men's loo at Simon Fraser University in Vancouver:

If God had wanted there to be homosexuals in the world, He would have created Adam and Fred.

It will be apparent that there is some confusion about the meaning of this particular form of sexual expression.

Are phenomena like homosexuality problems or not? Are they "perversions"? What, in fact, are they? If a man fantasises himself making love to another man, yet does not act out this fantasy, is he homosexual? If he has had homosexual experiences, yet does not find them to his taste, is he homosexual because he has performed the act? If he has a closer and altogether richer relationship with his best friend than with his wife, is he "latently" homosexual? And is he any more "latently" homosexual than we are all "latently" murderers, thieves, bigots, "savages", geniuses, or anything else among the infinite possibilities the psyche contains? It is time we thought hard about questions like these which at first seem easy to answer. Perhaps one might say to oneself: "If I am happy with my life, if it offers me fulfilment in those areas where I seek it, I am normal for myself. If I am unhappy with my life, if I feel that there is something wrong, if I feel trapped by the direction in which my desires move, I have a problem. I am neither normal nor abnormal; I have simply not yet become myself." Homosexuality, like so many other behavioural manifestations, is one of many possible ways of expressing a psychic state. In itself it is neither a cause, nor a sickness. It is a mode of expression, chosen by either conscious or unconscious, which the individual adopts because there is an inner symbol working itself out in his behaviour. And symbols are neither right nor wrong, neither normal nor abnormal.

There are many reasons for such symbolic expression. Some self-proclaimed homosexuals seem to gravitate quite naturally towards the characteristics of the opposite sex; perhaps they are truly "born" with their propensity, and could find happiness in it were they not subjected to the social ostracism of others. Sometimes, on the other hand, a real psychological problem seems to lie behind the homosexual's rejection of the opposite sex; the elements of fear, hatred and compulsion dictate his behaviour, rather than freedom of choice. Such cases can often be traced back to the parental relationships; but we must remember that the enduring effects of childhood experiences are as much a result of the former child — now become adult — clinging to them, as they are to parental power. A man whose mother-relationship has been distorted by hate, fear, rejection or will to power may develop a lasting, unconscious hatred or fear of women — both women in the world and the woman in himself. In consequence, he will be unable to function either emotionally or sexually with a woman, and this leaves him no alternative save his own sex. The violated anima, in revenge, may possess him, affecting his entire conscious psychology to the point where he thinks and feels and behaves like the inferior parody of a woman. Rather than label this individual homosexual, we would be more accurate in saying that he has a problem with the feminine principle. Unfortunately, however, he may label himself, for simple want of knowledge. There are many "normal" men who subtly abuse their women in a myriad unconscious ways, compelled by inner fear or resentment; the psychological pattern is the same as the "homosexual's", but if such men do not express it through overt desire for their own sex, then we do not stigmatise them with a label.

A man may never have severed the umbilical cord. He may be bound by ties of possession and devouring love to an over-devoted mother, who is happy to spare him the necessity of growing up. As a result, he may feel that no woman can ever match his mother — to whom he will remain psychologically wedded for the rest of his life. Here again, it would be more accurate to speak of a problem with the feminine principle. There are enough "normal" men about who assiduously seek wives patterned faithfully after their mothers, and we do not label them.

Problems with the father may also lie behind what we call homosexuality. A son who experiences the less attractive aspects of the male principle — brutality, violence, aggression, harshness, coldness — may develop a hatred of the masculine, both within himself and without. He may overvalue and identify with feminine values and feminine psychology, seeing his mother as a martyr — and this will impel him naturally towards relationships with men, in which he can enact his mother's role. Alternatively, it may draw him towards masculine women, some of whom are delicately disguised by the most polished patina of social femininity; and then we will say he is "normal". In this case, it would be more accurate to say there is a problem with the masculine principle. The man with a missing father, or a father who is obviously dominated by his wife, may seek his masculinity in symbolic infatuations for those he considers embodiments of manhood. A man who expresses this kind of hero-worship through conventional channels — by admiring a film star or football hero, or even a friend — is again considered "normal", while one who expresses it erotically is "abnormal". These examples should illustrate the ambiguity surrounding the entire issue; and the same ambiguity exists in other sexual anomalies or "deviations" as well. What we call homosexuality is really a meaningless term. There are simply individuals who have different ways of relating to their own balance of masculine and feminine. The same may be said of such things as voyeurism, exhibitionism, fetishism, narcissism, transvestism, frigidity, impotence and other "isms" which we call "abnormal". All are symbols of psychic states, and when one is dealing with expressions of the psyche one must be very careful about one's labelling.

If we try to put these things into perspective, what emerges is not a picture of normal or abnormal sexual drives, but a series of different images of how each individual relates to the male and female aspects of himself. Moreover, the balance between the two polarities changes constantly throughout life, so that actions performed at one given moment, reflecting a particular psychological constellation, may not have any meaning in the next. Unfortunately people tend to identify themselves with their own behaviour, and then to be puzzled, if not alarmed, by the inconsistencies they find. This does not apply to physical sex alone; it encompasses the whole of life. The same psychological components will also be expressed through a person's tastes, interests, choice of profession, religious convictions, and politics. A man may have a problem with the feminine principle, but this does not mean that he is homosexual; nor, Freud notwithstanding, is he "latently" homosexual. He is, however, likely to have many problems in relationships. He may be a real "macho" man, strong, decisive, aggressive, capable, scathingly critical about the "irrational" (which is how the world of the anima appears to him) — and

completely infantile about the subtleties of relating to the
women in his life through feeling. He and the mincing queen
may share virtually identical elements in psychological
composition — in consequence of which each will predict-
ably despise the other. But again, this does not mean the
he-man is a latent queen, any more than it means the queen
is a latent he-man. It means there is a central psychological
constellation expressing itself, as such energies do, through a
pair of apparent opposites.

Detailed consideration of any one sexual propensity could
fill a book. Many have already been filled in this way. When
we apply clinical terms to such matters, however, and
attempt to approach them wholly analytically, their real
meaning often eludes us. Ultimately one must ask what any
mode of sexual expression or sexual style — be it "normal" or
"abnormal" — means to the individual, and in what manner
it symbolises the inner psyche.

The problem of what we call frigidity is another
complicated issue. There are supposed to be "degrees" of
frigidity, presumably something like degrees of sunburn. And
there are enough manuals available on the engineering
behind the female anatomy to solve the problem, if it were
merely one requiring technical expertise. Some women feel
their lack of response is due to the "poor performance" of
their men. What is poor performance? Bad mechanics? Bad
feeling? Insensitivity? Why, then, choose such an inadequate
specimen as a partner? Qualities such as lack of sensitivity
are not confined to just sexual issues; they are personality
traits, and are visible in all the person expresses. Have
"frigid" women genuinely looked at the subterranean
currents in their relationships to discover what the psyche is
really saying through lack of physical response? By means of
such lack of response, many women express their unconscious fear, resentment or hostility towards men, while others
express their guilt for their own instinctuality. But both
resentment and guilt may be more connected with the
animus, and with the childhood, than with the particular
man with whom one is involved. Trying to "cure" frigidity
with technical manuals is like locking the stable door after

the horse has escaped. A woman must first understand, on a feeling level, what she is symbolically enacting when her body fails to be aroused. Perhaps it is nothing more than that she does not want a particular man. But then she must ask why she did not realise this before, and why she is with him now.

There are women who are capable of attaining orgasm physically, but are "frigid" on the feeling level. And this is as much a sexual matter as frigidity of body. The problem is particularly important today because women are becoming more conscious of their own creative potential. In consequence, the slights, insults and buried anger of centuries are pouring from the collective level into personal relationships. The collective animus has declared war, and he is unquestionably a dirty fighter; it is all the same to him if love and life are snuffed out, so long as he wins. If, as she develops her masculine side, a woman does not wish to lose her womanhood, she must understand the real psychological roots of her sexual responses. And one should not underestimate the kind of suffering this effort entails for a woman, who may often be bullied into feeling "abnormal", even in these "enlightened" times. Yes, she should perhaps possess the courage to instruct a man in what pleases her. But many men do not like to be instructed, and the instruction itself is irrelevant if the fear of psychic rape looms behind the merely physical coldness.

Since sexual prowess is lauded as much today as ever, one would hardly ascribe a problem to the man who metaphorically marks notches on the bedpost to commemorate his conquests. He is a figure for emulation by other men, and for much fantasising by women. But is he really what he seems? Might it be that he is really frightened by the degree of feeling intimacy which two nights with the same woman — let alone a lifetime of marriage — might entail? If so, he may possess a psychological constellation similar to that of the impotent man, whom his own secret fears lead him to despise — and who may be expressing in a different way the same anxiety about losing his manhood to woman's emotional rapacity. And because his insensitivity to feeling communicates itself to his partner, the Don Juan may be as unsatisfactory a bedmate, and suffer the same rejection, as the man who is unable to function. The "prevert"-hating general in *Dr. Strangelove*, who shuns all contact with women lest he lose his "precious bodily fluids", is in fact not confined to the screen. Many men are plagued by this secret anxiety, and withhold some part of themselves — although not necessarily sexual — from fear of being "unmanned". We are not talking here about Freud's idea of the castration complex, which is too abstract for the circumstances. We are again talking about the archetypes — the strange and numinous double faces of anima-mother and animus-father, dark and light, male and female, creative and receptive, performing their endless dance of magnetic attraction and repulsion which brings forth new life. And if we seek to penetrate the mystery of sexuality, we are ultimately confronted with the mystery of godhead, the mystery of life itself.

> Pleasure is not a corporeal joy, the mutual fulfilment of the two sexes, camaraderie and other such nonsense. Pleasure is a praying mantis, a pitiless struggle, an irreducible hatred of the two sexes, the two warring cosmic forces — the one that rises, the one that descends — engendering the Universe.[1]

*   *   *

These issues we have raised are intended to provoke thought, not to provide answers. No one can resolve such issues definitively; we can only attempt to explore and understand our own natures, so that we may express ourselves in ways most truly a reflection of psychic totality. But here, as in other situations, the astrological chart can be helpful by suggesting a direction, a point at which to begin.

In traditional astrology, the chief significators of sexual expression are Venus and Mars. Also linked traditionally with

1 *The Rock Garden*, Nikos Kazantzakis, Simon & Schuster, N.Y. 1963.

sexuality are the sign Scorpio, the planet Pluto, and the eighth house of the horoscope — which pertains to the emotional and sexual aspects of human relationships. Without the added dimension afforded by depth psychology, however, traditional astrology can only offer a limited and rather two-dimensional perspective on the matter. And this perspective is further circumscribed and distorted by popular sun-sign manuals, which proffer their well-known inventories of sexual characteristics for each sign. Scorpio, we may read, is always erotic, passionate and highly sexed, and one would think, from such descriptions, that Scorpio thinks of nothing else. Virgo is cold, chaste, prudish and unresponsive, Gemini is technically proficient but incapable of sexual fidelity, and Aquarius inclines to inventiveness, experimentation and even perversion. The absurdity of such generalisations is apparent to any serious student of astrology. Just as sexuality is an expression of the whole person, it is, astrologically considered, an expression of the whole birth chart. Nor can one ascribe to particular planetary combinations "responsibility" (as if they had malicious intent) for particular sexual difficulties. Sexual expression is so intimately connected with the anima or animus — which means with the entire unconscious life of the individual — that all the chart can do is suggest patterns or tendencies — in the feeling nature, the capacity for relationship, or the inner image of the opposite sex. It cannot disclose the specific sexual proclivities through which libido will manifest itself.

In a broad sense, Venus and Mars may be considered symbols of sexuality since they are connected with the masculine and feminine principles channelled into human relationships. As we have seen, they also pertain to the image of the inner partner. Psychic energy — which Jung calls libido, employing the term Freud thought originally applied to exclusively sexual energy — is symbolised by all components on the chart, but expresses itself in different fashion, or performs a different function, according to the meaning of particular planets and their contexts. Energy symbolically expressed by Venus is directed towards relating subject and object; it is stabilising, harmonising, unifying, and conducive to equilibrium. The particular mode of expression for each of these dynamic energies is reflected by the sign in which the planet is placed. For example, Venus in Libra suggests that the urge for relationship is expressed with a colouration of aesthetic balance, refinement, gentleness and "manners" — because of the light, airy quality of Libra. As a general characteristic of his nature, the individual with Venus in Libra will relate to things and people (whether the relation be physical, emotional, mental or intuitive) with a certain grace and style, adhering to certain aesthetic principles. Placed in Taurus, on the other hand, an earthy sign, Venus will tend to express the urge for relationship in a sensuous, earthy, physical, "natural", simple way. Such expression of a planet through a sign, then, will reflect certain qualities of the individual's psychological composition, certain values about particular aspects of life; and it is an important factor in chart comparison. Life is generally easier if one's partner is responsive to one's specific mode of expression, or is at least capable of accepting it. The woman with Venus in Libra may find herself sexually responsive amid candlelight, flowers, a harmonious atmosphere, a romantic setting, a poetic declaration of love; the woman with Venus in Taurus may find herself sexually responsive to a proximity with nature, to the partner's obvious love of pleasure, to the effect upon her senses of the sight, smell, feel of the healthy male body. These are stylistic matters; they tell us something about a person's values and natural inclinations in relationships, but only in a general way, and must be considered in the context of the chart as a whole. As we have seen, each temperament experiences life differently, and sexuality is an integral component of life.

No value judgments, particularly in terms of "normality" and "abnormality", can be imposed upon the sign placement of Venus on the birth chart. It symbolises a particular expression of energy, which the individual may utilise as he pleases — or, sometimes, as he is compelled to use by other, unconscious factors in the psyche. According to traditional astrology, sexual compatibility is usually indicated by one person's Venus contacting another's Mars in a harmonious way; the romantic refinement of the woman with Venus in Libra may elicit response from a man with Mars in Libra, who will express his masculinity with the same kind of refinement. But this will not tell us about the deeper currents at work within the relationship, or about the inner relationship each partner enjoys, or fails to enjoy, with the anima and animus. Both partners may like candlelight and satin sheets, but many a marriage has been wrecked in the bedroom by resentments and buried anger stemming from a totally different source — often not at all connected with the partner, but with the ghost of a parent.

In orthodox astrology, certain planetary configurations have a rather unsavoury reputation, purportedly signifying sexual "abnormalities". Reading old textbooks on the subject is rather like reading a medical compilation of diseases: by the time you have finished, you are convinced you suffer from every symptom listed. The following priceless aphorism appears in a textbook printed as recently as 1963:

> When Venus is in conjunction with Saturn and aspecting the ruler of the ascendant, the native is inclined to sodomy, or loves old, hard-featured women or poor dirty wenches.[1]

We must remember that the dubious objectivity of such a statement should not be blamed on astrology, but rather on the individual who has formulated his own peculiar interpretation of certain data. We may hear similar statements — but in psychological, sociological, medical, even theological, rather than astrological, works — from many other learned and enlightened modern minds.

In old astrology textbooks, Saturn and the outer planets — Uranus, Neptune and Pluto — are notorious for "causing perversions", particularly if they are found in aspect to Venus. In point of fact, these combinations *do* turn up with suspicious frequency among charts of individuals seeking

1 *Astrology and Human Sex Life*, Vivian Robson, W. Foulsham & Co., Ltd., London 1963.

counselling for sexual problems. But some aspects also frequently occur when the problem is expressed through some area of the feeling life, rather than through the sexual activities. Unless one is fettered to Freudian thought, in which everything is ultimately a symbol for something sexual, the implication is simply that contacts between Venus and these four planets affect the psyche's function of relatedness in a peculiar way. They are not necessarily indicative of sexual disturbance, although that may be one possible mode through which the energy generated is expressed.

Venus-Saturn aspects — especially the conjunction, opposition and square — and Mars-Saturn aspects as well — do appear to have some connection with impotence and frigidity. But why? The planets do not *make* us anything; they are symbols of particular patterns of psychic energy. But if one remembers the things to which these planets pertain, however, the enigma becomes more comprehensible; for while Venus and Mars are symbolic of male and female expression, Saturn is symbolic — among other things — of fear, the need for self-protection, the compulsion for defense. The woman whose birth chart shows a Venus-Saturn square may feel deeply inadequate and uncertain of herself as a woman, whether she is conscious of this feeling or not; her capacity to relate — especially as the loving companion represented by the planet's archetypal, mythological name-sake — has got caught by the shadow. It can therefore be used unconsciously by the inferior dark side of her nature as an instrument of control in relationships, an inhibiting factor rather than as a conscious expression of sharing and participation. Venus-Saturn does not say anything about a woman's sexual performance; but it does infer something about her attitude towards herself as woman, which is usually impaired in some way. One can thus easily understand frigidity when one remembers it is the physical symbol of an inner psychic state; the word itself is a descriptive image not of the body, but of the feelings, which have got frozen in some way and remain not only unconscious but often very childlike as well. To compensate, the woman may gloss this over, may mistake emotion or sentiment for feeling, may display apparent callousness, toughness and sophistication; at the same time, however, she will remain out of touch with the frightened, vulnerable child imprisoned in the darkness of the unconscious. It is no wonder the body does not respond. The sexual union is the most complete form of sharing we can know, but it requires a degree of maturity that the frightened child does not possess. On the other hand, a woman with Venus-Saturn may function quite adequately on a purely physical level, because the combination, as we have already noted, does not necessarily reflect a physical condition. Nevertheless there will often be some limitation, some constriction or self-defense in her relationships, some withholding of her ability to share herself with another. That Venus-Saturn has a reputation for selfishness will therefore be comprehensible, if we remember it is the selfishness of the insecure child — who, unsure of being loved, withholds until he obtains demonstrable proof that it is safe.

Mars-Saturn aspects in a woman's chart suggest something very different. Here the problem is not the relationship to femininity, but to masculinity; it is the animus which must be brought up into consciousness. In this case, the image of man as lover, symbolised by Mars, is coloured by the shadow. In consequence, a woman may perceive the image through the darkness of her own inferior side, so that the image and this darkness which taints it become synonymous; and, if both are projected onto men, then men will not appear very congenial. The animus may appear to be brutal, violent, repressive, tyrannical and callous, or, alternatively, weak, abject and ineffectual. Unless it is made conscious, the shadow appropriates for its own purposes the gifts inherent in the masculine side of the woman's nature, and employs them as instruments for authority or control. Sexual frigidity will then become a means of keeping the man from being a man, a means of immobilising his power, of cheating him of that ultimate submission which, unconsciously, the woman fears he seeks, never realising that for him, too, the sexual act can be an experience of submission. Venus-Saturn women may be cold because they have not learned to trust, to acknowledge or accept their own femininity. Mars-Saturn women, on the other hand, may be cold because they have never learned to trust men; they will constantly be confronted with the projection of their own rather untrustworthy animus figure. Or they may function with perfect ease in sexual matters, having learned the dubious achievement of disconnecting physical response from feeling; but they will seek to maintain control of the relationship on other levels, in order to protect themselves from projected domination.

Such Saturn aspects as these are rarely easy to deal with, and usually require much self-reflection and investigation of unconscious images and motives before the "trapped" planet — Venus or Mars — can be freed. Yet here, as always, Saturn plays the role of Lucifer. He often reflects frustration, loneliness and disappointment through sexual relationships which bring a woman to her knees, but this is done for a purpose: so that she may begin to look inward and learn the real meaning of her sexuality in a conscious way. As fairy tales tell us, the shadow is secretly a friend and guide; and when certain aspects appear on the birth chart, sexuality may be a realm requiring exploration for the sake of self-development. Seen in this light, aspects of Saturn to Venus or Mars can be valuable tools for growth and self-enrichment; and sexual expression, at first perhaps damaged, can become a path through which a woman can find much greater fulfilment and sense of meaning in her life.

On a man's chart, the situation reverses itself. Mars in a man's chart is a symbol of his virility, his masculine expression, and when Mars is connected with Saturn, it may be in the grip of his shadow. This might engender an ineffectual passivity with resentment secretly smouldering in the unconscious. Alternatively, it might provoke over-aggressiveness, which compensates for the debilitating feelings of inadequacy. Mars-Saturn aspects seem to have a connection with impotence, but once again we regard the term as symbolic of a psychological attitude — the impotence of the conscious ego to express the masculine principle in life. Physical impotence may be a by-product, but the Don Juan is not any the less characteristic. Nor is the bully, nor the man dominated emotionally by his women.

> Masculinity means to know one's goal and to do what is necessary to achieve it.[1]

It is this capacity to know and act which is damaged when a man has lost connection with his masculinity, or when it is being used by the shadow for power. But Mars-Saturn reflects difficulty with the masculine principle, not with the sexual performance — which, after all, is one symbol, among many, for a man's expression of manhood. To paraphrase the observation quoted earlier, even the penis is a phallic symbol.

Mars-Saturn aspects also seem to have some connection with violence and with that pair of opposites we call sadism and masochism. We must bear in mind the compensatory function of the unconscious; thus one pole of this duality cannot exist on a conscious level without its opposite being constellated in the unconscious, imprisoned in the darkness and projected. Again, both these manifestations of sexual behaviour are symbols of psychic states: if you feel impotent and helpless in the face of reality, you can either bow your head and call punishment down on yourself for your sins, or you can set out to conquer and if necessary destroy the world in order to overcome the sense of inadequacy. As sexual "perversions", sadism and masochism are rather ambiguous; they may also be discerned in many areas other than the sexual. They may be expressed through feelings and words, for example, and often in the guise of love. Ultimately they reflect a psychological attitude towards life and towards expression of the masculine principle; and specifically sexual behaviour is only one of many possible by-products. In any case, what all these patterns require is for the root of the attitude to emerge into consciousness, and then the whole personality will be transformed. To treat the attitude itself,

1 *Contributions to Analytical Psychology*, C.G. Jung, Kegan Paul, London 1928.

however, is like treating any other symptom. It merely compels the malady to find expression in some other form — which may be more destructive than the previous one.

Venus-Saturn aspects in a man's chart reflect an attitude towards the feminine which, because it is coloured by the shadow, will often be rather dark. A man with such aspects may perceive the anima, his inner image of woman and his capacity for relatedness, through the lens of his own unconscious inferiority. As a result, he will project this sinister quality onto his partner. There will usually be some element of fear or restriction in his relationships, and a distinct coolness; he may even manipulate his partner through feeling, in order to gain control, although he will usually believe it is the partner who is doing the manipulating. This may or may not be connected with problems of sexual expression. More often it will affect the feeling tone of the sexual act, rather than the actual physical performance; but women are highly sensitive to feeling tones, and may respond to their absence or deficiency in ways that threaten the relationship. Despite a conscious attraction to woman, moreover, a man peering through the lens of his projection may secretly see her as inferior or power-driven. If so, he will treat her accordingly, however subtly. All kinds of by-products may ensue, ranging from coldness, lack of feeling and withdrawal to eventual homosexuality. In all such cases, the anima must be disengaged from the shadow and both brought up to consciousness. Only then will the man cease projecting his curious marriage of dark psychic components onto his partners.

It will be apparent from these examples that certain planetary combinations symbolise a psychological image and a variety of possible responses to it, rather than a sexual peculiarity. As we have noted, sexuality is as difficult to pinpoint on the chart as the Self, and possibly for a similar reason: it is a great principle of creative energy, an archetypal exchange of male and female life forces; and upon the great striving for union of these forces the whole of existence is built. Human sexual attraction and its accompanying problems is a miniaturised reflection of what the ancients called the great marriage of Ouranos and Gaia, from whence issued all manifested things; it is also a microcosm of what the alchemists meant by the Sacred Marriage, the *Coniunctio*. Thus it pertains as much to the psychic striving for union of opposites within an individual as it does to the physical relations he establishes with others.

Until the discovery of Uranus, Neptune, and Pluto, orthodox astrology ascribed most sexual "aberrations" to Saturn. More recently, however, the three outer planets have become the primary culprits, and it is therefore worth considering them if only for that reason. If we remember that they are transpersonal, serving the collective rather than the individual ego, we may discern their connection with highly mythologised forms of behaviour. The person who, through sun, moon, Venus or Mars, is bound to one of the outer planets, will tend to act out, far more than his fellows, the archetypal myth with which the planet is associated; he is drawn by the pull of something greater than himself and must somehow sacrifice his purely personal viewpoint. So far as sexual behaviour is concerned, the three outer planets thus reflect something very different from Saturn — who has more bearing on the shadow, the personal unconscious, and parental fixations and complexes.

Uranus is a powerful collective animus figure. If, in a woman's chart, he aspects Venus or the moon — the two symbols of feminine expression — there may be some distortion of natural instinctual expression. Uranus is a god, compelling and numinous. As a component of the animus, he has far greater power than the more personal figure of the father, and may violently, even traumatically, invade consciousness, bursting apart a woman's connections with her instinctual roots and claiming possession of her psyche. Such an animus must be recognised and given creative expression; he can scarcely be ignored. But if a woman is to retain any relationship to her body and her feelings she must learn to walk a tightrope that allows her to preserve her connection to her feminine centre. With Uranus-moon or Uranus-Venus contacts on the birth chart, a woman may feel she must choose between her independence and creativity on the one hand and her need for relationship on the other; but she must learn to allow room in her life for the values of both, never permitting violation of the needs of the heart by the clarity of the intellect. If the animus, in this case, is suppressed, he will undoubtedly explode with destructive force; if the instinctual nature is repressed, the results may range from isolation and self-destructiveness to physical illness, particularly of the reproductive system.

Neptune and Pluto aspecting the sun or Mars in a man's chart reflect a mythic influence similar to that symbolised by Uranus. Both symbolise facets of the collective anima; and when they are linked to the personal conscious expression of masculinity, the archetypes they embody may invade consciousness. Neptune is the gentle, all-pervading, ocean-like Mother; Pluto is the devouring, voracious, inexorable and ruthless Mother, the earth as opposed to the sea. Both figures impinge on consciousness as collective images of the feminine, and are far more powerful than the personal associations with the personal mother. If a Mars-Neptune or sun-Neptune contact reflects homosexuality on a man's chart, the energy involved will be very different from that reflected by Saturn. The latter signifies fear, resentment and hostility. The former connotes seduction by the archetype, the magical and enchanting melusine who lures a man away from manhood and makes him her own.

When confronting the power of archetypes and the mythological images they bring to individual consciousness, one can hardly pronounce moral judgments. One can only try, as best one can, to maintain uneasy peace between the conscious psychology, rooted in the body's sexuality, and the transsexual unconscious energy symbolised by the outer planets. And if one fails, in a sense it is not really a failure; for along with the problems come many great gifts, of which the "normal" man may never be vouchsafed a glimpse. The animus may be a ruthless destroyer of feeling and feminine relatedness, but he is also a god, a lightbringer, a torch to illumine the consciousness of the world; and the anima may be a vampire who sucks away the lifeblood of manhood, yet she is a goddess who confers poetry, music, vision, prophecy,

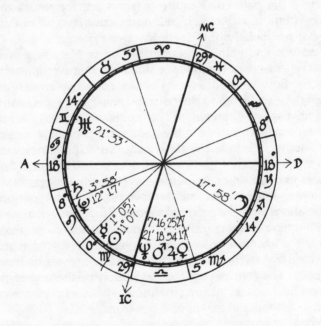

Victor

communion with the secret wellsprings of life. The ancients
believed that those whom the gods loved, they destroyed.
For some, the gifts are worth whatever price must be paid —
as they once were to the priests of Attis, who offered up their
manhood for love of the goddess and the secrets of her
mysteries. It is both puerile and presumptuous to hurl
pebbles against the breath of the numinous.

*   *   *

The chart shown above is that of a young actor named Victor,
who by his own definition is homosexual and has never been
anything else. With hindsight and once one knows something
about the individual, it is easy to point out on such a chart
configurations that pertain to sexual "propensities"; but if the
chart had been presented as an example of something else, it
is doubtful whether even the most learned of astrologers
could, without meeting the man, make any definitive
statement about his sexuality.

Victor came from a middle-class New York Jewish family,
and was dubiously blessed with that notorious figure
celebrated by *Portnoy's Complaint*, the Jewish Mother. (If
this figure is a myth, concocted by anti-Semites, she is also a
most emphatic empirical reality in the world.) Victor's father,
the owner of a reasonably successful chain of grocery shops,
was a shadowy figure who, on the rare occasions he was at
home, surrendered all domestic authority to his very capable
wife. The latter was a highly intelligent and perceptive
woman, gifted with an aptitude for emotional blackmail (a
peculiar talent of feeling-type women and anima-possessed
men); and she loved her only child with a ferocious and
devouring love. Nothing was too good for him, and he was
apparently given complete freedom; but she contrived
always to subtly manage his decisions for him, keeping him
in a state of perpetual boyhood and gently smothering his
right to make choices under a blanket of solicitous concern.
Victor accepted the passive role imposed on him, since it
did, after all, make life easier. As a child he was shy, gentle,
sensitive, and refined. He loved beautiful things and was very

attached to his home; and it was easy to manipulate him through his feelings, since he disliked hurting anyone and particularly detested violent emotional scenes. His mother's favourite ploy was to work on his sense of kindness, allowing him ostensible freedom yet always circumscribing it by making him afraid of bringing her emotional pain. Thus she seized the anima, the soul, and bound it to her.

By the time Victor was seventeen and ready to attend university, he had realised he hated his mother. This hatred for her was undeclared and obsessive; and she still possessed the power to make him feel guilty, for which he hated himself as well. What he did not recognise was that, in hating her so passionately, he was struggling against a secret identification with her; in effect, he was becoming her, for hatred is as potent a bond as love and the harder one opposes something, the more one is subsumed by it. Victor fought his mother with her own tactics; but, as the old saying goes, one needs a very long spoon to sup with the devil. By according his mother such immense power, Victor accorded increasing power to the anima-mother in himself, which slowly, by degrees, began to possess him. Unaware of the gradual change, he proceeded to become womanish, developed classic effeminate mannerisms which seem to be alike the world over among anima-possessed men: the limp wrist, the gentle lisp, the tossing of the head, the suggestive walk with swivelling hips and mincing steps — a parody, in short, of inferior womanhood. By the time he left home to study acting at university, at the age of seventeen, he had already had several homosexual experiences; such adventures were readily obtainable in New York, and Victor was a very handsome young man. Before long, he had developed into an unmistakable queen. His mother, however, appeared not to notice, although everybody else did; for in cases of this kind, the price of truth is the discovery of one's own responsibility, which is often very difficult to assume. She spoke frequently of her hopes that he would meet some "nice" girl at university, and it secretly pleased him to know that she would be forever disappointed. But on an unconscious level she wanted him as he was; it assured her that he belonged wholly to her. He, on his part, was quite happy to accept this unconscious collusion, which spared him any confrontation with the lost masculinity which his father had never helped him develop. In fact, Victor despised the man for his weakness.

Victor's romantic career was a predictable one. The particular "gay" social milieu of which he became a part — as an adolescent in New York, at university, and afterwards — possesses it own laws of relationship: the innuendo in a bar, the quick pickup, the brief fantasy, the quarrels between two touchy and vanity-ridden animas, the abrupt rupture, the search for a new affair. Victor had never touched a woman; the idea revolted and sickened him, although he could not explain why. In liaisons with men he usually played the feminine role. Yet the approval of women was terribly important to him, and he was deeply hurt when women avoided him because of his mannerisms. He had never perceived his own caricatured behaviour clearly, for it had possessed him unconsciously; had never realised that even the decor of his apartment, once he had secured his own independent living arrangements at university, was exactly like that of his mother — from the matching drapes and lampshades to the china animals over the fireplace. He was shocked when people whom he met socially pegged him immediately and treated him accordingly; he had thought his sexual life was a well-kept secret.

After he graduated from university, Victor's acting career was moderately successful. Because he was small and slender, with an open, ingenuous face, he was frequently cast as a child in various stage plays. He moved from New York to California, hoping to break into films; he worked hard, possessed a striking gift for wit and mimicry, a marked talent for singing and dancing. When not being catty, he also displayed a great sweetness of nature and an intense loyalty and generosity in relationships with friends. But the role he coveted was that of the leading man, the hero — for obvious reasons, if one understands something of his psychology. This dream remained inaccessible to him, not only because of his smallness of build, but also because, unconsciously and with uncontrollable exaggeration, he was so effeminate that casting him in such a role would have been a travesty.

As he neared thirty, Victor began to seriously question his life. Until then, he had managed to laugh at everything, thus avoiding any confrontation with his feelings. Now he began to see not only the limitations of his acting career, but also — and with some pain — those of his personal life. Social acceptance by other people meant a great deal to him, and their ostracism constantly wounded him. Because he was so totally disconnected from his feeling nature, he could not enjoy a meaningful or lasting partnership with either man or woman. Had he managed to open his heart to another man, he might possibly have established some genuine relationship; but to unlock his feeling nature would have been to open the door to the pit. Moreover, he was bound to the cult of youth and beauty, the darkest aspect of the "gay" scene, and at thirty one must face the fact that youth and beauty are only on short lease. Most naively for any mortal, Victor had sought to enact the ancient myth of the *puer*, the beautiful youth bound to the devouring mother-goddess, who is doomed to a brief flash of light and flight, then drawn back to the omniverous womb. Confronted by the latter prospect, he began to contemplate suicide. As this is being written, he is still acting and apparently enjoying his latest romantic fling. At the same time, however, he is desperately unhappy, refuses professional help of any kind, and feels convinced that the final resolution of his life — and the final act of vengeance on his mother — will be, some day, at some time, to destroy himself.

Victor's chart does not in any way reflect the rather depressive evolution of his life, or the crisis point at which he now stands. It is not a "bad" chart; there are no horrendous planetary configurations, no dreadful malign influences apparent. What is reflected is a gentle and refined temperament, exposed to the less pleasant aspects of motherhood, who has never forgiven either his mother or himself for his youth. One cannot but feel that Victor has had many opportunities along the way, and refused to seize them. Nevertheless, his chart is not "the chart of a homosexual"; it is that of a particular sensibility which has become fettered to a powerful archetype and cannot break free — or will not — because doing so would entail a painful confrontation with itself. His mother is certainly not a helpful figure, and one would probably be justified for disliking her. But no one has the power to destroy another in the way she did without some unconscious collusion. The figure which is truly controlling Victor is not his mother, but the feminine archetype within himself, whose dark Gorgon face holds him as if mesmerised. He continues to blame his disposition on his mother, as though she had afflicted him with a disease. Perhaps, in a sense, she did — at first — but he is a man now, not a child. Victor's chart may reflect blindness and reluctance to accept the responsibilities of choice — the difficulty in focussing his own will and his capacity for masculine decision-making to liberate himself from the Mother's bonds. But the fate he has created for himself is his own.

Victor's refinement and lack of aggressiveness, as well as the intellectual and aesthetic qualities of his temperament, are reflected by the sun in Virgo in the third house, that of mental development, and by the four planets — Venus, Mars, Jupiter and Neptune — in Libra. Five planets in air and an absence of water in the chart — although the ascendant (Cancer) and midheaven (Pisces) are in watery signs — suggests dominance of the thinking function and difficulty in expressing the feeling nature. For an individual with a lack of water, handling the feelings is often difficult; it is not that he cannot feel, but rather that the feelings are unconscious and therefore intense, primitive, archaic, and sometimes very dark. They also have an autonomous quality, which is frightening to a thinking-oriented type and often causes him to barricade himself behind intellectual ramparts; these keep the more disquieting aspects of his psyche at bay. The Cancer ascendant, functioning in a largely unconscious fashion, suggests that Victor himself has many qualities of the Mother within him. If undifferentiated, these qualities tend to be expressed negatively much of the time: smothering, devouring, manipulative, clinging, deceiving. And because they are completely unconscious, they are projected upon his mother who, most appropriately, has the sun in Cancer. She is thus an excellent hook on which to hang the projection, and absolves him of responsibility. On the positive side, the Cancer ascendant suggests a marvellously rich imagination, sensitivity, quick perception, response to the feelings of others, compassion, love of culture, an instinct to protect those who are weak and in need of help. Victor's aptitude for mimicry is also perhaps connected with the reflective and subtle rising sign. All these virtues he often expressed to his friends and in his work. But as he could not connect with his feelings, the same virtues — including the gift for mimicry — tended to function in a largely autonomous way.

Two planetary configurations are worth particular mention. One of these is the square of Venus to Saturn, suggesting that Victor's image of woman is rather unpleasant and coloured by his own repressed drive for power. Saturn in Leo is a placement which suggests a deep and urgent need for recognition, achievement, and adulation to compensate a fear of being ordinary and unloved. When these qualities are unconscious, as they usually are when connected to the shadow, they tend to produce unconscious inflation, self-aggrandisement and a craving for control over others, coupled with a profound sense of inferiority and a constant demand for reassurance and acceptance. It is these shadow qualities that Victor has linked with his image of woman; he secretly fears her as a huge, inflated, carnivorous dragoness ready to devour anything in her path. Had he recongised the same propensities within himself, he might have found room for the shadow in his conscious expression, thereby assuming responsibility for its transmutation and development. But this is a moral responsibility which many people find difficult to assume. Combined with the problem reflected by Venus-Saturn, there is the presence of the moon in Sagittarius and the grouping of planets in Libra, suggesting a Pollyanna-like quality to Victor's temperament. Both Sagittarius and Libra infer a predisposition towards the bright side of things; Libra in particular is notorious for its dislike of the dark, the sordid, the ambiguous and the irrational. This buoyant quality in

Victor's nature is in many ways admirable, and highly likeable. Carried to the extreme, it is a problem because it does not permit recognition or expression of anything which is not "nice". Mars in Libra, even at its most aggressive, is only mentally self-assertive; it is too refined for the kind of direct self-salesmanship Victor needs to feed his Saturn in Leo, the shadow so hungry for love. Moreover, Mars is also widely conjunct Neptune, the second important indication of Victor's sexual expression. It suggests that his will, his power to actively pursue a goal, is affected by the collective anima — that is, by fantasy, moods, emotional states, and a subtle atrophy of energy which renders him impotent when confronted by life's problems.

These few pertinent points on the chart — and they are by no means the only terrain one could explore — reflect a very clear picture of a multifaceted psychological problem. But nowhere on the chart is there a specific indication that Victor would attempt to resolve this problem through homosexuality. On the contrary, there are many paths he might have chosen, and many modes of expression — some of which are more productive than others. In order to imbue his life with meaning and a relationship to others — both of which are essential for a temperament reflected by the grouping in Libra and the watery ascendant — Victor must become more conscious of himself, and particularly that aspect of himself which is manifested by the male body in which he was born. The trines of Uranus to Venus, Mars and Jupiter suggest that Victor possesses a capacity for originality, self-determination and freedom; and the balance of eight masculine signs to two feminine suggests the balance he would find most natural if he could unshackle himself from the grip of the anima. Because of his physical limitations, acting is not necessarily the most productive choice of profession, but some aspect of the arts certainly is. This is reflected by many points on the chart, and the many gifts with which Victor is endowed would bring him far more fulfilment if they were not being usurped by the shadow. Victor's is so much a situation which dictates the individual choosing to become himself. The chart has not damned him, his mother has not damned him;

it is he who has damned himself, not because his stars have
fated him, but because he has accepted a particular path. In
many ways the path of the *puer* is an easy one because one
need never really confront life. On the other hand, the man
who lives out a myth is the chosen of the gods; in a deeper
sense Victor's pattern is perhaps the appropriate fate for the
purposes of the Self. One cannot know these things, or pass
judgment on them in any conventional way, according to any
conventional standards. Victor's sexuality is only one aspect
of a life pattern which is part of a myth; and, like the good
actor he is, Victor plays his part for all it is worth.

VII
Honour Thy Father and
Mother ... with Reservations

Parents are Patterns.
                                    — Thomas Fuller

Do not think that there is more in destiny than
can be packed into childhood.
                                    — Rainer Maria Rilke

In the early days of psychoanalysis, it was assumed that every
man secretly wanted to bed his mother, and every woman her
father; and the entirety of the unconscious life of the psyche
was thought to be directed towards this one end. According
to Freudian thought, psychological problems were invariably
linked with the expression of infantile sexuality. At some
stage, this sexuality had been arrested or fixated through some
kind of trauma, the consequences of which continued to
manifest themselves in the adult's psychic and sometimes
physical life. Psychology has grown more sophisticated since
Freud's great pioneering work, but the undeniable power that
the parent exercises on the child's psyche remains an obvious
reality to anyone working in the field of human growth. How
many of us can take what we call our identity and be certain
that it is truly ours, that it is not permeated throughout with
the values, ideas, needs and attitudes held — consciously or
unconsciously — by our parents?

Freud believed the bond between child and parent could
always be reduced, in the end, to "nothing but" a sexual tie.
It is now apparent, however, that there is more, far more,

than simple desire for sexual gratification involved in the mysteries of the unconscious parent-child relationship. On one level, granted the sexual tie may indeed exist as a reality in childhood; but sexuality, as we have seen, may encompass something much more comprehensive than the act of copulation. And while many adult individual problems may derive from sexual sources, this occurs only where natural energy has been distorted or mischannelled in childhood. Nonetheless, one may say with Homer:

Never did any man of himself know his own parentage.

We must remember that mother and father are not only concrete human beings associated with our earliest experiences, but also symbols who embody the numinous power of archetypes; and the enormous dynamic strength of mother and father within the individual psyche stems not only from the personal relationship with the parent, whatever its nature, but also from the archetypal significance attached to that parent from the first coalescence of consciousness.

Among all possible ghosts that haunt man, the spirits of the parents possess the greatest significance. When father and mother become inner factors, they are no longer fantasies of childhood projected upon persons, but parts of the psyche that hinder advance.[1]

Because the experience of the parents is universal and archetypal, we may expect it to be represented in some way on the birth horoscope. And parents are indeed part of the pattern of the chart, for an individual is not only himself but the flower of the tree of his heritage. Neither mother nor father, however, is reflected in any objective sense; neither is depicted with any accurate delineation of individual character. What the chart *does* reflect is how the individual may experience his mother and father, and what emotional,

1 Quoted from Jung's conversations with Frances Wickes in *The Inner World of Choice*.

mental, physical and spiritual values he may attach to them. It will also reflect whether the parent-child relationship, apprehended from a completely subjective point of view, is likely to facilitate or oppose the individual's personal drives and development. Behind the relationship to the actual parents stands the relationship to the symbolic parents — and this, once again, returns us to the world of archetypal images and the great polarity of male and female, the cosmic mother and father. Mother in this sense is earth, matter, feeling, the cycle of birth and death, the all-giving and all-destroying, the instinctual life of the body and of the earth itself. Father is heaven, spirit, fire, will, meaning, purpose and purposeful development, order, structure and law. As in dreams, everything we experience — if it has the power to change us, or to create change within us — is both literal and symbolic, and this applies to parental figures as well. How we experience these archetypes is what the chart infers, and what we project of them onto their actual, personal, concrete representatives. Like a caul over the head of a newly-born child, the veil of the personal relationship, with all its nuances of feeling, thought and sensory experience, conceals the deeper psychic energies. Before we can freely penetrate the veil, however, we must first deal with the personal relationship and all its inevitable problems.

We have seen again and again how the inherent disposition of the individual is present at birth, and is reflected in the patterns of the birth chart.

> There is an *a priori* factor in all human activities, namely the inborn, preconscious and unconscious individual structure of the psyche. The preconscious psyche — for example, that of a new-born infant — is not an empty vessel into which, under favourable circumstances, practically anything can be poured.[1]

It is this "preconscious psyche" that gives us the free will to

---

1 *The Archetypes and the Collective Unconscious*, C.G. Jung Routledge & Kegan Paul, London 1959.

become what we are instead of what others have made of us. The child is not a mere receptacle for the psychic life of the parent; although he is susceptible to the unconscious forces which surround him in childhood, he also brings something of his own to his experience of them. Because of this, we cannot really attach moral blame to any parent, even if his or her neglect, rejection, harshness, absence, overpossessiveness or lack of understanding appears to have engendered psychological conflict. Such factors certainly leave their mark, and much brutality often occurs in the name of love. But whatever the mentality exhibited by the parent, something in the child meets it halfway, so to speak, accepts it and absorbs it; and the value he attaches unconsciously to one or another parental attribute determines the parent's effect upon him. Without ever realising it, one may become permeated by certain attitudes that are not truly one's own — attitudes deriving from a parent who, well-intentioned but unconscious, treats a child in a particular way because the child evokes this treatment from him.

The most important factor in the problems of difficult parent-child relationships, particularly those involving the mother, is not what the parent did or did not do. It is the interaction between the two parties, the combination of the two chemical substances; both are contributing factors to the product that results. In short, it is not only what the parent did, but what the child expected him to do, and the discrepancy between action (or lack of it) and expectation.

> In treating patients, one is at first impressed, and indeed arrested, by the apparent significance of the personal mother. This figure of the personal mother looms so large in all personalistic psychologies that as we know, they never got beyond it, even in theory, to other important aetiological factors. My own view differs from that of other medico-psychological theories principally in that I attribute to the personal mother only a limited aetiological significance. That is to say, all those influences which the literature describes as being exerted on the children do not come from the mother

herself, but rather from the archetype projected upon her, which gives her a mythological background and invests her with authority and numinosity. The aetiological and traumatic effects produced by the mother must be divided into two groups: 1) those corresponding to traits of character and attitudes actually present in the mother, and 2) those referring to traits which the mother only seems to possess, the reality being composed of more or less fantastic (i.e., archetypal) projections on the part of the child.[1]

This extremely important postulate of Jung's must be considered if we are to work constructively with parental images in the psyche. In our present society, it is unlikely that there are many individuals unscathed by the ambiguous imprint of the parents. This is partly because the undervaluing of relatedness, and of the feminine principle in general, during the last two thousand years, has created universal problems within marriage which are bound to leave scars in the child's psyche. Because that psyche is so susceptible to the parent's unconscious life, the impress of the latter will be far more confused and destructive if a couple conforms to model "normal" behaviour, never confronting their secret desires, impulses and drives. In primitive cultures, for example, where there is little individuality and less value attached to the sanctity of individual parents as personalities — the parents, rather, are embodiments of age-old archetypes — we do not find the kind of mother- and father-complexes to which the Western psyche is so prone. Through the injunction of the Ten Commandments, combined with the increased ego-consciousness of developing man, we have both gained and lost. Our obsession with the personal aspects of family life has offered us the richness and depth of individualised relationships. It has also rendered us vulnerable to all manner of new psychological influences, many of which may be inimical to growth.

1 *Ibid.*

Your children are not your children.
They are the sons and daughters of Life's longing for
   itself.
They come through you but not from you.
And though they are with you yet they belong not to you.
You may give them your love but not your thoughts,
For they have their own thoughts.
You may house their bodies but not their souls,
For their souls dwell in the house of tomorrow,
   which you cannot visit, not even in your dreams.
You may strive to be like them, but seek not to make
   them like you,
For life goes not backward nor tarries with yesterday.[1]

These words of Kahlil Gibran eloquently articulate simple
truths. Yet can we honestly say that our parents understood
these truths — or that we ourselves, as parents, understand
them? If an individual has not dared to live his own life, he
will unconsciously attempt to live it through his children. We
cannot blame him because he is unconscious, but we must
usually recognise the violation and the damage his blindness
often entails.

In order to make some sense of these difficulties, and to
utilise them in a constructive way, we must first separate the
real parent from the archetypal projection. If this is done
gently, and with respect for the parent, whatever his failings,
no bond of love will be violated. Violation only occurs in the
unconscious, when the separation is not effected and the
resentment accumulated over a lifetime spills over into a
man's waking existence, poisoning his relationships with
those around him. Esoteric doctrine offers a convenient
principle worth remembering. Of our own accord we choose
our parents, but not as "punishment" or "reward" for "good"
or "bad" deeds in other lives. We choose them because these
parents are of our own substance, are connected with us by a
unity of psychic composition — whether we recognise the
link or not. Our parents are therefore both objective people

1 *The Prophet*, Kahlil Gibran, Alfred A. Knopf, New York 1971.

in the outer world, and symbolic figures in the inner psyche.

It is easy enough to recognise that mother is the first woman we meet in life, and that she will therefore imprint upon the child's psyche his initial and most powerful experience of everything the feminine will come to mean. Likewise, father is the first man we meet in life, and he will also leave his mark upon the unconscious of the child as the embodiment of the masculine. We are born with the collective heritage of several millenia's experience of mother and father, and the collective configurations of these symbolic figures are inherent within us; but the personal "I", the ego, does not know any of this until it is objectified in the external world as the family into which the child is born. And even then, one rarely knows it consciously.

> Children are so deeply involved in the psychological attitude of their parents that it is no wonder that most of the nervous disturbances in childhood can be traced back to a disturbed psychic atmosphere in the home.[1]

If the child, bearing within him the archetypal images of symbolic mother and father, encounters, instead of solicitude and stability, a welter of unconscious chaos, hostility, aggression, violence, envy and destructiveness, he will very understandably display "neurotic" traits — which in one form or another will perpetuate themselves into adulthood. And all too frequently the parents of such a child bring him to the analyst's office, or even to the astrologer, asking why he is so disturbed and what can be done to "cure" him. This places the counsellor in a most difficult position. Few parents (particularly if they are conscientious) care to be told that it is they, not their children, who belong on the analyst's couch. Yet that is the only thing the conscientious counsellor *can* tell them.

What then happens if — all conscious efforts and appearances notwithstanding — a mother unconsciously resents having had to bear a child in the first place, or

1 From Jung's introduction to *The Inner World of Childhood*.

desperately wanted one of a different sex, or possesses a deeply submerged drive to power which has never found expression by virtue of the demands of society and upbringing? The archetypal mother, full of warmth, compassion, sympathy, solicitude and nurture conflicts violently and discordantly with the child's perception of the real mother, who may not be any of these things. The dark face of the archetype will then be constellated — for all archetypes are a duality of light and dark — and mother, as a result, will become devourer, dragon, witch, destroyer, castrator. Moreover, the child's own disposition, which causes him to be more or less sensitive to the abyss between mother and Mother, will itself colour his reactions to this abyss. If the child is male, how will his unconscious attitudes towards women be affected? How will the constellation of the anima be influenced, the subterranean image of woman which he carries within him? And if the child is female, what will happen to her own emerging femininity, if it is patterned on the model of such a mother? If the latter unconsciously despises or fears men, what will this do to the daughter's unconscious image of them?

If there is no father to whom a child can in some way relate, what will provide him with a symbol of strength, support and purpose? Such a child may be subjected only to his mother's view of the absent father, which, if the marriage has failed, may be badly distorted. Alternatively, a child may be confronted with a mother who attempts to play father and assume the masculine role. The fantasy image a child creates in his father's absence will inevitably assume gigantic proportions, for Nature abhors a vacuum and so does the psyche; and where there is a personal vacuum, the archetypes will flood in. Should he be present, on the other hand, the father will also exert an influence through what he is unconscious of within himself. If he is frustrated and dominated by his wife, what will his unconscious anger and bitterness do to his child? If he is unable to acknowledge or express feeling, how will this affect the child's trust in the healing and binding power of love? Nothing dies that is not lived out; but if it has been unlived in the parent, it may live a secret life in the unconscious of the child, and "fate" his life accordingly.

These are simple enough questions, and the answers are fairly obvious. Unfortunately the questions are not usually asked until adulthood, and the answers then come too late. In addition to all these questions, moreover, there must be another. What does the child unconsciously expect of the parent? Ultimately, perhaps, we can only do as the *I Ching* suggests, and work on what has been spoiled — always accepting our share in the responsibility.

There is a most uncomfortable phase through which the evolving individual must inevitably pass, a phase at which he discovers an ambivalence of emotion towards his parents and recognises the darker, more destructive elements in his relationship with them. This phase will therefore be characterised by a natural and — in some sense — thoroughly justified resentment and recrimination which, with the dawning awareness of "what has been done to me", burst angrily into consciousness. Yet this phase is only a preliminary to the work that must be performed. It is like an abscess collecting all the toxins which have previously infected and circulated through the whole body. And the advantage of an abscess is that it can be lanced, the poisons can be drained away, and the body can be given an opportunity to heal.

When the resentment and recrimination subside, one gradually becomes aware that what the parents "did" occurred many years ago, and that it is only oneself who has allowed the ghosts to remain alive within the psyche, feeding on one and directing one's choices from one's own underworld. As an individual begins to see that he has himself endowed certain images with their continuing power, he can disengage himself from them; and he will also recognise that many unattractive qualities in his nature, which he had formerly attributed to parental influence, in fact belong to him. As he develops compassion for his own darkness, moreover, he will begin to feel compassion for the darkness in his parents. They will emerge as human beings, not monsters, who will be washed clean, as it were; and their gifts of love and loyalty, however small, will be accorded an appropriate due. Thus the child gives new birth to the parent; and at the same time, becomes aware of the deeper energy which stands behind the parental figure and constitutes his own true source. By freeing ourselves, we free our parents. Only in this way can we truly honour them — with the honour which any human being is due. It is very different from paying lip service with a burden of guilt and a heart full of secret resentment, for which we make our own partners and children pay.

The problem of clashing psychological types must also be considered here. It is nobody's "fault", yet it can wreak havoc through unconscious rejection of another's most precious values. Because one sees what one can see best oneself, the thinking parent may undervalue the feeling child's feelings; the sensation-oriented parent may be frightened by the perceptions of the intuitive child; and in many families the child is made to carry the burden of the parent's projected shadow, animus or anima, regardless of whether he is temperamentally suited for the role. Children project the archetypal parents on the living ones, and parents, in the same way, project the archetypal child — the new life full of creative possibilities — on their own progeny. When this occurs, the image of the child may become tinged with the parent's secret inferiority — the secret drive, the clandestine ambition which has never been granted access to consciousness. How many mothers, striving to be domestic, caring and faithful to the world of feeling and relating, harbour unconscious animus ambitions which they project onto a child, hoping he will become the intellectual genius, the creative wonder, the worldly success? In such cases the will to power wears the mask of love. In the name of "what is best", the mother commits a psychic rape of her child, then recoils, astonished, when he violently rebels or withdraws into "abnormal" behaviour. In other cases, the child, desperate for love, may model himself on the parent's projection; he may spend half his life trying to be the prodigy he is expected to be, measuring himself against standards of perfection that are superhuman and, in consequence, perpetually falling short. And, not surprisingly, the sequence of successive failures will engender a profound sense of inadequacy and guilt. In adulthood he must eventually confront the demon which has driven him, must recognise that it is not his own, must recognise also that he has accepted it as his own and consequently damned himself. Chidren provide a splendid vehicle for many parents to live out the unlived sides of their own psyches; and this can occur even when the unlived elements are abhorrent to the parent's conscious values. The ambitious, successful father may produce a wastrel or effeminate son, the proper and chaste mother a promiscuous daughter. Whose is the effeminacy, whose the promiscuity? It belongs to both. How many mothers are jealous of their daughters, because of vanished youth and unseized opportunities? How many men are jealous of their sons, or threatened by them? How many father desire their daughters, or mothers their sons? Yes, Oedipus lusted after Jocasta, but Jocasta also encouraged him, and took him voluntarily into her bed. We can only conjecture about these things until we meet them within ourselves; and on the way down to such trysts, it becomes darker and darker. Yet amidst this darkness, within the morass of unconscious swamp and quicksand, a flower, so to speak, has sunk its roots and glimmers like a talisman. It is the limitlessness of possibility latent within human nature, an infinite potential which includes love, compassion, sympathy and forgiveness, a sense of the continuity of life and the nobility of the soul. And it compels one to recognise that, had one been one's own parent, with the latter's anxieties, needs, limits, conflicts, dreams and aspirations, one might have been guilty of the very things one condemns. Our parents' "sins" — both of commission and omission — may indeed have been visited upon us, but we always retain the option of transmuting curse into blessing — the blessing of being able to say, open-eyed and gratefully, that "there but for fortune go you and I". The purposeful patterns of the psyche, reflected by the purposeful patterns of the birth chart, suggest that we have chosen whatever experiences "befall" us. And what we choose is in some way appropriate and necessary, although the ego may sometimes find it painful,

shocking, confusing, frustrating, and destructive — at least
until we possess sufficient insight to discern its meaning and
coherence in the overall configuration of our lives.

*   *   *

On the birth horoscope, there are two primary areas from
which we may obtain some understanding of an individual's
parent images. One of these is the chart's vertical axis, with
the midheaven or MC (*medium coeli*) at the top or south
point, and the IC (*immum coeli*) at the bottom, or north. In
the rich tapestry of symbology we have inherited from our
past, north is often the place of spirit, the point of rebirth,
the abode of the gods. South is the place of the heart, of
earth and matter. The northern and southern points of the
horoscope are connected with the deepest mysteries: the
roots from which a man springs and draws his unconscious
life, and the mission he is called to perform in the world of
which he is a part.

In addition to this vertical axis of the horoscope, we must
also consider the moon and sun, symbols of the feminine and
masculine principles within the psyche. These, too, are
connected with mother and father. Not only are they
intimately associated with the roots and the flowering of the
individual tree of life; they are also the most basic essence of
woman and man. The two houses of the horoscope which
follow the MC and the IC are the tenth and fourth
respectively. The tenth house is said to be connected with
profession, career and place in society, the fourth with the
home and domestic attitudes. Both, however, are connected
with parental relationships as well. It is possible that the
meridian — the vertical axis of the horoscope — and the
polarity of sun and moon suggest two different aspects of the
parental experience. The houses seem to reflect the material
reality in which an individual finds himself, while the planets
reflect currents and directions of energy within the psyche. In
other words, the two "parental" angles of the chart are
perhaps more of an indication of one's relation to one's own
father and mother, while sun and moon mirror the

individual's inner experience of his archetypal parents. It is difficult to say which is more important. Certainly both pairs of opposites must be considered.

In orthodox astrology texts there is much argument about whether the fourth house, connected with the IC, should be associated with the mother or father. Older books state definitively that the tenth house rules the father, the fourth the mother. Some more recent authorities contend that the issue depends on the sex of the individual, others that it depends on which parent is playing the masculine or feminine role. The problem is further complicated by the fact that a person may manifest the characteristics of one sex physically and the other psychologically; and matters become more complicated still by the compensatory function of the unconscious, which guarantees that the conscious personality of a parent will be counterbalanced by its subterranean antithesis. And it is usually the parent's unconscious which affects the child most powerfully. As in any polarity, of course, each pole will complement and compensate for the other, so that some equilibrium is attained. Thus the relationship with one parent will engender its opposite with the other. One cannot separate the parental couple, since they affect each other reciprocally and both affect the balance of opposites within the child. Parents, in short, are a unitive experience. It is never a question of either-or. Rather, it is one of and-and. Like other dilemmas in the study of astrology — the problem of house systems, for example, or the question of co-rulers of signs connected with the three newly discovered planets — one cannot speculate in the abstract; theories may be plausible, logical and aesthetically satisfying, but they simply may not work out in practise. It is also extremely difficult to do statistical research on such uncertainties, because one is dealing with the psychic experiences of individuals — and psychic experience does not lend itself to black-and-white analysis. Ultimately, one must work with what seems to work, always recognising that what works for one astrologer might not for another; and this applies to the subject whose chart is being studied as well. The following interpretations of the parental houses are

not theoretical, but empirical; and they may not necessarily
be universally apt. To some significant extent, however, they
have proved valid, and they therefore warrant consideration.
The relationship with the father seems to be reflected most
clearly by the north point of the chart (the IC) and by any
planets which fall in the fourth house. The relationship with
the mother seems to be reflected most clearly by the
midheaven, the south point (the MC) and by any planets
which fall in the tenth house.

The sign at the midheaven generally suggests the particular
factors which predominate in one's relationship to one's
mother. It often — too often for coincidence, too often for
anything perhaps save the mysterious principle Jung calls
synchronicity — corresponds to the mother's sun-sign,
ascendant, moon-sign, or the dominant influence suggested
by a strongly placed planet on her chart. The sign at the MC
mirrors that facet of the mother's nature which affects the
child most strongly, because something in him is especially
receptive to it. One could amost say that this sign, and its
opposite at the IC, are symbolic reflections of our heredity,
for they often recur repeatedly among the charts of close
family members. It is as though the meridian and the horizon
(the ascendant-descendant axis) formed the cross upon
which the individual psyche is "crucified" in matter — the
corporeal structure in which he must incarnate as a conscious
individual, bound by the limitations of his heritage. No
matter what components exist within the birth chart, he is
fixed to this cross which obliges him to express what he is
through the specific and unique channels it affords.

A Virgo midheaven, for example, suggests that the
qualities primarily associated with the mother are earthy; she
may be seen as a practical, earthy person, committed to
individual productivity, service, work or material security.
And she may represent also a strong emphasis on duty, on
order and structure. All these attributes are likely to be
incorporated into the conscious values of the individual
himself, as he sees himself through the world's eyes. A Leo
midheaven, on the other hand, might imply a powerful
creative impulse in connection with the mother, a powerful

maternal personality, an insistence on self and the desires of self. A Cancer midheaven might suggest a dominant feeling life, possessiveness, adherence to the unity of the family and the values of the past. These, of course, are oversimplified examples. But in some way the mother, or what the child experiences through her, is connected with the attributes of the sign which falls on the "maternal" angle of the birth chart. Needless to say, no value judgment can be pronounced, positive or negative, about the sign on the midheaven. It is simply a symbol for both a complex and a mode of experience, which the child absorbs unconsciously — not knowing that it sets a stamp upon him, shapes the values he will express in relation to his subsequent environment. The sign on the midheaven signifies how an individual would like to be seen by the mother, or how he sees her. His social values ultimately derive from her, as well as those concerning relationships with others. The sign on the midheaven is also often a statement of the lesson to be learned through the mother, the obstacle which must be made conscious so that one may integrate it into his own creative life. Or we might say that the MC's sign suggests that part of the inheritance from the mother which is also within the child, and which he must develop for both of them.

The tenth house has other meanings, although they are all associated with the archetype of the mother, that which issues from the womb of earth and crystallises in matter. Traditional astrology regards the tenth house as a significator of career, achievement, and status in society. It seems to be connected with the *persona*, the mask of social adaptation which every individual develops in order to mesh smoothly with the environment of which he is a part. Often it suggests the kind of endeavour in which the individual is most happy, or a set of attitudes which he espouses in his working life. Generally this is because it defines his values, values to which, through his work, he will seek to impart form. Thus the Leo midheaven, through the experience of the mother, may have to learn something about personal power and expression of individuality. Accordingly, he may seek work which involves him in the creative arts, or puts him in a position of responsibility and authority. In these activities he can express that which he has learned to value, through the mother-relationship — the experience of individual creativity. At the same time, however, we must not forget that one may come to value certain things the hard way, by having to assert and validate them in the face of opposition.

The MC is often a very conscious point on the chart, a point with which a person readily identifies himself. He may often be heard to espouse the sign's values as he describes himself to others. How he acquired these values is not usually so conscious, but some investigation will usually disclose some aspect of the mother-child relationship.

In contrast to the MC, the IC is usually a deeply submerged and unconscious point of the chart. It symbolises the source and roots of one's being, those elements lying silently at the base of the psyche, pumping sap into the tree which eventually flowers in the world through the midheaven and the social attributes the midheaven implies. Perhaps the values of the MC are often the most dominant in conscious life; but the spiritual source of being is the Father, personified by the father, who confers his name and lineage, as well as the structure and support which enable the family to exist. There is a mystery about this south point, which the sun crosses at midnight at the end of one day and the dawn of the next. Here the sun is at its lowest ebb, and the ego is rooted in the unconscious forces of past and future. Orthodox textbooks call the IC the beginning and end of life; it seems to reflect the deeply buried source of meaning which is never displayed to the world, yet which nourishes the identity from within. Just as the ascendant always has its opposite sign at the descendant, the MC always has its opposite at the IC. If mother-anima-woman provides the key to experience, father-animus-man provides the key to the meaning behind experience, the plan, the purpose, the direction, the seed from origin to ending. The sign placed at the IC often represents a quality which the individual seeks in others — hence its importance in chart comparison — yet which can — albeit with some effort — be found within himself. It is the secret unconscious value which ultimately motivates the choices one apparently makes through one's consciously adopted goals.

When a planet is placed in either the fourth or tenth house, the relationship with the parents immediately assumes greater importance. Such placement suggests that the archetype or psychological impetus symbolised by the planet in question is somehow associated with the parent. It may be projected upon him, but it is also experienced through him: the projection evokes some quality inherent in the parent, through whom the child apprehends a particular planetary energy. This applies even if other personality traits are more dominant in the parent's makeup; what the planet symbolises is what exercises the pivotal influence, because both parent and child share it. In short, it is the point of connection between them. The energy symbolised by the MC or IC may be unconscious in the parent, and may be so in the child as well. But only by bringing this energy into the orbit of his own conscious experience can the individual free himself from the unconscious umbilical cord that fetters him to his progenitors.

The problem is most obvious, and most complicated, when a masculine planet (sun, Mars, Jupiter, Uranus) is placed in the tenth house, or a feminine planet (moon, Venus, Neptune, Pluto) in the fourth. Such placement implies that some masculine component in the mother's psyche, or some feminine component in the father's, has provided a hook upon which the child can project; and confusion may then result from discrepancies between the psychological sex of the particular parent and the archetypal qualities naturally associated with him. The sun in the tenth house, for example, is a most interesting placement, for it implies far more than honour and success in one's profession. It implies that the mother may be possessed by a drive for power, conscious or unconscious, and that she may seek to live out her masculine side through her child. And the child, for his part, may project his own capacity for self-direction and self-expression upon the mother — or upon suitable objects in the outer world which symbolise mother — so that he concurs in living out her goals, never realising he has failed to develop his own. This placement — the sun at the MC — often occurs in charts of ch'ldren who are expected to bring honour to their mothers by their success in the world. And frequently, such children will indeed attain success in the world, but without realising why they want it so badly. The same chart configuration may also occur when — in the death or absence of the mother — the unconscious fantasy assumes an autonomous power. Then mother may become Mother and the individual's goals may be directed towards actualising some demand issued by the compound, semi-archetypal figure. The sun in the tenth may also indicate the absence of the father — in which case the mother must assume the masculine role, whether she wishes to do so or not. As with all astrological placements, specific circumstances will vary, and no blame is involved. Problems symbolised by the positions we have discussed may, for example, exist concurrently with a very profound love. Once again, it is the psychological meaning of the placement, the individual's own experience of the mother-relationship, that matters, not events or circumstances; and when the sun is in the tenth house, one's identity is often entangled with that of the mother. He must first free himself from the umbilical cord, must find his own goals in the world, must make his own choices about what he contributes to life. Only in this way can he fulfil that drive most precious to him — to become a whole, balanced and integrated individual who can express himself in a genuinely creative way and realise the infinite potential within him.

Another extremely significant placement, and one which often causes enormous problems, is Saturn in the tenth house. In this case the shadow, the inferior dark component of the psyche, is somehow associated with the mother. She may then come to symbolise restriction, pain, rejection, frustration or loss of a kind which inhibits the individual's expression and denies him the gift of faith or trust in his own destiny. When Saturn is placed in the tenth house, there is often a destructive element involved in the mother-child relationship. Because Saturn is connected with frustration, crystallisation, atrophy and constriction, there is often some component of the individual's nature which was "seized up" in childhood, subsequently undermining his confidence in himself and his capacity to create a meaningful reality. A statistical analysis of male homosexual charts shows a suspicious frequency of tenth house Saturns. We must remember, however, that this placement does not "cause" homosexuality; rather, it indicates something about the way in which an individual will relate to women and to the feminine element, coloured by the mother-experience, within himself. If a man experiences Saturn through his mother, the dark side of his own personality may be fused with his image of her. Then it may seem that she "restricted" him, "rejected" him, "emasculated" him, "made" it difficult for him to feel a part of society. He may become inordinately ambitious, yet secretly fearful and self-doubting, constantly assessing himself, his abilities and limitations through what he thinks are his mother's eyes. Here, too, one cannot distribute blame; the problem has resulted from a collaborative effort. But the individual must become conscious of his bondage, must free his own projection from what was acted out around him. When he has done this, he can develop his own sense of support and inner strength — also a facet of Saturn — without depending unconsciously on mother.

A very different dilemma is reflected by Neptune in the tenth house. When this placement occurs the mother may be experienced as the martyr, the sacrifice — and she may nourish such a projection by exhibiting excessive passivity and self-abnegation. By doing so, she may provoke a deep sense of guilt, or unconscious obligation, in the child, to whom she has apparently "given so much". As a result, the child may come to idealise his mother, to see her as perfect and install her on a pedestal. Alternatively, he may become severely disillusioned; he may unwittingly blame his mother for not attaining the perfection his own guilt has conferred upon her. In consequence, he may find himself devoid of direction or purpose, wandering aimlessly from one career to another, never realising that he has made of himself the sacrifice he ascribed to her.

When Pluto is placed in the tenth house, the experience of

the mother is often invested with some element of the devourer, the archetypal destroyer, the dragon who possesses the child and wields absolute tyrannical power. Not infrequently, something within the child will "die", or, in other words, go unconscious — his own capacity for transformation, his ability to accept and adapt to the cyclical changes which occur within his life. He may be deeply afraid of death, deeply afraid of change, and may — overtly or unconsciously — seek power in order to preserve himself. In some fashion, the experience of the mother will be connected with power, control, possession and submergence of self; and this is often linked with extreme submission or bondage on a feeling level. At risk of oversimplification, we might say that Mercury connects the experience of the mother with the life of the mind, with understanding, negative criticism or both; Venus connects the mother-image with the ideal feminine, the hetaira, who can provoke jealousy in a daughter and adoration in a son. Uranus, forceful and disruptive, may indicate alienation, separation or violent rebellion in the mother-relationship, the need for the individual to break free and express his own individuality. Mars, god of war, connects the mother-experience with will and desire, aggression and dominance. And the moon at the maternal angle suggests a deep and instinctual bond which may tie the child's unconscious feeling life to the mother's and compels him to express her feeling values as his own.

These are very brief analyses of terribly complex situations. When there is more than one planet in the tenth house, the issue becomes even more complicated — and one must also consider the aspects such planets make to other planets. The same principles obtain, of course, for planets in the fourth house, save that they reflect the experience of the father rather than the mother. In consequence, they will impart a completely different colouration to the situation by virtue of the different roles played by each parent in the individual's development. In the end one must explore the placements of planets in the fourth and tenth houses through one's own personal experience. We must remember, however, that the circumstances surrounding the parents are only half the

picture. It is primarily the unconscious life of the parents —
what they have not expressed either to each other or to the
world around them — which the child experiences in his
early years. The presence of a planet in either the fourth or
tenth immediately focusses attention on a parental tie. This
tie need not necessarily be negative. All such ties, moreover,
are meaningful and lead the individual to greater understanding of himself. But we must be aware of the indications that
some portion of the individual's psyche is bound to the
parent, and he must become conscious of the relationship's
deeper aspects if he is to reclaim that crucial fragment of
himself. We all have parents, and there has never yet been
one that is perfect. If a specific individual develops an
enormous complex, an intense identification or a highly
charged spectrum of emotional reactions in relation to one of
his parents, the responsibility resides as much with him as
with them. The two halves of the equation can never be
separated. Nor is there ever any question of "fault", no
matter how brutal the parental experience may be. On one
level we might argue that one should not bear a child if one is
going to abuse it; but such an argument does not allow for
the general problem of unconsciousness in people. We must
be wary of attaching blame. One can only work on what has
been spoiled.

As well as being individuals, mother and father are the
embodiments of archetypes. To the growing individual, they
thus afford an opportunity to gain deeper understanding of
some aspect of a particular planetary energy, which he may
eventually incorporate into his own conscious life. The
absence of planets in the fourth or tenth house suggests that
there may be less direct identification of the parent with an
archetype. If this is the case, the parent becomes associated
with that area of life symbolised by the house in which the
ruler of the MC or IC is placed. For example, if Virgo is at the
midheaven, and if no planets fall in the tenth, one must
consider Mercury, ruler of Virgo, and his placement on the
chart. If Mercury is in the second house, which reflects the
individual's attitudes towards stability, security, durability
and permanence in himself and in his life, his experience of

the mother will be connected with these values. She may, for example, support her child even into adulthood; or her own values about material things may become part of his conscious hierarchy of values. The possibilities are endless. Moreover, the aspects of the midheaven ruler to other planets must also be considered. These will suggest how the experience of the mother is "digested" in the chart as a whole — with ease, or with conflict.

Along with the testimony of the meridian and its two angles, one must consider the sun and moon — their signs, their houses and especially their aspects to other planets. The sun-moon dyad symbolises the masculine and feminine balance within the individual in the broadest sense. Thus its placement in the context of the chart will reflect his particular attitudes or experiences or images of male and female. At the same time, the sun and moon do not seem to be as closely linked to actual circumstances as the MC and IC; they are connected more with the deepest level of the individual's interpretation of male and female, as he lives these opposites out within his own life. The sun conjuncting Uranus, for example, will indicate more about the father one embodies than it will about the father one had; and although one may project the former onto the latter, it will originate within himself, from his own substance. The moon in conjunction with Saturn will infer more than what kind of mother one has. It implies what kind of mother one is, regardless of one's sex. The inner image of the maternal, the feminine, lives within the individual and its attributes are symbolised by the moon's sign, house position and aspects. These are one's feeling values, one's anima, one's interpretation of the myth of Mother which exists in all human beings. Again, one may project it onto one's own mother; but the substance of the projection lies within oneself.

These mechanisms are often unconscious, although sometimes all too obvious to others. One may listen to a person with Saturn, Uranus or Pluto in the tenth proclaim how marvellous his mother is, and what a splendid relationship he enjoys with her. And she may indeed be marvellous. She may also love him. Nor may there be any question of a "bad" relationship. There may, however, be a question of power, and of how much power the marvellous mother exercises — whether deliberately or not — over the psyche of her child. Or a question of how much of his own hierarchy of value, his own identity, his own attitude towards both the women within him and around him are affected by her imprint. And it is often a question of how long it will take him to make this imprint conscious, so that he can reclaim it, reintegrate it and make it truly his own.

Because the study of the parents on the birth chart is a complex matter, some points may be clarified by an example. When one is seeking to understand depths such as these, no step-by-step definitive guide to precise chart interpretation can be offered. The keywords fail us, and to decipher the central symbols of meridian and planets one must rely on the testimony of the individual — spoken and unspoken — as well as on one's own intuitive understanding. It is impossible to be literal. Chart interpretation is an art, and derives as much from one's own sensitivity on the feeling and intuitive level as it does from delineation of logical principles.

The best place to begin is with an individual's chart, and that of one of his parents. The image one holds of the parent must first be weighed against the inherent temperament reflected by the parent's chart, and the result should yield much in the way of insight. Such insight will not in itself solve any problems. It may, however, constitute a valuable and enlightening guide.

* * *

Howard, whose chart is shown below, is a man endowed with brilliant intellectual capacities and a remarkable facility of verbal expression. As professor of philosophy at a prestigious university, and an acknowledged authority in his subject, he has ample opportunity in his career to utilise his intellectual gifts. Within the structure provided by academia, he has always easily achieved his goals. Being highly differentiated in both the realms of thinking and intuition, he can quickly make connections, synthesise ideas, juggle systems like an

Relating

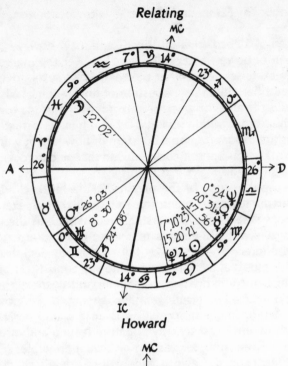

Howard

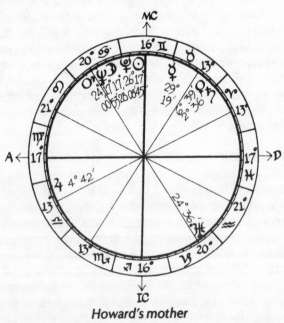

Howard's mother

entertainer and make them appear both philosophically and psychologically relevant. His professional success is therefore assured, and his undeveloped sensation function renders him oblivious to the world of objects. In consequence, he is not unduly concerned about living accommodations, clothes and other "mundane" things. His salary exceeds his needs and he spends it prodigally.

Howard is the product of a middle-class suburban family subjected to typical pressures of conformity. His mother was a highly intelligent woman who excelled in academic pursuits, earning a university degree a full three years before her peers — and at a time when such accomplishments were extremely rare for women. She herself was the product of a cultured continental family, with musicians, composers and artists blossoming prolifically from her father's genealogical tree. As a result, she chose to forget her mother's antecedents, who had been lower-class industrial workers. Her greatest ambition was to provide her son with the best education possible, then to see him achieve recognition in the scholarly world. This would compensate for the career she had herself abandoned when she assumed the responsibility of raising a family. Endowed with numerous talents, but never having allowed them to develop, she sought to realise her own unlived potential through her gifted son.

Howard's father, on the other hand, came from a working-class background. As a young man, he had displayed a certain academic promise, but his family lacked means to provide him with the education he probably deserved. In consequence he came to distrust and disown his intellectual faculties, became deeply introverted and felt more comfortable in the world of craftsmen and artisans than he did in the world of the mind; and by the time Howard was born, he had already discovered an intense satisfaction in such activities as carpentry and woodworking. Not surprisingly, his marriage proved disastrous, an exhausting and paralysing bond, like that of two stags with locked antlers.

Confronted by financial problems, Howard's mother clung all the more fiercely to her academic credentials. Incessantly, she would brandish them in her husband's face,

never letting him forget that he was uneducated, her
intellectual inferior. He, for his part, withdrew increasingly
into himself, intimidated and with waning self-confidence. In
mounting desperation, he embarked on enterprise after
enterprise, vainly trying to prove himself a responsible
breadwinner; and with each successive failure, he would be
subjected to his wife's denigration and scorn. This drove still
deeper his already subterranean but powerful erotic drive,
and distorted it into a dormant yet smouldering propensity
towards violence. By the time Howard needed him, he was
too turned in upon himself to offer any valid relationship to
his son.

Howard thus grew up in an atmosphere of withering
coldness and bristling hostility, never seeing his parents
express any affection for each other. Moreover, both fought
over him, and over the manner in which he was to be reared.
Projecting his own dreams of material success onto his son,
Howard's father insisted that discipline and hard work were
the prerequisites for manhood. Howard's mother, on the
other hand, obsessed by fantasies of what her son should be,
emphasised academic achievement and rewarded it with gifts
of money. Neither she nor her husband offered any feeling to
the child, only approval or disapproval; and these were
translated into money granted or withheld.

Having unconsciously absorbed the brutal antipathy
between his parents, Howard recoiled from it by dissociating
himself from his own feeling life. To counteract the
destructive atmosphere surrounding him, he displayed an
increasing susceptibility to illness — asthma, sinusitis,
stomach trouble, even pneumonia, from which he nearly
died. These maladies at least elicited some demonstration of
warmth and solicitude, some display of feeling which he
could not otherwise obtain.

As an adult, Howard found he could not really experience
feeling as a reality. There was a coldness within him, a
disinterest so far as others were concerned. This forced him
to invest his relationships with a calculating quality, which
made it impossible for him to relax, to enjoy himself or an
experience without dissecting both to pieces. To protect

himself from emotional pain and the profound sense of inadequacy that gnawed at him, he applied his intellect to his feelings, thus hoping to establish control over them and subordinate them to his will. Not surprisingly, his romantic life was riddled with disappointments; his undifferentiated feeling function made it difficult, if not impossible, to open himself and risk the vulnerability that doing so would entail. Increasingly, therefore, he came to rely on his incisive intellect, with which he found he could always impress others, particularly certain types of women. At the same time, he shrank from women who could meet him on his own terms. Instead, he turned to those who displayed a tempestuous wildness, a volatile unpredictability, an instinctual and irrational response to the nuances of situations; and through these qualities he sought to compensate for his own inhibitions. Such women invariably brought him pain, casting him repeatedly in the role of Professor Rath, enamoured of Lola Lola. As a further bulwark against any threat to his feeling nature, Howard consistently involved himself with married women. Such women were "safe"; their situation would circumscribe the relationship from the beginning, would establish predetermined limits to it, and would thus absolve him from any serious commitment he might not wish to incur. Although capable of profound depths of feeling, he distrusted them; and, to neutralise them, he constantly subjected them to the bright beam of his cold intelligence. Despite his brilliance and the interest he awakened in others, his inner world was one of intense loneliness. To escape it, he would immerse himself ever more deeply in abstruse philosophical treatises. When they failed to answer his inner needs, he would seek distraction in popular crime novels and television.

In deference to his mother's ambitions, Howard had embarked on an academic career and quickly attained one success after another. Before long, he had distinguished himself in scholarly circles for his perceptive commentaries on great philosophers of the past. While still in his twenties, his published two books, both of which received generous critical praise; and by the age of thirty, his university department had awarded him tenure. Howard, however, was dissatisfied; he had tired of analysing the thoughts of others and longed to produce something genuinely his own. Again and again, he would re-read the works of Nietzsche. His dream was to publish an opus that would articulate his own vision of reality with the same passionate intensity, the same vital urgency, the same dynamic energy as that of the German philosopher. Without knowing it, he was seeking through this project to re-establish the severed connection with his unconscious and his badly damaged feeling nature. But when he began his opus, his prose did not flow, did not possess the organic quality to which he aspired. Rather, it was ground out, sentence by sentence, carefully structured, brilliantly polished, unerringly precise, yet somehow arid and devoid of life. And although his edifice of ideas satisfied the standards of the most rigorous and exacting criticism, it failed to provide the link with his own inner life which he had sought from it. During the course of his project, moreover, Howard experienced recurrent periods of sterility, which brought the work to a halt. At intervals, a relationship with a woman would trigger a new burst of creativity. No sooner would this occur, however, than Howard would withdraw, shrinking from commitment to a living human being and preferring to lavish his affection on images of fantasy — images that lay beyond the perimeters he had established for the relationship. As a predictable result, none of these superficial liaisons could break through the carapace in which he had encased himself; none of them could lead him into the realm to which he sought access, the realm that would enable him to tap the collective source of inspiration.

Howard was particularly repelled by feeling-oriented women, whom he contemptuously dismissed as "gushy" and sentimental. At the same time, his secret image of womanhood conformed to this type — smothering, sloppy, dripping with insipid and trivial emotion, incapable of participation in his world of exalted ideas. When dealing with women who embodied this image, Howard was capable of uncharacteristic cruelty. What he failed to recognise was that his cruelty was actually directed at his mother, and at an aspect of the anima figure within himself.

Howard's inferior sensation function led not only to inhibitions in sexual relationships, but to difficulties with his health as well. He was constantly plagued by colds, influenza, stomach pains, headaches and sinus trouble. And something within him actually seemed to invite these maladies. Indeed, he seemed unconsciously bent on destroying his body through every excess that came to hand, including alcohol, cigarettes, and an imposing spectrum of drugs, licit and otherwise. And if he displayed irresponsibility towards himself, he displayed even greater irresponsibility towards his money, squandering vast sums on trifles, running constantly into debt, bouncing cheques like tennis balls. To the observer, however, none of this was apparent. All of it was concealed behind the glitter of his ideas, his scintillating presentation of concepts in both books and lectures. In short, people were so fascinated by Howard's mind that they failed to see Howard; and it is not surprising, therefore, that the human being hidden within him began to long for some personal warmth. When he finally consulted an astrologer, he had not been involved with a woman for some time and his creative energy had all but dried up. In consequence, he had begun to feel concerned. Although conversant with psychological theory, he could not translate it into practise, could not apply it to himself.

Several important points are suggested by Howard's birth chart. The grouping of planets in Leo in the fifth house, that of creative expression, reflects his intense need to fulfil himself through creative endeavour. The dominance of fire on the chart — both the sun in Leo and the Aries ascendant — suggests the powerful intuition which is the dominant quality among Howard's mental gifts. Mercury conjunct Venus in Virgo in Virgo's house, the sixth, suggests the analytical scalpel of his intellect; Saturn in Gemini in the third suggests the structuring and fine differentiation of ideas, as well as the difficulty he has expressing or understanding anything that cannot be accommodated by his intellectual scaffoldings. The moon in Pisces, buried in the twelfth house and the only water on the chart, indicates how deeply unconscious, and how vulnerable, his feeling nature is, how isolated and cautiously withheld in his human relationships. Moreover, the moon stands in opposition to the Venus-Mercury conjunction. This implies that Howard's constant critical evaluation of relationships opposes his yearning to lose himself in the flow of feeling that these very relationships might release. Unconsciously, he aspires to lose himself in another; consciously, however, he is terrified of emerging from the ivory tower of ideas, within the safety of which he works and lives. Venus in square to Saturn suggests the problem Howard experiences in expressing his feelings. It also suggests isolation, fear of rejection, a sense of being unwanted and unloved, reluctance to allow himself emotional exposure to another. As a characteristic Leo, Howard has strong ideals, and prides himself on a strong sense of loyalty, integrity and honour in relationships. But these virtues are often only abstract concepts to him, and he cannot always express them at the appropriate time. With women, he is sometimes rather less than honourable.

This is a very rough sketch of the dominant themes in Howard's birth chart. As our subject is the parental relationship, we must now ask what clues Howard's chart might divulge of his mother, who has influenced his life in a very powerful, often destructive, and totally unconscious way.

The sign at the midheaven of Howard's chart is Capricorn, which suggests that authority, structure, ambition, status and material achievement are the dominant themes in the mother-relationship. This is certainly confirmed by the fact that Howard's mother saw him primarily as a fulfilment of her own ambitions. She wanted status, and she wanted it desperately. Despite her efforts to do so, she could never quite forget that her own mother was the product of an urban slum. Thus her son's every achievement was immediately trumpeted to neighbours, friends and colleagues at work: *her* son had earned his PhD, had won an academic prize, had published a highly praised book, and all these accomplishments somehow resounded to her greater glory, as though she had performed them herself. That she loved Howard is beyond question; but there is love and love. Moreover, Capricorn at the midheaven of Howard's chart suggests that he was particularly receptive to this aspect of his mother, and tended not to register any others. She never wondered whether Howard actually *wanted* to accomplish what she deemed so important; it was simply taken for granted that he did. It was also taken for granted that he could want to be a showpiece, and this was an unwarranted assumption. Although typically Leonine in his need for acceptance and admiration, Howard was a shy boy grown into a shy man, sensitive, dwelling in secret romantic fantasies, intensely self-conscious about the public exposure his success entailed. This never occurred to his mother. After a while it never occurred to Howard either; for Leo, if he cannot achieve self-esteem, will often try to obtain esteem from others. Lest one judge too harshly, however, it may be said that, through his mother, Howard was able to discipline his intellect and accomplish something with it which constituted a valuable and important contribution. His philosophical work and his teaching were enlightening and inspiring to both students and readers. He was able to kindle the minds of those with whom he came into contact; and his natural laziness — reflected perhaps by Mars, the ruler of the chart (Aries is on the ascendant), in Taurus — was counteracted by his mother's influence. This impelled him to utilise his gifts productively.

The ruler of the midheaven, Saturn, is placed in Gemini, in the third house, that of education and intellectual development. It is a clear reflection of what the mother-relationship meant to Howard. Both dark and light aspects of this placement are apparent — in the thoroughness and depth of his mind, and in his capacity to value anything else. Somewhere within himself, Howard no doubt felt a sense of deep inadequacy — one cannot avoid this, when one is expected always to be a genius. Some of his intellectual development thus probably involved a kind of compensation, as is often the case with Saturn. And we might justifiably suspect that the shadow side of Howard's psyche would reveal a thoroughly ordinary, nonintellectual, perhaps inarticulate person, conventional, "Philistine", eminently human. It should immediately remind us of Howard's father as perceived by his wife. Having witnessed what his mother did to his father, Howard dared not permit himself the luxury of being human and expressing ordinary human stupidity.

Saturn's squares to Venus and Mercury express something else important about the mother-relationship. In some way, this relationship constitutes an obstacle to the development not only of Howard's feeling life, the values reflected by Venus, but also to his mental development as reflected by Mercury. Bound to the theories and intellectual constructs suggested by Saturn in Gemini, he could never really express Mercury — which, being in Virgo, an earthy sign, is naturally disposed towards concrete, earthy experience and seeks its realisation through the rituals and immediacies of everyday life. Work, in any shape or form other than thinking and teaching, was anathema to Howard. It did not appeal to his sense of intellectual glamour, was therefore demeaning and had to be avoided at all costs; and this attitude, of course, is intensified by Leo, which brings its sense of pride to bear on the question. Situated in Virgo, Mercury is basically modest. Through quiet labour, through assiduous application and a low profile, it seeks to employ its gift for refinement, discrimination and distillation of experience to establish contact with ordinary life. But none of Howard's thought really pertained directly to life. Rather, it comprised an elaborate hypothesis *about* life; and Howard could not always discern the difference. Unable to utilise the earth on his chart, his philosophy, when he attempted to articulate it, did not strike that chord in the reader which resonates from the true archetypal experience. One could not say, "This is real to me, because it is human."

The moon in Pisces suggests Howard's unconscious image of the deeper archetypal experience of mother and anima. Symbolised by Pisces, Mother is all-giving, all-sacrificing, all-loving, devoted, selfless, sensitive, feeling and redeeming. That Howard's mother might have embodied some of these qualities is entirely possible; every human being probably embodies some of them. But she did not express these qualities in her personality, save for the financial sacrifice she made to send Howard to university; and even this sacrifice was contaminated by her own ambitions. Moreover, it is doubtful that Howard would have recognised Piscean qualities even had his mother displayed them, for because of his own psychic composition he projected the figure of Saturn on her. The anima in Howard is a poet, a dreamer, a mystic, a romantic and an idealist. This is the archetype whose deep source of collective feeling life he must tap if his work and thought are to come alive and speak immediately to his audience. But between Howard and his experience of the archetype stands his mother — and he cannot surmount or circumvent that obstacle until he becomes fully conscious of the damage done to his own feeling nature. This he is reluctant to do, continuing rather to aggravate the damage by refusal to relate to his feelings except through his intellect. There is much of Howard's mother in Howard, and his conscious values make it even more difficult to build a bridge between himself and the source of inspiration he seeks. He is dedicated to the world of thought, and sees himself as a Philosopher, in the classical sense of the word. Nothing which cannot be encompassed by the orbit of this ideal enjoys reality for him. Because he cannot acknowledge those experiences which involve simply living, he perpetuates the dissociation of this thought from life — a dissociation he frequently condemns in others, never realising he exhibits it himself.

An examination of Howard's mother's chart provides some interesting additional material. From the sun conjuncting Pluto in Gemini at a Gemini midheaven, we might expect her to possess a powerful masculine drive — linked perhaps with her own mother-experience and all that it lacked — as well as imposing overbearing personal power. This can be either transforming or destructive. With this pair of powerful planets at the MC, Howard's mother identifies with the masculine principle and seeks her identity through recognition in the world, undervaluing the feminine and her own feeling life. Her ascendant in Virgo, another Mercury-ruled sign, suggests that her intellect is highly developed; and Mercury in the ninth house suggests that the refinement and discimination of her nature are directed towards "cultured" channels, higher education, spiritual aspiration. Her own difficulties in relating are reflected by the conjunction of Venus and Saturn in the eighth, and here is an example of that "inheritance" of substance which one often sees in family relationships. It is as if Howard, possessing a certain problem within himself, has chosen a mother with a similar problem; and as if his mother has chosen him. They are of the same substance, and each hurts the other because of an inherent fear of vulnerability in personal relationships. Howard's father, whose sun is in Aquarius and moon in Virgo opposed to Saturn, also has a Venus-Saturn conjunction. It is like the curse of the House of Atreus — a group of people, sharing great artistic and intellectual gifts, brutalising each other on the feeling level because each possesses the same problem. And each blames the others for his difficulties.

The watery element on Howard's mother's chart should have perhaps been developed, but she is so wholly under the sway of the animus that it remains undifferentiated and unconscious, and displays itself as sentiment. Howard's mother is that most unhappy of creatures, a feeling type *manquée*, a basically sensitive and emotional woman who has violated her own nature. She is kind to dogs and children, as though her feelings had become congealed into a stereotyped mould, but she is completely insensitive to the feelings of others. She despises "overly emotional" and "impulsive" people, and her own repressed but powerful emotiohs have found expression in a variety of unpleasant physical symptoms — from high blood pressure to a chronically disordered gall bladder. She is also lonely, finds it difficult to make friends, and wonders why others reject what she calls her love and her sacrifices. With the fixed conviction that a woman's goal in life is to be a mother (a glance at Uranus, symbol of independence, in the fifth house connected with children, implies otherwise, but she would hardly be conscious of this) she attempted to express her Cancerian planets in a conventional way; but she did not express them with the gentleness and sensitivity that are characteristic of Cancer at its best and most differentiated. As these planets are opposite Uranus, moreover, her powerful animus — the creativity she never lived out — perpetually interfered, making her possessive, overbearing, critical, clinging, demanding, and secretly resentful of having her life "ruined" by being reduced to a mere female. And she excelled at manipulation through emotional blackmail. Her need to care and be cared for was distorted by her drive to power, and she could not offer anything without attaching strings to the gift. Deeply disappointed in her marriage, she ascribed the lack of love to her husband. He dared not contradict her. Before he met her, he had loved another woman, and married Howard's mother on the rebound; and in the way that some people do, had spent all of himself, exhausted his store of love. There was nothing left for him to give.

The contacts between Howard's chart and his mother's are worth exploring. Her sun-Pluto conjunction falls on his Saturn, the midheaven ruler. This suggests that, despite his wholly black image of her, she is in fact a perfect hook for his projection. For Howard's mother, intellectual development was a vehicle for ambition and, when conducive to this end, a source of joy; for Howard, however, it was the onerous fulfilment of an obligation and a responsibility, a duty imposed upon him. Because he could not genuinely identify with them, he hated his mother for her pretensions, forgetting how truly necessary and meaningful to her they were. Nor could he appreciate that for her, a Gemini, knowledge was not to be taken seriously in itself, only used as a key to popularity and contact with others. When she displayed less interest in his thinking than in the prestige it earned him, he therefore felt betrayed. She seemed to him a hypocrite, who had coerced him into activites she felt intrinsically devoid of value. In other words, he was projecting his shadow on her.

Howard's mother's chart completely lacks fire. Thus she could not relate to the intuitive element in her son; she thought his idealism and indifference to mundane affairs both foolish and impractical. For her, philosophy was a means to an end, a stepping-stone to financial and material security. Having experienced an economic depression and two world wars, Howard's mother attached immense significance to such security. Howard, a child of the post-war era, could not understand her obsessions. Because money was unimportant to him, he could see no reason why she should not help him with his constant debts, and felt no compunction about turning to her. It was as though he were saying: You never gave me anything except money — and I will bleed you of that now for the rest of your life. Pay, and pay more.

It will be apparent that Howard is unconsciously bound to his mother by some rather destructive ties. Although he lives within relatively short travelling distance of her, he tries to assert his independence — and to flaunt it in her face — by only visiting her once or twice a year. Nevertheless, her ghost still haunts his psyche. It makes things difficult for him in the material world, incessantly throwing him back on the real woman for financial aid. It also affects his emotional life. His sensitive feeling nature has been so violated — by both of them — that he cannot find it, and both his relationships and his creativity constantly threaten to run dry. Were he to start working with his feelings, to start seeing and experiencing himself as something other than a perfect intellect on two legs, he might begin to evolve as a whole human being. For the moment, however, the parental ghost still rattles her chains within him, ruling as Saturn, aided by the unconscious voice of his insecure shadow. Together they twist and manipulate his potential so that it earns him acclaim but keeps him divorced from life. As Howard nears his mid-life crisis, the unconscious earth-water element in him, the moon-Venus axis, will begin to surface. It is possible that the goals and ambitions he has hitherto espoused will no longer mean so much to him. Because Leo is eternally seeking its own heroic potential, and because his Aries ascendant perpetually seeks a better future, it is probable that Howard will manage to free himself. In his search for his own Self through the creative impetus within him, he will, at last, perhaps rediscover the lost anima, the lost Mother and Beloved, the lost figure of Woman in his own psyche, now buried beneath debris of the personal mother-image. And yet this very debris, if reconstructed and reintegrated, can constitute a portal to the archetypal Mother — the Woman who must ultimately speak through him if his vision is to be truly alive.

*   *   *

To receive their appropriate due, the parental relationships would require a volume in themselves. We begin and end with both matter and spirit, those great parents of all life; and whatever the personal relationship to the personal parents, the greater archetypes attend us along the way, comprising the very root and fabric of our inner being. It is worth untangling the mire, the illusions, the sentimentality, the guilt and the resentment in order to rediscover these two Parents, for we are eternally in their hands. And if we acknowledge this, it will at last become possible not only to see one's mortal parents as people with their share of dark and light, but as people who might — or might not — be worthy of real human love, rather than the empty gestures we generally offer them. Mother-love can be black and stinking as the pit, or cleansing and redeeming as divine grace. Father-love can be searing and self-shattering as the torturer's fire, or bright and vivifying as the sun. In the end it is the individual's responsibility to discover these possibilities not in the personal mother and father, who can hardly wield such awesome power, but, through them, in the Mother and Father. In this way, we honour them all.

VIII
The Infallible Inner Clock

Freedom of will is the ability to do gladly
that which I must do.

— C.G. Jung

Pear seeds grow into pear trees, nut seeds grow
into nut trees: God seeds into God.

— Meister Eckhart

The conundrum of fate and free will has perplexed the
greatest thinkers throughout man's history. No less than
philosophy and religion, astrology has grappled with this
enigma and attempted to articulate in its own language an
answer to the question of whether there is truly such a thing
as choice. In their various ways, individual schools of
psychological thought are also exploring aspects of the same
problem — how much of human behaviour is conditioned by
heredity, how much by environment, how much by
conscious volition. And here, as in other spheres of man's
enquiry, one may see the inevitable clash of opposing
viewpoints. The conundrum of fate and free will is probably
like many other profound questions, whose answer ultimately consists of a paradox. Both astrology and analytical
psychology describe this paradox, each in different phraseo-
logy:

Man is bound to the wheel of fate until consciousness of
his God-given choice dawns upon him. Then he glimpses
the paradoxical nature of the force that has both bound
him and given him power to break the bonds *if* he will

choose the pain entailed in the struggle and accept the perils of freedom to be encountered on the spiral way that sweeps upward from the broken wheel.[1]

Fate and free will are major philosophical issues; yet they are pertinent not only to metaphysical speculation, but to our relationship patterns as well. What kind of choice is at work when an individual falls in love? What kind of choice is involved in the birth of a child, who carries within him his own inherent temperament — a temperament which may or may not develop according to the parent's designs? What kind of choice does one have when one's partner abandons one, despite one's noblest efforts to preserve the relationship intact? And what role does choice play in the damage so often incurred by a difficult childhood, which we must sometimes struggle for a lifetime to disentangle?

There are people who prefer to believe that everything in life is random, subject purely to the whims of chance; and this is to some extent comforting because it mitigates the burden of personal responsibility. There are also people — and they number millions in the East — who believe that life flows wholly in accordance with the predestination of one's karma, the effects of causes rooted in past incarnations; and this too is comforting because it absolves one of present responsibility. Finally, there are people who believe that one's own will is the determining factor of one's fate — a position somewhat less comforting because life habitually confronts us with things which cannot be altered by an effort of even the most powerful will.

There is obviously an inherent reluctance in many of us to tackle this question of fate and free will creatively, for exploring it too closely would be tantamount to assuming a responsibility we are not prepared, perhaps not equipped, to assume. Yet we must have some belief in the power of choice, without which we sink into helpless apathy, and some faith in the guiding laws of life itself, lest their

1 *The Inner World of Choice*, Frances Wickes, Prentice-Hall, Inc., Englewood Cliffs, N.J. 1976.

workings leave us irreparably shattered.

The problem of fate and free will underlies one of the most common popular misconceptions about astrology. This is largely because there is so little popular understanding of what astrology has to say on the matter. We have already seen how an individual's unconscious projections will lead him into confrontations, relationships and situations which assume the guise of fate, yet which reflect his own struggle for self-awareness. Some consideration of the workings of the shadow, the parent-images which dwell in the depths of the psyche, the dynamic energies of anima and animus, can help to illumine the strange paradox Novalis utters when he declares fate and soul to be one and the same. The birth chart is the seed, and pear seeds do indeed grow into pear trees; we should be astonished if they did otherwise. It is not difficult for even the pragmatic thinker to appreciate that the birth horoscope reflects only a reservoir of potentialities which, depending on his level of awareness, the individual may utilise to actualise the myth that is his own life.

But when we begin to explore progressions and transits — the sphere of astrology which is essentially the predictive art — there is much ambiguity and not a little confusion, even on the part of astrologers. Eastern astrology, for example, is almost wholly fatalistic in dealing with prognostication. This is understandable since Eastern astrology has its roots in Eastern philosophy, which rests largely on the laws of karma and the wheel of rebirth. To the Indian astrologer, a transit of Saturn over the sun often means that you *will* have bad luck, ill health, or relationship problems, because it is dictated by your karma. Western astrology, on the other hand, is permeated not only by Judeo-Christian doctrine — which allows for voluntary redemption and the caprice of God to proffer grace — but even more deeply by pagan beliefs, classical philosophy, Gnostic and Hermetic thought as well. Implicit in these latter traditions is the "heretical" but profound premise — of which the modern astrologer is often unconscious — that man is not just "fated" by God by virtue of the fact that human nature is not self-created. Man is also both God and the instrument of redemption of God, Who, to become conscious of Himself, depends upon man's voluntary choice to grow in consciousness. This Gnostic underpinning is usually buried beneath newspaper sun-sign columns. But if we exhume it and bear it in mind, it will help explain why Western astrology, as a consulting tool, is so largely devoted to the development of individual consciousness. To the Western astrologer, this development is not only worthwhile, but absolutely essential to the meaning and unfolding sentience of life. The Western astrologer is therefore brash enough to consider both the individual and his potential claim to the exercise of free will.

Few astrologers with any cognisance of their art would claim that the same transit, involving the same planets yet affecting two different individuals, will produce precisely the same effects. Not only are the individual's charts different, but one must also consider the environment, the current circumstances, the sex, the particular psychic constitution, and the present level of awareness for each. All that can be said is that the *inner meaning* of the transit is the same. And as soon as we begin talking about the meaning of an event to the individual, we are no longer dealing with external circumstance but with the psyche. We thus find ourselves in the domain of analytical psychology, which attempts to explore the laws governing and regulating the psyche's activities. It is in the study of planetary transits and progressions, and what they indicate of the individual's development, that astrology and psychology have most to offer each other. Psychology can provide astrology with a framework that renders its symbols comprehensible and relevant in specifically human terms. At the same time, astrology can offer psychology a blueprint of the individual's potential, which not only determines what kind of seed, but what timing and what patterns of growth must be considered. In the sphere of human relationships, the paradox of choice implicit in both astrology and psychology becomes most evident, most easily observable, and most universal.

The word progression is self-explanatory. There are several different technical methods by which one can progress a birth chart, but the basic principle is the same: the motion of the planets after birth reflects the motion of the individual's development after birth — reflects, in other words, the growth pattern and inherent timing of the seed. One can reasonably expect a lentil seed to sprout in two days, and yield lentils in three months, because that is its nature and in a sense constitutes its "fate". An avocado seed, on the other hand, may take three months to sprout and ten years to bear fruit. The same parallel applies to individuals. Life is eternally in motion, and so are human beings. There is a natural progression of development, both psychologically and physiologically, from childhood to adolescence to adulthood to mid-life to old age and to death. We are not able to stop this clock. We experience the process because we are part of it; yet we prefer not to examine it too closely. If we do, death looms too largely in our consciousness as the ineluctable conclusion of the cycle. And so intimidated are we by its spectre that we fail to recognise it as the prerequisite for rebirth, the commencement of a new cycle.

There are collective biological laws which govern many aspects of the growth pattern. The archetypal experiences of human development — birth, puberty, the awakening of sexuality, fertility, mating, the birth of children, the slow decline of the body, and death itself — we assume we have documented carefully, because they are universally observable. But it would be more accurate to say that we have documented the physical manifestations of these experiences, because such manifestations are obvious and irrefutable. The collective psychological laws of development are not so well-documented, however. This is because we have hitherto tended to ignore the life of the psyche, preferring to believe it is somehow an accidental by-product of body and brain. Among his peers, Jung alone devoted to the inner pattern of development the time and insight it demands.

There are problems and conflicts which are characteristic of each phase of life, aspirations, dreams and tensions unique to one phase of development and superfluous to others. It is natural and fitting for a child of two to be dependent on its mother, yet we are understandably dubious when a thirty-year-old man exhibits the same dependency.

We may expect a woman in her twenties to be concerned with childbearing, yet we do not expect her to be so at eighty — not only because her biological development renders the issue irrelevant, but also because she has psychologically left that phase of life behind. Similarly, we may expect an individual in the autumn of age to devote himself to inner realities, to the meaning of his experiences and to a retrospective appraisal of the patterns according to which his life has evolved — patterns that might afford some glimpse of its deeper significance. Yet we would hardly expect to witness such activity in a child, who possesses few objective experiences upon which to reflect, and little continuity of individual consciousness to do the reflecting.

We accept — or attempt to accept — these basic human cycles of development because they are inevitable, in accord with nature, and common to the whole of life. The cyclic pattern of growth is within us and all around us; and one of the few definitive things we can say objectively about life is that it changes. Often we feel surprise or distaste at individuals who cannot leave one phase of life behind and allow themselves to grow into a new one: the young man too afraid of losing the psychological comfort of his mother-complex to risk a serious relationship with a woman; the young woman choosing to remain an emotional six-year-old, eliciting favours from a surrogate Daddy; the older woman who — hidden beneath layers of paint and powder — dares not look in her mirror, because her youthful face and body have hitherto been her only understanding of her own femininity. But perhaps we should be more tolerant of those we are inclined to call "neurotic" for such reasons. There are few individuals who, in some secret area of their lives, do not cling to something which has outlived its purpose and its usefulness. On the progressed horoscope, the objective representation of the deaths and births of phases of awareness is a great help and clarification. But one must first take the time to learn the requisite symbolism.

Woven against the rhythmic patterns reflecting cycles of collective human development, there hangs the tapestry of individual development which differentiates the pear tree from the nut tree; and if we are not yet fully cognisant of the collective cycles, still less are we cognisant of the individual. In part this is a consequence of our education and our social conditioning, for certain things are expected of civilised Western man which may not at times conform to the individual blueprint. We are expected, for example, to be ready for university at seventeen, equipped to venture out into the world and choose a profession at twenty-one, mature enough as a woman to marry and bear children at any time after seventeen, determined enough as man to be established in one's profession at thirty-five, stable enough to be settled with a house and at least one automobile by forty-five, exhausted enough at sixty-five to retire and begin thinking about pensions and death. Whether or not these conventional expectations are realistic in theory, they are often disastrous in practise. Each individual has his own inherent temperament, burgeoning with individual creative possibilities. Each individual also has his own natural pattern of growth and his own timetable for development. This alone can determine what phases are appropriate at a given moment for the expression of different aspects of his psyche.

Some women are psychologically fit for childbearing at twenty-one, others not until thirty-five, still others not at all; some men know what they wish to do in the world at eighteen, others at forty-five. Some people reach intellectual maturity at seventeen and have no problem adjusting to the demands of higher education. Others do not attain their intellectual peak until fifty and would profit far more from academic study then. And some people are emotionally mature at twenty while others remain emotional infants even into old age. The world, however, laughs at the person who wishes to begin a new profession at forty; he is regarded as a fool for throwing aside all he has built. The world is perplexed by the career woman who, at forty-five, decides marriage is a desired goal; she is "over the hill", people say, too old for the marriage market and should learn to live with the unfortunate choice made in her youth. Through blind acceptance of collective opinions, we cripple ourselves and our own potential for meaningful growth and change, and we rarely understand how closely such debilitation is linked with depression, physical illness, neurosis, and death. People change, and yet we do not seem to like it. The engineer may turn poet in the middle of his career, the housewife turn business manager, the doctor turn gardener. If these changes are truly spontaneous products of the psyche's inner development, they should be encouraged and nurtured. We should not laugh at them because we lack the courage to perform them ourselves. We should not thwart them because they force us to adjust our own projections. We should not despise them as idle dreams and foolishness because we think that at a certain age one should be "realistic". Each phase of expression in life is appropriate and necessary for its time, which may be long or short; but if each is not allowed to pass and yield to something else when its time is fulfilled, it becomes a suffocating cage in which the soul begins to atrophy.

The individual progressions of the horoscope depict symbolically the inner timing of psychic events. They indicate in succinct form what areas of the basic potential expressed by the birth chart are going to be "constellated" — that is, afforded opportunity for conscious recognition and integration — at different periods of life. As with other aspects of astrology, one may well ask why it is necessary to consult a horoscope to find out what one's psyche is up to. Probably it is necessary because we have so little contact with, so little awareness of, the matrix of life from which the conscious ego springs — and so little understanding of the currents at work in the unconscious, shaping our lives and making our choices for us in accordance with the imperatives of the Self. Admittedly, some highly intuitive people have a great sensitivity to the inner timing that regulates the endings and beginnings of phases, a knack for divining the moving forces of the unconscious; and as one of the intuitive's basic characteristics is his love of flux and possibility, changing cycles do not surprise him. In such cases, the information yielded by the progressed horoscope often provides confirmation, rather than new insight. For those oriented towards the other functions of consciousness, however, astrology can often be a great aid — not because it can predict what will happen, but because it can identify in symbolic form the patterns of inner growth aspiring to the surface of consciousness at a given moment. Many people become terrified at the first breath of impending change; in consequence they project it onto the enviornment, rather than acknowledging its true origin within themselves. As a result, external things begin to appear unstable and unreliable, and strenuous efforts are required to nail everything down, to ensure the immutability of one's personal habits, viewpoints, and property. And repression of natural psychic events of course provokes the unconscious, which, diverted from its natural channels of expression, must resort to indirect channels. These channels lead the individual to unconsciously invite the destruction of the very thing to which he clings. And the ensuing upheaval, which he has invoked himself, he proceeds to call adverse or hostile fate.

In *The Secret Doctrine*, H.P. Blavatsky describes karma as "substance", and this is a key to understanding why certain events occur in association with particular progressions or transits. The external event is composed of the same quintessential principles as the individual; it is a living symbol of the energies at work within the psyche. The individual will therefore attract to himself circumstances and phenomena which correspond in their intrinsic meaning and coherence to the forces activated within himself. Thus, the person and the event are identical — and we are back to Novalis again, and the maxim that fate and soul are two names for the same principle.

The progressed horoscope confirms what we should know about ourselves, but have become too civilised to discern. The primitive can sense and accept changes because he looks for omens and portents everywhere; he knows that life is always in flux, that nothing is permament, and he sees harbingers of shifting patterns in the turn of a leaf, the flight of a bird, the "mood" of the spirits in trees, rocks, streams and animals. In this respect the primitive is wiser than civilised man; he is not fettered to the illusion that his precious ego can freeze time and alter the quality of life itself, crystallising and imbuing with artificial permanence the forms he personally esteems. The primitive is unaware of changes as occurring "inside" or "outside" him because, being unconscious of himself as an individual, he draws no distinction between the two, recognises no frontier between self and non-self. We are both blessed and cursed with a greater ego consciousness, and have lost the primitive's capacity to respond spontaneously to the quality of the moment by apprehending its symbolic resonance.

> Whoever hunts deer without the forester
> Only loses his way in the forest.
> The superior man understands the signs of the time.[1]

Like our own ancestors, the primitive also knows that things are changing because his dreams tell him so, for dreams are the spontaneous communication of the unconscious to consciousness. Archaic man respects dreams because he regards them as messages from the gods, informing him of the life flow of the cosmos around and within him. We no longer believe in either gods or dreams and have, in consequence, lost one of the most valuable means of contact with the ceaselessly changing and creative roots of our being. Now, ultra-civilised as we are and so near self-strangulation by our own cleverness, our need is all the greater for vital symbolic alphabets. Only through such alphabets — astrology, for example, or dreams as they are utilised by psychology — can we obtain some glimpse of the patterns governing the development of that organism which is oneself.

The progression of a planet, moving forward in the days after birth and arriving at an exact contact with the birth placement of another planet, is, in a sense, like the bell indicating coffee is ready. The progression does not "make" anything happen, for progressions are purely symbolic and

1 *The I Ching*, translated by Wilhelm/Baynes, Bollingen Foundation, N.Y. 1950.

have no basis in objective reality. Rather, they are synchronous with some psychic event, some constellation of a specific configuration of energy — the archetypes — in the unconscious. What a progression indicates is that the time is ripe for certain things to become conscious, in accordance with the basic growth pattern of the seed. Inherent in the seed are both the essential qualities and the growth pattern — they are, in fact, the same thing — and both are represented symbolically in the horoscope. In the unconscious, there is no time; past, present and future are simultaneous and the seed and the fruit-bearing plant are one. Thus the pear seed contains and is the pear tree — although a more literal mind, cutting the seed open, would find only pulp. On a conscious level, we need linear time — time as the ego recognises it — to unfold the pattern.

> O chestnut-tree, great-rooted blossomer,
> Are you the leaf, the blossom or the bole?
> O body swayed to music, O brightening glance,
> How can we know the dancer from the dance?[1]

It is only through the filter of the conscious ego that past, present and future enjoy a semblance of distinction; and it is the ego's stubbornness in clinging to this sequential continuum that impairs our understanding. It precludes our recognising the meaning of an outer event and the appropriateness of the time at which it occurs, as well as the opportunities such events afford for developing consciousness and the power of free choice.

When, therefore, we try to predict an event from a progression or transit, we cannot always do so. A progression does not reflect a concrete occurrence so much as it does the need for inner recognition of something, for integration of some dormant quality into conscious awareness. It is not impossible that if we knew more about these things we would have some choice of the vehicle — the event — through

1 "Among School Children", *The Collected Poems of W.B. Yeats*, Macmillan, N.Y. 1933.

which recognition becomes accessible. On the other hand, the event is generally so perfectly apt for the moment that, having once deciphered its meaning, we could not improve upon it. In the absence of such insight, however, we are at the mercy of events, failing to realise that we have drawn them to ourselves through the magnetic attraction of our own essence. Nothing happens to a man which is not contained within him. Events, moreover, will often take the line of least resistance — the energy released will find egress through whatever door the individual leaves open; and the nature of this door depends upon the possibilities available at a given time. If a train is moving at a certain speed from one station towards another, one can be fairly certain that — unless the engine breaks down or someone plants a bomb under the tracks — it will reach its destination at a scheduled time. No one would accuse British Rail of fortune telling; yet the astrologer or analyst employs the same principle when he assesses the probabilities implicit in a particular progression or a particular series of dreams. The faulty engine, or the bomb under the tracks, may be likened to the intrusion of transpersonal or collective factors which impinge — as they constantly do — upon the individual growth pattern. A pear seed may grow into a pear tree, but if a drought or flood occurs, it will suffer — regardless of its inherent potential for growth. Likewise, careful watering and tending will allow it to achieve possibilities which it might never have exhibited if left alone. For the individual, a progression will express itself through whatever channels he allows. Hence the obvious importance of understanding both the meaning of the inner event, and the outer circumstances attending it.

The sun progressing to contact Venus, for example, is traditionally supposed to portend marriage. This was the fatalistic view of astrology in the past, when destiny was undoubtedly as much the property of the psyche as now but was deemed an act of God; and God at that time resided exclusively in Heaven, disdaining to occupy any place in man's consciousness. If we look closely at the sun-Venus configuration, it may indeed have relevance to external events — or it may ostensibly have none whatsoever, for an inner realisation is not always accompanied by dramatic or even readily discernible external effects. The sun, symbolising self-expression or self-realisation, in configuration with Venus, symbolising the aspect of the feminine principle we call relatedness, suggests that in some way there will be an activation of the latter archetype within the psyche. As a result, the creative power of the unconscious will generate or be drawn to an objectified experience which — because it embodies the same qualities as the archetype (or is a reflection of the same archetype) — provides access to consciousness for the experience of relatedness.

A three-year-old child with a sun-Venus progression can hardly be expected to marry. On the other hand, he may well be in the right place at the right time, and thus exposed to an experience which produces some increased awareness of human relationships. He may form a close and meaningful friendship; he may learn something of the world of feeling and personal affection through a cherished pet; his father might remarry, or his parents divorce; his mother might embark on an extra-marital affair which profoundly affects the atmosphere of his home. One can never be certain of the specific circumstances; one can only make educated guesses about them after knowing something about the overall situation. And even then they are only guesses and perhaps better not made — for people are eminently suggestible. The only certain thing is that an archetype is being activated within the psyche, that it is connected (in this example) with the experience of relatedness, and that it will seek expression through whatever channels offer themselves at the moment, depending upon the individual's experience, sex, environment, and inherent temperament. One may or may not appreciate the significance of his experience at the time. It will inevitably affect him, however, and its repercussions will inevitably surface later in his life.

A twenty-one-year-old might be expected to fall in love or marry under the progression of the sun to Venus, but this progression often signifies divorce as well, or the birth of a child. It may also signify the blossoming of the aesthetic sense, or even death — which to some individuals is an act of love in the most profound sense, and a true union with the soul. The experience is not predictable; and, to some extent, it can often be shaped by conscious choice. What the progression indicates is the meaning of the experience to the individual; and it is most illuminating to retrospectively consider progressions which coincided with such important events as marriage, birth of children, job changes, crucial self-revelations conducive to growth. In instances of this kind, the progression will elucidate the essence of what a particular experience meant in the context of the overall growth pattern.

Consultant astrologers are frequently inundated with requests to prognosticate the time of marriage, or the possibility of divorce, or the outcome of a triangular love affair. As we have seen, the horoscope cannot in itself predict anything, and such prognostications are therefore impossible. It is unfortunate that public opinion persists in believing the contrary. As a result, some people are frightened away from astrology, lest it prove that their lives are indeed "fated". Others become childishly dependent upon astrologers, incapable of making decisions for themselves and abdicating their responsibility of conscious individual choices. Astrology cannot make a man's choice for him, any more than a road map, of its own volition, can choose whether or not one will undertake a journey. But there is much insight to be gained from the progressed horoscope about what energies are at work within the individual at a given time. This insight can clarify the meaning of the situation in which one finds oneself, and enables one to make his own choice — or to live with someone else's — with a more lucid understanding. It is ultimately the total psyche which makes our choices, not the ego. If it recognises the significance of the choice, the ego can decide to cooperate, in which case it will reap the richness of greater growth and comprehension. Alternatively, the ego can oppose the choice, remaining blind to its value — in which case pain, frustration and a sense of meaninglessness will often ensue. If we wish the freedom to make choices, we must learn something more about ourselves —

both about our inherent disposition and the timing that regulates its functioning. Only then can we discover why a particular choice has appeared at a particular time, what its implications are, and what opportunities for growth it can provide. Undoubtedly we will still suffer from some of our choices; but we will no longer suffer blindly. And this is perhaps the most we can ask, given the conflicting elements of which we are made and between which we struggle to maintain equilibrium.

A transit differs from a progression in that it represents the actual position of a planet orbiting around the sun, while a progression is a purely symbolic movement with no direct relation to the planet's physical position in the heavens at the time. Both progressions and transits appear to operate in a similar way — they indicate that something is being constellated on a *psychic* level, which may or may not manifest itself in a physical event. Unlike progressions, however, transits, being reflections of actual planetary movements, reflect actual forces or energies in the external world which impinge upon the psyche from without, producing a reaction according to the individual's constitution. Progressions, on the other hand, are wholly subjective reflections of the individual's inner growth pattern. A transit cycle is the return of a planet to the position it occupied on the chart at birth; and each planet has an orbit of its own and its own interval for completing its cycle. The moon requires just over twenty-eight days; the sun requires one year to make its return; Pluto requires two hundred and forty-eight years.

There are two transit cycles which are of considerable importance to the subject of human relationships, and these occur at approximately the same age for all individuals: the cycle of Saturn, which takes approximately twenty-nine years, and the cycle of Uranus, which takes approximately eighty-four years and reaches its critical midway point at the age of forty-two. Both these cycles symbolise collective patterns of development for the whole of humanity, but the personal form such patterns assume will vary according to the individual. No one escapes them, however, any more than anyone escapes puberty, or old age. And because the Saturn and Uranus cycles often coincide with periods of crisis, reorientation, and the making and breaking of relationships, it is worth exploring something of their general implications. We can then apply what we learn to the individual horoscope.

The Saturn Cycle

As we have seen, Saturn is connected with the primitive, "inferior" side of human nature which Jung calls the shadow. It may be regarded as a symbol for all that is base, crude, undifferentiated, inchoate and unconscious within the individual; and it pertains, as we have also seen, to the past, to parent images, and to crystallisation and identification with what has gone before. Alchemical symbolism portrays Saturn as the base material upon which the Royal Art is performed — the raw, unformed substance of the world, perpetually in conflict with itself, unconscious, in need of redemption, yet containing within it all the potential seeds of the future, from which can be wrested the life-giving spirit, alchemical gold.

In its natural orbit around the sun, Saturn attains a critical relation to its position on an individual's birth chart every seven or so years, and forms a conjunction with its natal place at about age twenty-nine. Each time the transiting planet touches its original birth position is significant. The completion of every such cyclical return indicates that the dark, undifferentiated and unconscious side of the personality is activated and accorded an opportunity to grow through the medium of some situation requiring struggle or pain. At age twenty-nine, the culmination of the first Saturn cycle, it is possible for the individual to face and free himself from painful feelings of inadequacy, spheres of overcompensation, parental ties, and values borrowed from the past. He can then begin a new twenty-nine-year cycle as a developing individual rather than as a product of his background, his family and his unconscious shadow.

The transit of Saturn to its birth place is called the Saturn

return; and the year immediately prior to this crucial moment
is often one of gradual breaking down, disintegration,
disillusionment, as well as recognition of all that is false,
one-sided, dependent, and unrealised within the personality.
This year may comprise a period of depression and painful
self-evaluation, discouragement and difficulty, but it need
not be so — unless one fails to recognise that it heralds the
true end of psychological childhood and reflects a concerted
thrust from the unconscious to liberate the developing
personality from the pull of the past, thus launching one on a
true quest into the future. Because we project outward that
which is unconscious within ourselves, the inner constellation of the shadow is often accompanied by apparent
difficulty and opposition from other people. Thus many
marriages tend to disintegrate during the Saturn return, while
the individual — not realising it is his own darkness
confronting him — lays his discontent with himself at the
feet of his partner. In some sphere of his life the skin he has
occupied has grown too tight. It must either stretch or split to
accommodate the new elements emerging from the unconscious; and the pain of this adjustment is all too easily
blamed on a "restrictive" mate.

Sometimes the constellation of the shadow is attended by
feelings of helplessness and inferiority; a person's self-
confidence may prove more fragile than he had assumed,
while the old wounds, anxieties and sense of inadequacy —
which he thought he left behind in childhood — often
surface, making him feel he is suddenly cast adrift, without
any props, landmarks or instruments to guide him. Often, he
does not recognise himself, becoming suddenly aware of
needs he has hitherto scorned in others. And much of what
he has unquestioningly valued may begin to appear false,
narrow or insufficient. This reappraisal of former values will
depend on the extent to which they were too one-sided, or
secretly those of his parents rather than his own.

A great many marriages undergo a crisis at the time of the
Saturn return, either because the marriage itself was based on
values now outgrown, or because one projects one's
disillusionment on one's partner. On the other hand, a great

many marriages are also made under the Saturn return. Often they derive from the sense of helplessness — the sudden recognition that childhood is ended and that there is an unknown future ahead, in preparation for which one has created very little of one's own. As a result, one may be propelled into a marriage because it offers some sense of security, some assurance of stability at a time when everything in the psyche is in upheaval. Such marriages are not necessarily "wrong", nor should they necessarily be avoided. On the contrary, they may be precisely what is required. But, like Parzival in the Grail Castle, one should perhaps ask why, so that one enters one's compacts with open eyes and an understanding of one's true motives.

Marriages may also occur during the Saturn return because they reflect the psyche's need to free itself from the past. Thus the choice of a partner in some way entails crisis or struggle, or an important but difficult choice. And a few — a very few — of the marriages contracted during the Saturn return are contracted in full consciousness, with an awareness that the road to the future is now free of at least one major obstacle — one's illusions about oneself. In such cases, a mature commitment is made between two sentient and responsible adults exercising the power of individual choice — rather than by unconsciously desperate, clinging and dependent children.

The Saturn return does not always pertain to marriage. What it pertains to depends upon Saturn's position on the birth chart. For some individuals, the Saturn return may be connected with the work life, with a sense of growing dissatisfaction concerning one's choice of goals and the uncomfortable realisation that one's motives have been spurious. Sometimes great external benefits come with the Saturn return, but these may be accompanied by inner dissatisfaction because the original goals, to which such success would supposedly lead, have changed. Often one discovers the real secret master in the house, the shadow, who has used one's natural abilities for purposes of its own — usually to satisfy the undernourished unconscious child. When this occurs an individual's confidence about his own integrity of choice may suffer severely. But a man cannot make any choice without being aware of his shadow; otherwise it will inevitably do the choosing, while he pays lip service to his exalted ideals.

Much depends on how much of the individual is truly individual by the time the Saturn return occurs, for the transit is only a reflection of what one has truly earned. Handled properly, it can be an opportunity for great change, consolidation of long-desired goals, constructive self-realisation, and the planting of seeds which mature in the second half of life, engendering a whole individual as their fruit. Badly handled, it can entail a collapse of virtually everything. Then the individual must recognise that what has collapsed is not himself, but what he thought was himself — but which is better discarded because it retarded his future growth. For some people, a child may be born under the Saturn return; for others, monetary changes may transpire, or illness, or a shift in religious beliefs. For the meaning of these experiences one must always look to the individual. If change occurs under Saturn, it is connected with the need to integrate the formerly scorned but vital unconscious elements of the shadow into one's conscious personality.

The nature of Saturnian experience under the return will be suggested by the house, sign and aspects of the planet on the birth chart. A seventh or eighth house Saturn may point to the sphere of relationships; a tenth house Saturn may point to ambitions and career goals; a ninth house Saturn may point to the individual's *Weltanschauung* or "world-view"; a fifth house Saturn may point to one's attitude towards children, or one's creative enterprises. Sometimes, moreover, several areas of experience will be linked by the same significant changes. What a person commences under the Saturn return will often prove a vehicle which offers him room to grow and develop his own inner strength for the duration of his life. Saturn usually digs its roots deep, and Saturnian experiences have a quality of permanence. The Saturn return is ultimately a process of death and rebirth, the sloughing of the old mask and the discovery of the real — and often less "perfect" — individual who has been growing all along, hidden beneath the scaffolding of conscious identifications. How much or how little of this newly discovered self is acceptable depends on the way in which the ego perceives it. Usually the shadow is not easily digested. But whether palatable or not, it is reality, and must be integrated into one's life. One cannot be other than what one is. If this is not voluntary, it will usually be involuntary, because the ego is less invincible than it would like to be. In the end it has the option of cooperation with or opposition to the unconscious. Either way the final choice is inherent in the seed; but the form this choice assumes, and the awareness of its implications, remain the individual's responsibility.

The Uranus Cycle

Uranus takes eighty-four years to transit around the sun, and forms an opposition to its natal place on the birth chart when the individual is between forty and forty-two years of age. In doing so, it coincides with the phase of psychic development Jung calls the mid-life crisis. This critical point does not involve the Uranus cycle alone. Saturn, we must remember, makes its cycle every twenty-nine years, moving into significant aspects with its natal place every seven. Fourteen years after the Saturn return, the planet will have completed half of another cycle. In our forty-second year, it will thus be in opposition to its natal place. At this age, then, we must deal with the impact of two important transits. It should not, therefore, be surprising that the synchronous changes within the individual's psyche during the mid-life crisis are perhaps the most important he will ever experience. They are reflected by the most important of collective cycles.

As we have seen, Uranus is connected with liberation, freedom, forcible breaking through into new spheres of expression, expansion of the mental perspective. He is a planet which has much to do with the rending of the veil, and his mythological associations with the thunderstorm, the wind and the heights suggest that he operates much more at a transpersonal level than do the planets within the orbit of

Saturn. Through Uranus, one may be brought face to face with the great archetypal images.

Jung describes the mid-life crisis as a time when the unlived aspects of the psyche — the anima or animus in particular, as well as those functions of consciousness which have remained "inferior" or undifferentiated — begin to knock loudly on the door of the ego and demand expression. If the ego's previous configuration has been very one-sided, these unconscious contents will erupt with much dramatic force, and the individual may commit some abrupt and inexplicable actions — he may walk out of a seasoned marriage, out of a stable career, out of a country in which he has lived all his life. Such behaviour reflects the need to burst free from the ego's fettering confines, the need to begin exploring the depths and heights which have never been lived. An intense restlessness often accompanies this time in life, in both men and women; although here, too, the individual may project his reality outward and become the apparent victim of someone else's inexplicable actions. For women, the menopause is approaching and the childbearing years are over. Children are now approaching adulthood; they no longer need maternal support. A woman is thus free to confront, willingly or not, what she has built of her own individual life, thought and identity — that which she intrinsically is, independent of family relationships. In consequence, many women for the first time begin to explore a field of work which affords mental stimulation and involvement with the outside world. The animus is constellated and mind, spirit, objectivity, impersonal contribution to the group life, begin to take precedence over personal satisfaction or feeling commitments to husband and family. For men, "success" has often been attained by age forty, or at least acceptance of failure; stability has been achieved, and the mysterious inner world of the anima begins to beckon. Many men who have enjoyed scrupulously conventional marriages will suddenly find mistresses, or fall desperately in love with women much younger than themselves. Alternatively, a wife's infidelity or departure may rudely shock them into recognition of their own inability to relate. All these situations are symbolic of the inner search for anima values, for deeper understanding of human relationships, for exploration of the creative, imaginative, inner world of the psyche.

The opposition of Uranus to its natal place symbolises the release of that which has been unlived with powerful force. Everything depends on how much of this unlived life has accumulated, and on how much awareness of its implications the individual possesses. The Uranus cycle can release a person into the most creative, productive period of his life; but if he resists the changes occurring within him, it can shatter him mentally, emotionally or physically. We may have to learn the steps of a new and unknown dance; but they, like the rhythm to which they move, are already within us, and in repudiating them we only do violence to ourselves.

The transit of Uranus, moreover, is accompanied by Saturn opposing its natal place. This suggests a further opportunity to work with the inferior side of the personality, the functions which are not valued or developed; and such work can yield wonder and excitement for the individual who understands the propitiousness of the time and can therefore make constructive choices. On the other hand, Saturn, like Uranus, can reflect agony, disruption, uncertainty, confusion — or all these things combined. Once again, we do not have any choice about whether growth will occur; but we can choose to understand it and try to work with it cooperatively.

The Individual Progressed Chart
The ambiguities and the insight implicit in the progressed horoscope are best illustrated by an example. In this way, some of the most important statements posited by astrology on the matter of choice will become self-evident. We would do well to summarise these statements. Firstly, a progression or transit does not signify an external event; it implies that some new content is emerging from the unconscious which must be integrated into consciousness. Secondly, external events, seemingly dissociated but containing the same intrinsic meaning, may occur synchronistically within the

period of time involved — one to three years. Thirdly, the
occurrence of a specific event is not necessarily coincident
with the peaking of the progression, since such events are
part of the inner working through of unconscious material;
they usually occur *before* the progression is exact. The peak
of the progression usually suggests the period when
understanding of what has transpired, however tenuous,
begins to dawn; it thus marks a time of *inner* change, based
on apprehension of the change's meaning. The outer events,
if there were any, have usually already occurred. And the
fourth, perhaps most important, statement posited by
astrology is that there are many choices available for
integration of unconscious forces. But the ego cannot
prevent these forces from asserting themselves, or deny the
unconscious its needed self-expression. One may select a
particular mode of expression in lieu of others — sometimes
— but the inner reality nevertheless demands recognition.

Jean-Pierre, whose chart is shown on the next page, is a
highly creative and volatile man whose past pattern of
relationships includes three marriages and a particularly
dynamic love-affair occurring towards the end of the first of
them. This pattern thus provides an excellent illustration of
the working of the progressed horoscope in the field of
human relationships.

Jean-Pierre's birthplace was a small French village, his
background one of poverty. During his boyhood, he was
raised by his mother and grandmother, who remained in their
native village until their deaths. He never knew his father, a
Hungarian emigrant who passed through the town one day,
enjoyed a brief liaison with a shopkeeper's daughter, then
went on his way, leaving behind him a child and great
emotional pain. Jean-Pierre's early life entailed an inner
struggle to establish a sense of manhood and identity in the
face of his ambiguous and socially unacceptable parentage;
and this struggle was rendered more difficult by his mother's
and grandmother's devout Catholicism, which fostered the
conviction that he was a child conceived in sin.

He worked at a series of unrewarding jobs, then met and
married his first wife, Liliane, when he was twenty-five. She

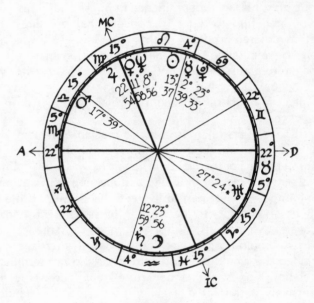

Jean-Pierre

was eleven years older, and the wedding was largely at her instigation. That Jean-Pierre accepted the arrangements suggests his own unconscious collusion and his need for a mother-figure, but most of the obvious dependency was on Liliane's side. Being of a strongly intuitive temperament, he could sense many possibilities within himself which he could not at the time express; yet his background, his strong sense of principles, his lack of confidence in himself, and his guilt all prompted him to defer to conventional pressures. He therefore entered wedlock with many half-acknowledged feelings of reluctance, and a nagging intuition that he had not begun to realise his full potential — that he was not yet an individual, and that he was signing his life away in exchange for a superficial security, which might easily turn into a cage.

Nearly two years later, Jean-Pierre met an American girl, Carol, at a party, and the ensuing affair was both compulsive and tormenting. For the first time he felt he was truly in love, yet his sense of marital infidelity and ensuing guilt not only made it impossible for him to live with his passion, but also paralysed his capacity for decision. After some eight months of covert assignations, Carol returned to America; as Jean-Pierre could not be pried loose from his marriage, she concluded she would be badly hurt if she did not terminate the relationship. After her departure, Jean's domestic life progressively deteriorated. Having discovered the clandestine affair, and recognising that her husband's feelings were directed elsewhere, Liliane became more and more destructive, finally attempting suicide. Jean, in the meantime, had resolved to extricate himself from the marriage to resume his relationship with Carol and marry her. The final rupture with Liliane occurred almost three years after the marriage ceremony, when Jean-Pierre was twenty-eight.

For six years after, the volatile and explosive relationship between Jean-Pierre and Carol continued. During this time, both had other affairs, and Carol married someone else, then left him to return to Jean-Pierre. The two of them could not live together, yet could not leave each other. In the meantime, Jean-Pierre had found his way into a *métier* which would eventually become his life work — the film industry. Initially, he was involved in commercial distribution for a small film company, travelling about Europe and America as a salesman, gradually acquiring experience in the field. Despite his bond to Carol, he was therefore subjected to periods of prolonged isolation, finding himself in strange cities with no companionship other than that of prostitutes and call-girls. Then, when the opportunity presented itself, he would resume his involvement with Carol — although this was now losing the magical quality with which it had formerly been endowed. In short, Jean-Pierre was always compulsively driven towards women, yet could never quite find the woman he was seeking — for this Woman existed only within himself. Unwittingly, he was searching for his anima, and, in the process, lived out fantasies which many men only experience safely in their daydreams. But although he had a great number of women, he remained incapable of sustaining one relationship for any length of time.

The termination of Jean-Pierre's relationship with Carol occurred when he was thirty-four. At this point, he left France and settled in England, determined to sever himself from his past and create a new life. Gradually, he began to establish himself in his profession, rising to executive status on the distribution side of a large film company. His income increased, he developed confidence in his abilities, but he was still frustrated, finding no outlet for any creative efforts of his own. Moreover, he had difficulties relating to the English temperament. Nevertheless, he was determined to succeed, both to prove his manhood to himself and to demonstrate that he was capable of sticking to something. The spectre of the father he had never known haunted him, and he was determined not to become the wandering and untrustworthy wastrel his mother and grandmother had portrayed to him as his progenitor.

Shortly after his move to England, he met Sara, an English woman employed by his company. Within three weeks of their first encounter, they married. Sara was thirty at the time, four years younger than Jean-Pierre. For a few months she enabled him to dwell in his romantic illusions; her calm and rational temperament, and her sense of orderly solicitude, allowed him to experience the mother-relationship he had lacked in childhood. But once the marriage had settled into a pattern, problems began again. This time Jean-Pierre was determined to suppress them, having decided that the new marriage *must* "work", regardless of the currents buffeting him in his unconscious feeling life. As an intuitive thinking type, he possessed the capacity to sever his feelings from conscious awareness, and managed to survive for some time without acknowledging that anything was seriously wrong. Eventually, however, symptoms began to appear. He began to eat too much, and gained too much weight; he began to sleep excessively, particularly when he was at home on weekends. As he became more and more successful, he was becoming more and more frustrated. Finally, he and Sara moved back to France, where he opened an office for his film company. He was happier there, but Sara was not.

After three years of marriage, Sara gave birth to a son, who for a while provided Jean-Pierre with new hope and a burst of creative energy; he projected his own deprived childhood onto the boy and this developed into an intense and profound attachment. And for a while too, the prospect of the happy, stable family and the quiet, orderly life afforded him some sense of peace. But this prospect existed wholly as an image within him, and did not allow for inconsistencies either in his own feeling nature or in Sara's. Beneath the surface, therefore, the marriage continued to disintegrate, with a concurrent loss of emotional and sexual contact. It had now become a hollow form, with carefully prepared meals and a beautifully kept house and appropriate friends entertained at well-organised dinner parties.

After six years of marriage, Sara succumbed to a prolonged period of severe depression. This was accompanied by a dawning recognition of the mother-projection she had elected to assume and the implications attendant upon it. As a result, she resolved to terminate the marriage, a decision which caused Jean-Pierre considerable pain. Although he himself had unconsciously helped to create the rupture, he could not for a time acknowledge this fact, and tried desperately to restore the relationship. The domestic edifice was necessary. It had become for him the symbol of an unfulfilled childhood and a bulwark against his own psyche's need to grow. And his attachment to his son made the situation all the more difficult. Eventually, however, Sara left with the child and returned to England. During the two years between the separation and the final divorce, Jean-Pierre could never wholly accept the fact that the marriage was definitely over. Although he engaged in numerous affairs, he retained in some part of himself a secret bewilderment and an unconscious hope that somehow something would magically occur to resuscitate the past. That this past had been primarily his fantasy only dawned on him slowly. As he began to understand Sara better as an individual — which he had to do in order to understand why she had left him — he began to discern the basic incompatibility of their respective temperaments.

At approximately the same time as the marriage began to collapse, Jean-Pierre had grown increasingly discontent working for other people and stifling his own creativity in the process. He decided to form his own film company, and — despite Sara's opposition and conviction that the venture would fail — he accepted the risk, made the requisite gamble and invested most of his capital in the new project. There followed long and arduous struggle to render the new company financially viable. Just before his forty-second birthday, Jean-Pierre discovered the "growth movement", which constituted a new world for him. With a mounting sense of awakening, he began delving into psychology, alternative healing and esoteric thought and proceeded to read voraciously. At the same time, he established contact with many rather unconventional people and attempted to explore his own unconventionality, seeking some under-standing of the motives which had propelled him into so many unsuccessful relationships. His abandonment of a secure but stultifying career, his venture into the unknown and its attendant growth in consciousness led to his meeting with Katherine, a Canadian artist and illustrator living in France. She, too, was deeply involved in the esoteric movement on which Jean-Pierre had stumbled, and it provided a sphere of shared interests and visions that drew them together. By now he was beginning to appreciate his need for individual creative expression, regardless of the difficulties he might encounter along the way; and he recognised in Katherine, despite her rather forceful personality, a respect for that need. Despite certain conflicts of personality and the fact that each possessed a similar intuitive, temperamental and self-willed character, they married. The results of this union remain to be seen; but for our purposes, it is not necessary to pursue Jean-Pierre's "case history" any further.

There are several important points suggested by Jean-Pierre's birth chart, and we must consider these before we proceed to the progressed horoscope. The dominant motif in the natal chart is growth of consciousness, suggested by the sun in the ninth house and by the ruler and Mercury in the eighth. Pluto, the ruler, widely conjunct Mercury, suggests a powerful drive towards self-understanding, digging into the depths to shed light on one's own motives. Moreover, Scorpio rising further accentuates the need to understand oneself. This kind of emphasis immediately suggests an individual driven to seek knowledge of himself and of life through creative expression. Leo as a sun-sign also suggests that one's need is to discover one's Self; and in the ninth house, it implies a quest for meaningful experience which can engender a *Weltanschauung* of as much depth and breadth as possible.

The exact opposition of the sun and Saturn reflects Jean-Pierre's lack of confidence, the sense of inadequacy and failure triggered in part by his difficult childhood. But although this opposition suggests many anxieties and feelings of limitation, it also suggests a determination to confront them, surmount them and become one's own self at any cost. The intuitive temperament is reflected by a fiery sun in a fiery house, and also by Uranus in Aries, another fiery sign, in the fifth house, that of creative expression. The dominance of the thinking function is reflected by the third house moon in Aquarius — an airy sign in an airy house — and by the similar placement of Saturn; and Mars, the co-ruler of the chart, is likewise in an air sign, Libra, in an airy house, the eleventh. In contrast, the feeling function is undifferentiated. This is suggested by the Scorpio ascendant, a watery sign whose primitive and intense feeling orientation is not easily digestible by the dominant functions of consciousness. In consequence, it is likely to be projected upon others. Sensation, too, is a weak function, and the grouping of planets in Virgo at the midheaven suggests qualities Jean-Pierre might seek from a partner: earthiness, stability, order, structure and refinement. Venus conjunct Neptune in Virgo in the ninth house implies a particular kind of anima image: dark, earthy, "foreign", and highly mysterious. Because of the relative balance of elements, one could not easily type this chart; but if one knows something of the temperament involved, it is possible to examine the chart and understand how the elements of earth and water have been suppressed and projected upon the partner.

Having noted these basic temperament traits, we must also appreciate that fixed signs like Leo, Scorpio and Aquarius — all of which figure significantly in Jean-Pierre's chart — are always slow to grow. They forge their values slowly, through direct experience, and do not usually blossom until mid-life. Resistant to change from without, the fixed signs as a group typically cling to values and experiences that have outlived their usefulness. On Jean-Pierre's chart, moreover, the sun-Saturn opposition suggests many obstacles which Jean-Pierre must confront within himself before he is free to express his individuality. Chief among these is the split between his ego and his shadow. Ultimately, he must make peace with the inner darkness. Reflected by Saturn in Aquarius, this darkness threatens to keep him trapped in a sense of his "ordinariness", and consistently seems to confront him from without in the form of an obstructive society or an obstructive individual. Until he can accept without judging both the "inferiority" within himself and in the external world, he will find himself pitted against an apparently hostile environment. His powerful feelings, suggested by the Scorpio ascendant, must also be accepted as they are and integrated, rather than being structured into categories of "good" and "bad" by his thinking function. There is great tension reflected between the sun, moon and ascendant, and this no doubt contributes to Jean-Pierre's vitality and intensity — in the terms of analytical psychology, he is full of "Eros". But he must learn to adjust his ideal image of himself and others to the reality of human nature, which is both dark and light. Like many people with highly developed thinking, Jean-Pierre is extremely emotional and therefore confuses Eros with feeling. Most of his relationships have involved powerful emotion and intense passion, but the feeling has remained largely undifferentiated. Jean-Pierre has a real problem understanding the feelings and motives of others; he perpetually projects the darker side of his Scorpio ascendant outward, believing that others are brutal, aggressive, controlling and suspicious, and desirous of obstructing his own development.

Venus in quincunx — a 150-degree angle — to Saturn suggests a problem in relationships; it is a contact frequently concurrent with the childhood wounds of a cold and unsympathetic home life. Jean-Pierre's mother was a hard-working but undemonstrative woman, and his grandmother, too, had great difficulty in expressing feeling. Jean-Pierre is basically afraid of exposing his very vulnerable and childlike feeling nature in close relationships; yet these very relationships, suggested by the Venus-Neptune conjunction in the ninth house, must be for him a means of self-transcendance and a pathway to his own soul.

At the time of Jean-Pierre's first marriage, several interesting progressions were just beginning to gather. Because it was encouraged by so much pressure from Liliane, his first marriage may have seemed her decision; but it takes two to collude, and Jean was unconsciously staging for himself a situation through which he would be forced to acknowledge the power of the anima and the strength of his own unrecognised feeling nature. During the first year of that marriage, the sun was progressed to conjunct Neptune. This latter planet symbolises a peculiar passivity, a temporary inertia of the individual will, a paralysis from which one can obtain freedom only by sacrificing some aspect of oneself.

As the sun gradually moved towards conjunction with Venus Jean-Pierre met Carol. The progression of sun conjunct Venus symbolises constellation of the anima, the archetypal feminine; and it is hardly surprising, therefore, that at this time he would not only marry and divorce, but also become involved in the most passionate affair of his life. The sun's progression over Venus continued throughout the collapse of Jean-Pierre's marriage and the first two years of his travels. During this time he was compulsively seeking a woman who embodied the inner image dominating his consciousness, which the energies reflected by the progression had activated. At the same time, Venus also made a progression over Mars, another symbol of the passional, erotic side of the anima being constellated. During this whole period of his life, Jean-Pierre was completely dominated by his erotic and emotional nature. Nothing else really mattered to him. While these progressions were occuring, Jean-Pierre also experienced his Saturn return, which completed itself when he was twenty-nine and a half. As a result, the old self was broken down and disintegrated, and a new one emerged, burdened with new questions and new disillusionment yet at last free from the structures and values of the past.

We must remember that the progressions did not make any of these things happen. Nor can we moralise, or assert that Jean-Pierre should have made different choices. Both his marriage and its bondage were a necessary part of the experience; they caused his relation with Carol to be an authentic crisis instead of a pleasant love affair, and tore him apart in a way that forced him to become conscious of his feelings. Through this kind of suffering, the anima leads a man to experience life. Moreover, Jean-Pierre's choice of love partner was a disastrous one, since Carol, because of her own emotional problems, could not sustain a stable relationship; and here too one can see the imprint of the anima, which entangles a man in emotional bonds, drives him into the jungle of his own feeling life, and confronts him with choices which madden him because they are neither black nor white nor clearly definable as right or wrong.

Jean-Pierre thought he could make his feelings submit to his thinking principles. The entire period during which the sun progressed over Neptune and Venus comprised an experience which brought to consciousness a side of his nature he had never known existed. It is pointless to say that one should or should not make certain choices because people will be "hurt". The unconscious decides such things for us, and only the individual who has been overwhelmed by the activation of its forces can know what power they have. And in the face of these forces the rational intellect, with its precise structures of appropriate behaviour, must remain mute.

At the time of Jean-Pierre's wedding with Sara, Venus was progressing into a trine to the moon, which became exact during the first year of this second marriage. At the same time, the progressed midheaven had also come into a trine to the moon. Initially, the marriage was a homecoming, a return to a blissful fantasy childhood; the moon is a symbol of the mother, and Jean-Pierre at last thought he had found a woman who could provide the calm and stable solicitude he had never experienced in childhood. These progressions, in short, symbolised the constellation of another aspect of the anima: the mother-image.

The marriage's disintegration coincided with two important progressions in Jean-Pierre's chart: Venus progressed to an opposition with Uranus, and Mars progressed to a square with both the sun and Saturn. The first of these symbolises Jean-Pierre's awakening realisation that something was lacking in his marriage, something that had been lacking in all his relationships with women: the transpersonal element, the capacity of the anima to act as psychopomp, guide to the spiritual depths. Not even his involvement with Carol had constellated this aspect of the feminine archetype. His passions then had certainly been aroused, but Carol had corresponded to the anima's Venus phase, the hetaira, the ideal courtesan and playmate. Now, however, he needed something more profound. His creativity was being activated (Uranus is in the fifth house of creative expression) but it was virtually impossible to express this hitherto dormant side of his nature within the framework of the marriage he had made

with Sara and, indeed, at first wanted. Mother-son relationships do not permit either mother or son to grow into man
and woman. There was a meeting of habits between Jean-
Pierre and Sara, and often a meeting of minds, but not one of
feeling, and certainly not one of spirit. Moreover, in his
marriage with Sara, as in his other relationships, Jean-Pierre
tended to live out the different aspects of his anima through
the woman, rather than developing them within himself
through the stimulus of the relationship. The progression of
Venus to Uranus suggests it is time for him to awaken, to
become conscious of the potential of the feminine aspect of
his own psyche, to express this potential through his own
creativity.

Mars progressing to trigger his natal sun-Saturn opposition
symbolises the stirring of Jean-Pierre's need to develop
himself as a man, to seek something of his own, to meet
challenge — in short, to grow up in the deepest sense. The
suffocating quilt of secure salary, nice house, garden and
Sunday papers was seriously rumpled under this progression.
A new unconscious constellation had begun: Uranus, the
Awakener, was prodded into motion, and slowly proceeded
to emerge into consciousness. It took Jean-Pierre some time
to recognise his collusion in the collapse of his second
marriage to Sara. Eventually, however, he was compelled to
do so, for he had planted the seeds of it himself. He could not
remain a child in his feelings forever, nor could Sara remain
the devoted and caring mother-wife. The verbal decision to
separate may have been hers, but the groundwork had been a
collaborative undertaking. Like many mother-son relationships, Jean-Pierre's and Sara's had not been devoid of
affection and answered their joint needs at a specific time.
But needs change with growth; and the progressions of Venus
to Uranus, Mars to the sun and Saturn, heralded the
severance of the umbilical cord.

By this time Jean had reached his "mid-life crisis". Uranus
arrived in opposition to its natal place and he began to
expand his thinking, to become involved in a new movement
with new people whom he had never encountered before. Although his intuitive temperament had afforded him glimpses

previously, the broader significance behind events began to
dawn on him now in a conscious way. His mind and his spirit
were awakening, and he had the problems and joys of his
new child — the film company — to occupy him. He met his
third wife, Katherine, when Uranus was stationary in the sky
opposite his natal Uranus. At the same time the progressed
moon was in trine to Uranus, and the progressed midheaven
had come into opposition to Uranus as well. One can see the
immense power of this planet being activated within his
psyche. His goals, his self-image, his entire conscious
outlook on life were undergoing radical change.

This very brief outline does not do justice to either the
individual chart or to the events reflected by it. The
implications of each progression are enormous, and involve
far more ramifications than it is possible to explore here. For
one thing, we could ascribe each of Jean-Pierre's four
important relationships to four different planetary energies.
His marriage to Liliane was reflected by the progression of the
sun over Neptune; his meeting and subsequent affair with
Carol bore the imprint of Venus; Sara coincided with
progressions to the moon; and Katherine was connected with
the activation of the energy symbolised by Uranus. On the
basis of this perhaps over-simplistic schema, one might say
that Jean-Pierre's four women were symbols to him of four
different facets of the feminine, four different archetypes
operating within his own psyche and seeking expression in his
life. The additional circumstances surrounding each relationship also partake of a particular, and corresponding,
archetypal energy.

That of which we are unconscious, we project. Because
Jean-Pierre's relationships, like most people's, were largely
unconscious, the attributes of the archetype were projected
on the individual women. No human being, of course, can
literally be an archetype, but if one examines the charts of
the women in question, one can see how much of the
relationships were purely projection on Jean-Pierre's part,
and how much the women themselves conformed to his
internal image. Carol's horoscope, for example, shows very
little Venus influence, although she appeared as Venus to

Jean-Pierre when they met; and some of the ensuing disappointment no doubt resulted from her inability to fulfil the demands of the projection imposed upon her. A similar discrepancy occurs in Sara's birth chart, which reflects no lunar qualities; no planets fall in Cancer, and the moon is cadent and hidden, poorly aspected, in the twelfth house. Here again, Jean-Pierre projected qualities which did not coincide with the object of the projection. Such "errors" — if that is the appropriate word — are neither "good" nor "bad", however. Had Sara indeed been a lunar type, the mother-son marriage might have endured far longer, and with greater suffocation for both partners involved. Ultimately, one can only accept one's experience as Experience, live with it and grow through it into knowledge; it is neither "right" nor "wrong". All one can say is that each of Jean-Pierre's relationships was necessary, productive and inevitable, because something within his psyche made it so. During the course of this trial-and-error process, moreover, Jean-Pierre has become more conscious, so that his chosen partner conforms more closely to the anima within yet is not made to carry the burden of living this inner image out herself. Katherine's chart, for instance, shows a dominant and angular Uranus, which aspects every planet on her chart including the sun and moon. It is the focal point in a "bowl-shaped" horoscope. Perhaps she will prove capable of fulfilling the needs which governed his attachment to her.

Not everyone lives out the release of energies symbolised by progressions in the obvious external way that Jean-Pierre did. His temperament is perhaps responsible for the drama in his relationships; for other men, successive aspects to Venus need not entail a perpetual change of partner. Under progressions, however, every man's image of his partner will change, and so will what he seeks from a relationship. If a union is conscious on both sides, such changes can be handled cooperatively and a new and richer facet of life introduced into the relationship. If both people are unconscious, the consequences will usually be explosive and destructive. But some individuals choose the high road, and others the low. For some it is necessary to act out an experience, in defiance of all obstacles. For others, it will be lived within an existing structure. One cannot predict the mode beforehand; one can only wait until growth inaugurates change. When this occurs, the progressed horoscope has much to say about why.

IX
Relating in the Aquarian Age

Not only of cyclic Man
Thou here discern'st the plan,
Not only of cyclic Man, but of the cyclic Me,
Not solely of Mortalities great years
The reflex just appears,
But thine own bosom's year, still circling around
In ample and in ampler gyre
Towards the far completion, wherewith crowned
Love unconsumed shall chant in his own funeral
pyre.

— Francis Thompson

It is perhaps time to return to that *Zeitgeist* under whose auspices this book began, and to determine what bearing it, and the widely proclaimed advent of the Aquarian Age, have on the problems of becoming conscious in our relationships to other human beings. The large is reflected in the small, and the new era of consciousness symbolised by the Aquarian Age is not a phenomenon which "happens" somewhere out there, its effects eventually reaching us through the environment. It is an occurrence within the psyche of each individual, and must be recognised as such. Only then can we understand the connections between our changing needs and values in relationships, and the groaning and heaving around us which signify the new era's birth pangs.

In the summer of 1967 the first "love-in" was staged in California, a congregation of hundreds of under-thirty "dropouts" making their personal statement about what they deemed a stagnating, tottering and dehumanised social structure. At roughly the same time, the rock musical *Hair* became a hit in the United States, and one could hear its theme on every radio station around the country:

> When the moon is in the seventh house
> And Jupiter aligns with Mars,
> Then peace will guide the planets
> And love will rule the stars.
> This is the dawning of the Age of Aquarius ...

Prophets, seers and exponents of utopia appear at the dawn of every era, and their proliferation, dramatic as it has been in the last decade, has been seen before. It occurred at the dawn of the Piscean age, when the new religion, embryonic and unrecognised, was kept tenuously alive amidst the Roman catacombs by the devotion of a handful of believers. In another form, it also occurred at the advent of the Arien age, around 2000 B.C., when hordes of blue-eyed, yellow-haired tribes, with their hierarchies of warrior gods, swept down from Northern and Central Europe and overran the great matriarchal agrarian cultures of the Mediterranean. We possess no coherent record of the dawn of the Taurean age, which coincides with that period, between 5000 and 4000 B.C., when nomadic desert tribes began to till the land and established the foundations of the river-valley cultures of the Nile and the Tigris-Euphrates. Nevertheless, we regard these cultures as the beginning of Western civilisation. There have also been lesser flowerings of vision during each astrological age. The Hermetic Renaissance of the late 15th and early 16th Centuries, the Rosicrucian Enlightenment in the early 17th, the "Romantic Movement" with its burst of creative genius embodied in such figures as Blake, Goethe, Swedenborg, Novalis, are a few examples of these smaller melodies during the last age. Important as they are, however, they carry the dominant theme of the great archetypal energies ruling this last two-thousand-year cycle.

Astrological ages appear to commence with great heaves

and groans, like the birth of any new thing into the world, and they are accompanied by the death pangs of the old era which engendered them. There also appears to be a basic cyclical pattern within each age, which corresponds to the pattern of development underlying individual consciousness. Plato called the cycle of the astrological ages the Great Year, an epoch of 25,000 years divided into twelve eras or aeons of 2165 years each. He believed that each of these eras was a different incarnation of the macrocosm Man renewing the cycle of death and rebirth — in much the same way that the individual microcosmic man, according to esoteric doctrine, enacts the cycle of successive incarnations on his spiralling path to greater consciousness. And we must remember, too, the cherished principle of alchemy — that God is not only man's redemption, for man is also God's. If this is so, the successive eras of consciousness are the development of God, as well as of man's god-image. Or perhaps there is no distinction between the two.

With myths and prophecies rampant about the advent of the Aquarian Age, it is worth considering the phenomenon from the astronomer's point of view, and then from the astrologer's. The latter, particularly, whose symbolic system has endured for so many thousands of years, has much to complement the findings of depth psychology. With the aid of these two disciplines, we can attempt to understand the great cycles of human development and their effect on the individual.

The precession of the equinoxes was first discovered by a Greek astronomer-astrologer named Hipparchus around 150 B.C. and is caused, apparently, by the earth wobbling on its polar axis as it orbits around the sun. Because of this wobbling, the north point shifts; and while we now site due north from Polaris, the North Star, that heavenly compass reference for true magnetic north did not always exist. In fact, the polar axis describes a circle which takes some 25,000 to 26,000 years to complete, and during that time it perpetually changes its orientation towards the stars in space. These changes can be measured each year at the vernal equinox, when the sun crosses the meridian at noon over the equator and enters what we call the zodiacal *sign* of Aries, the start of the new astrological year. At the present vernal equinoctial point, the backdrop of stars behind the sun is the end of the *constellation* of Pisces and the beginning of the constellation of Aquarius; and it is into the latter that the vernal equinoctial point is now slowly moving. Two thousand years ago, this vernal equinoctial point passed from the constellation of Aries into Pisces. Two thousand years from now, it will move into Capricorn, and another new age will begin.

We do not know why the physical phenomenon of a wobbly and not quite spherical earth, uncertain as to its orientation in the heavens, should have any connection with the growth of human consciousness. Perhaps it is a manifestation of synchronicity on a titanic scale. In any case, the new age seems bent on tearing the veil from nature's hidden face and its secrets; and if we sustain the pace of the last few years, we will no doubt acquire some understanding of a good many ancient mysteries, couched in suitably scientific language for the disciplined Aquarian mind. But whatever the reason, the correlation between the precession of the equinoxes and the changing eras of man's development appears to be symbolically valid, even if we do not yet know the laws governing the enigma. This correlation is inescapable if one studies history, and particularly the development of religion and myth throughout history, since it is man's religious symbols that express most clearly the energies at work from age to age. At the close of an era, many old gods die or are subordinated, and new gods — gods who are symbolic of energies which have not emerged into human consciousness before — are born. For example, the cult of the Great Mother, at the end of the Taurean age, was displaced by the cult of the sky gods. The explanation offered by esoteric thought warrants consideration: the universe as we know it is one living organism, and the physical and psychic patterns through which, at any given time, that organism manifests itself reflect symbolically the same quality of meaning. Or we could think in terms of our *Zeitgeist*, and suggest that certain great archetypal energies, "time spirits", both physical and spiritual in nature, are activated or constellated at the beginning of an age, imparting to both outer and inner reality the same pattern and the same meaning, from major world events to the private lives of individual men.

An exhaustive study of religion and myth in every era and in every country in the world would be required to delineate precisely the manifestations of each of these great archetypes or *Zeitgeists*. The reader is referred to Frazer's *The Golden Bough*,[1] Joseph Campbell's four-volume study, *The Masks of God*,[2] Neumann's *The Great Mother*,[3] and Jung's *Aion*[4] for further exploration. We may summarise, however, by suggesting that the meaning of the astrological sign presiding over a particular age seems to permeate the religious values of that age. What man worships as the highest possible ideal, the highest good and the highest mystery behind life, appears to be in some way symbolised by the governing astrological sign, and this mystery always embodies something entirely new, something previously unknown to man's consciousness. Thus, over the ages, the macrocosm Man expands his awareness, and becomes more whole.

With the advent of the Taurean age, man discovered the fertility of the earth, and his vision of deity was embodied in the Great Mother, symbol of the power of procreativity, a reflection of the earthy, feminine sign of Taurus the Bull. The many representations of this presiding feminine power may be found in virtually every culture during this age, along with the Mother's consort, the Serpent. In considering any astrological sign, we must always consider its antithesis. Taurus is opposite to Scorpio; and whether it is expressed through an individual or an age, the simplicity and passivity of fertile earth strives towards the dynamic spark of fertilising life — which of course entails death and rebirth. This regenerative principle is symbolised by Scorpio, and the Serpent — the ancient symbol for the sign — becomes the

1 *The Golden Bough*, Sir James Frazer, Macmillan, N.Y. 1922.
2 *The Masks of God*, Joseph Campbell, Viking Press, N.Y.
3 *The Great Mother*, Erich Neumann, Bollingen Foundation, N.Y. 1955.
4 *Aion*, C.G. Jung, Routledge & Kegan Paul, London 1959.

Mother's consort. The Serpent embodies wisdom, and the
knowledge of choice; only through choice can man die and
be reborn. Without it he remains as the vegetable kingdom,
passive, acquiescent, and without knowledge of his origins or
his destiny. The *Zeitgeist* of the Taurean age, reflected by the
symbols of the Great Mother and the Serpent, seems to have
been that of the mysteries of sexual union, procreativity,
death and rebirth; and all these aspects of the archetype were
dramatically expressed through the various forms of worship
during this age.

Astrological ages do not begin and end abruptly; the
decline of one fertilises the birth of the next. At the dawn of
the Arien age, the matriarchy and the supremacy of the
Mother began to give way before a new pantheon of deities,
sky gods who lived high on their mountain tops and kept their
feminine consorts in line. A very striking feature appears in
many myths originating in the Arien age: the gods, who
previously had not concerned themselves directly with
human fate, now became involved with man, and coupled
with living women to produce a race of heroes and demigods.
God, or the gods, are slowly approaching the domain of man.
During the Taurean age, the gods were symbolised as
daemonic powers of nature, who must be propitiated and
placated, but never directly approached. Nor were they
always — or even frequently — anthropomorphised. But with
the emergence of the divine patriarchy, the gods began to
condescend to be concerned, even worried, over human
affairs.

Aries is a masculine, fiery sign, and the dawn of this age
reflects the next step in man's evolving consciousness: he has
begun to subjugate the powers of nature with the creative
tool of his will. His vision of diety was embodied in symbols
of the power of the masculine principle, most significant of
which is the symbol of the Hero. Aries is the antithesis of
Libra, and this polarity is reflected in the development of
systems of thought, law, philosophy, military strategy,
mathematics and the development of ideas. In the Arien age,
if God was embodied as a warrior and a hero, he was also a
God who could think.

At the beginning of the Piscean age, the fiery pantheons of sky gods were not overthrown in any overt way. Instead, they were infiltrated, disintegrated, and subtly cloaked with new names — characteristic of Pisces — by a benign God of love and compassion and sacrifice. The next stage in man's developing consciousness is an increasing awareness of his fellow man: the development of feeling values. Pisces is a watery, feminine sign which embodies a sense of the unity of life; it is also a naturally dual sign, portrayed in the symbol of the two fish struggling to swim in opposite directions yet bound to each other by a golden cord. It may be this duality which is in part connected with the terrible split between the opposites which has occurred during the last age. During both the Taurean and Arien ages, there seems to have been a relative unity or harmony between the antithetical principles symbolised by the opposite signs. Perhaps this is a reflection of man's instinctual state during these ages; for unconsciousness possesses its own unity. But the values embodied by Pisces and its opposite sign, Virgo, have been inimical to each other for the last two thousand years; this enmity is very similar to that experienced by an individual at war with his own shadow. The qualities embodied by Virgo were forcibly repressed during the Piscean age. In consequence, the highest value — that absolute love for and forgiveness of mankind of which Christ is the most significant symbol — has not been given balance and form by the realistic earthy consciousness of Virgo. The enormous gulf between man's spiritual aspiration to purity, perfection and union with God on the one hand and his daily life on the other is still evident now as it has been for centuries. It is best personified by the Sunday church-goer, who is totally sincere in his religious convictions yet who, every other day of the week, spews out hatred, jealousy, violence, cruelty and spite over his fellows until the next Sunday's visit with God.

Miracles and visions are very much an aspect of the Piscean mode of expression; so is mass emotion, receptivity to the collective feeling needs of the group without individual discrimination. Blind faith, belief without question, and even fanaticism are expressions of Piscean energy.

Virgo, with its emphasis on discrimination, discernment and self-refinement, is a natural counterpoint to the Piscean urge for disintegration of the individuality in the sea of the mass; but Virgo's values, which are humbler and more concerned with living daily life within the framework of the limitations of personality and time, were denigrated in a rather forcible way. Virgo, although discriminating, allows value to the impure; it is concerned with what is useful, practical and within reach. It is not an idealistic sign, as Pisces is. One may see the obvious traces of the repression of Virgoan values in the accent on purity, celibacy, and the inherent evil of matter; it is also observable in that highest of Christian ethics, "good works", often performed without any realistic assessment of whether the recipient wishes to be offered these services or not. Virgo is an earthy sign, like Taurus, but the personification of the feminine principle is not the primitive, fertile earth symbolised by the bull; it is a differentiated female figure, the Maiden, who is receptive but also possesses the power of reflection and discrimination, and the ability to say no. It is here that we can begin to see the enormous implications in this terrible split in the collective unconscious of man during the Piscean era. Virgo is a symbol of Woman, who during this era has become charged with the projection of the collective shadow. The devil, who is also an embodiment of the same principle of matter — "Rex Mundi" — always works through a woman in the Piscean age, and the once sacred serpent in the garden, having lost the value of instinctual wisdom he once possessed during the Taurean era, has become the Lord of Darkness pursuing his ends through the weakness and inherent inferiority of the feminine. The symbol of the Great Mother, once an embodiment of the wholeness of Woman, has split in two and become Mary the Virgin and Mary Magdalen the Harlot; and the happy, ribald pantheons of gods and goddesses now become the Holy Trinity of masculine godhood while woman, matter, earth, remains below, in the grip of the Lord of the World, incapable — until very recently, when the Church has at last permitted Mary entrance into Heaven complete with body — of full redemption.

The collective values of an age find their way into the psyche of the individual; for individuals are individuals only to a certain level. Beyond this, they are part of the larger group. The meaning of this psychic split on a collective level has far-reaching implications in the sphere of human relationships, which has been one of the central problems of the Piscean age. The dominant value of an age may be compared to the masculine pole of the opposites, for it seems to be the function of the masculine principle — whether in man or in woman — to give form, coherence, structure and meaning to the values embodied in the governing sign. On the other hand, it seems to be the function of the feminine principle to provide connections, intuitions, inner significance, human application, practical expression for the values embodied by the opposite sign. In other words, woman has been the carrier of the archetype symbolised by Virgo during the last age not only because Virgo itself is a symbol of Woman, but because it is the opposite, the complement, to the ruling theme of the age. The whole sphere of human relationships belongs to the feminine principle, and the devaluation of the feminine — which means not only of woman but of matter, flesh, instinct, the art of the small — has virtually destroyed our capacity to relate to each other. We are paying the price now for this complete ignorance of such an important facet of human life, as we become progressively more embroiled in attempts to "make good" the damage through projecting the redeeming symbol on sexuality — which is hardly equipped to carry the whole of relationship values. The collective anima has suffered badly during the Piscean age, and it will be a long time before she is able to be redeemed from her darkness. And this process of redemption cannot be done on a collective level through changes in legal status, or movements. These are the product of inner change, not the cause of it. Regaining the value of the feminine principle will never be accomplished through acts of force, or riots, or legislation. It can only be done within the individual, who must first learn to reclaim these values himself — whether the individual is a man or a woman. Society is made up of individuals, and this is an individual task.

When an individual represses the dark side of his nature completely, it tends to break out during the middle of life in full force, and he will often flip into the opposite of all he valued and live his life out in total contradiction to what he was before. It would seem that this same principle is at work on the collective level as well as the individual. In fact, small outbreaks occur at regular intervals on the collective level just as they do in individuals: little puffs of steam which reveal the rumblings underneath and help to keep the entire structure — whether of society or of the ego — from toppling with a resounding crash. During the Piscean age, for example, one of these outbreaks occurred at the time of the Crusades, and was counteracted to some extent by Courtly Love; one occurred with Luther and Calvin and the Renaissance. The major outbreak, the *enantiodromia* as Jung calls it, the mid-life crisis of the age, occurred at the dawn of what we call, for some unaccountable reason, the Age of Enlightenment. The emergence of the shadow has taken the form of blind materialism, and complete rejection of spiritual values by material science. We are still plodding through the mire of this eruption, as we build bigger and better weapons without any sense of the humanity for whom we are supposedly building them. The so-called sexual revolution, as well as dialectical materialism, also appear to be outgrowths of suppressed Virgo blindly reaching out for some light. Anything which has been kept locked in the basement for fifteen hundred years is likely to be rather unprepossessing when it emerges, and also rather angry.

Attempts were made before this *enantiodromia* to restore balance to the increasingly lopsided values of the Piscean age. These attempts were promulgated by alchemy, devoted to reclaiming the God in matter; and also by the development of the Grail legends, which were devoted to reclaiming the values of the feminine. As Jung has shown, both these attempts erupted from the collective and were an attempt at balancing a hopelessly one-sided Church dominated by masculine values. They sowed seeds which engendered the Italian Renaissance, the flowering of Elizabethan England, and most significantly, the Romantic

Movement, the single most important objective of which was to repudiate reason run amok and reclaim intuition, feeling and a feminine-suffused numinous. However, these movements did not permeate to the extent that they could reverse the calcification which had already set into Western culture.

We are now in transition between two ages, and a new *Zeitgeist* has arisen, a new time-spirit and a new symbol of the godhood which once, in man's distant past, was so aloof and so remote that he could only bow to its power but which is now so imminent that it would seem God is at last incarnating not as One Man, but as men. Where then are we going, and what is our new *Zeitgeist* about? Who are the new gods?

> If, as seems probable, the aeon of the fishes is ruled by the archetypal motif of the hostile brothers, then the approach of the next Platonic month, namely Aquarius, will constellate the problem of the union of opposites. [1]

Aquarius is an airy sign, which suggests that the sphere of the intellect and of knowledge is becoming the dominant value. According to the pattern, it is the function of the masculine principle to provide structure and form for this urge for knowing. It is not strictly material knowledge, embodied in material science; that is a manifestation of decaying Pisces and rampant Virgo. Ages do not begin and end suddenly; they overlap, and amidst the crumbling ruins of one can be seen the slowly germinating seeds of the next. Aquarius symbolises an attitude of consciousness which is interested in knowing and understanding the laws by which the energies which stand behind manifested life operate. It is science, but not science as we have seen it in the last hundred years with its refusal to concede anything except what can be held in the hand. It is science in the sense of the word's Latin root, which simply means to know. We can see the beginnings of this as further and further exploration

1 *Aion*.

occurs into the nature of sub-atomic particles and the nature of light; we can see it in the new field of parapsychology, "psi" phenomena, no longer regarded as "weird" or "supernatural" but rather as natural functions of life whose nature operates according to logical principles which we do not yet fully understand. Fields like alternative healing, acupuncture, radionics, Kirlian photography, telepathy, telekinesis, the exploration of the etheric or bioplasmic body, are all subjects for the probing Aquarian mind and thirst for tearing the veil from the face of the mysteries. Astrology is receiving new attention as well, not in the old event-predicting way, but as a map of the system of laws by which the energies of life operate — an astrology vindicated by statistical research and scientific investigation. The human body itself, with its energy field and its system of seven "chakras" or energy centres, each correlating with a planetary energy, is no longer a laughable subject in the West; and psychology as well is rising from its infancy as a study of sexual complexes and behavioural mechanisms to a true study of the laws by which the psyche operates — a study, as the word suggests, of the soul. We now talk about archetypes and energy rather than gods; to Aquarius, everything is energy and operates according to natural laws, and these energies exist within as well as outside man. God, to Aquarius, is the intelligent principle by which these laws, both physical and psychic, operate. God, in fact, is alive and well in the Aquarian age and is hiding secretly not only in matter but within the human psyche as well, disguised in psychological parlance as the Self.

We must now consider the sign opposite to Aquarius, for this will provide us with a key not only to the role of the feminine principle in this new age, but also to what we must develop within ourselves if we are, as Jung suggests, to heal the terrible split between the opposites which has occurred in the last age. During the Piscean age, Virgo/matter/woman was the shadow, and we know what happens to an individual who suppresses the dark side of his nature. We should not be surprised at the violent rebellion of both woman and of materialistic science after so much time spent in the darkness. Leo is now the shadow with which we must contend, and this sign is a symbol of the creative individuality. As a fire sign, Leo is connected with the intuition and the perception of the intrinsic value of the individual. If we are able to take these values and integrate them with the ruling dominant of Aquarius, we will see a renaissance not only in the field of the creative arts, but in relationships, in the place of woman in society, and in individual consciousness as well. It is towards this synthesis that we are now moving.

Aquarius is primarily a group-oriented sign. It is impersonal, operates according to thinking principles, and is concerned with the energies of the group rather than with the personal creative unfoldment of the individual. Leo is individualistic and is uninterested in the group; he seeks above all else to become what he envisions as his own heroic potential. Aquarius is logical, consistent, and principled; Leo is dramatic, intuitive, and seeks myth rather than fact. The value of the individual, and his right to be himself, is a fine counterpoint to the collectivisation which we are already experiencing in such early and crude Aquarius experiments as communism, expansion of large corporations, and other manifestations of impeccable organisation at the expense of individual freedom. Organisation is a keyword for Aquarius, and the inner development of the individual — which, we must assume, is likely to be of far more importance to woman — must balance this massing occurring under Aquarius, with its belief that the whole is more important than the parts which compose it. Aquarius seeks hard facts, logical principles, consistent behaviour according to principles of right and wrong with the benefit of the group in mind. Leo seeks joy, self-expression, spontaneity, the right to believe in magic and to bring fairy tales to life by living one's life creatively. We may see words leaking into common speech which show us how far the new values have progressed: in the Piscean age, one spoke of love, compassion, selflessness and sacrifice, while now we speak of group consciousness, energy, organisation, and discovery. Aquarius, with all its nobility, will wipe out the individual if it runs rampant; Leo, if it is suppressed and erupts, is the dictator, the megalomaniac, the true figure of the antichrist, whose individuality is the supreme value. Somewhere between these two we must steer our course.

There is a new god emerging under Aquarius, although he is no longer projected upon the heavens; we know that he is living in man, but he is a god nonetheless. He is thrice-greatest Hermes the Magician, straight from the Tarot deck and clothed in a laboratory smock. A new archetype is emerging into human consciousness, and its effect on the individual is to enlarge his consciousness — which means the unleashing of both dark and light. In the end, this task of bringing to birth a new age with new values lies where it has always lain — in the hands of the individual.

We are no longer psychological children. All the pomp and pageantry and mummery and glamour and violence of past ages has been our childhood, and we have passed through a childhood no better and no worse than the childhood of any individual. It has had its moments of beauty and vision and discovery, and its moments of darkness and horror and brutality. The adult Man is beginning to emerge, and beginning to exercise his gift of reflection at last. It is beginning to dawn on him that he has created the world in which he lives, and that his psychic reality is the only reality he can ever know; there is no objective observer and no object to be observed, for they have become the same thing. He can no longer blame his political failures on the ruling government, for he has elected it himself. He can no longer blame his employer for his unhappy work life, for he has the freedom to choose it. He can no longer blame his love problems on his partner, for he is discovering that they lie within him as well. He is learning that there is more to his psyche than he had thought, and that he is responsible for bringing to birth the potentials which it contains. Aquarius offers him the sacred injunction, "Man, know thyself"; and Leo, in contrast, offers him another: "Man, be thyself." Caught between these two, he can no longer plead the excuse of unconsciousness for his failures. He has passed through earth and fire and water and is now learning to breathe the air

— and one can only hope he does not become so inflated by it that he blows himself up.

Our new *Zeitgeist* is a synthesis of these two injunctions. Man, led by science, is exploring the world only to find that it is composed of the same substance as himself. He explores himself, led by psychology, only to discover that he has shaped the world. No one can help him decide what to do with his discovery. In the end he must place his allegiance with the Self, and the gatekeeper to the centre of his own being is that inner partner which lives within his own psyche and serves as psychopomp and guide to the mysteries. And in the end the only way he will ever discover and bring to consciousness this inner partner is through understanding the outer one, the human beings with whom he lives and shares his planet. He will only find himself in the looking glass. Perhaps then he can fulfil the myth of the sign which rules this dawning age:

Water of life am I,
Poured forth for thirsty men.[1]

1 *Esoteric Astrology*, Alice A. Bailey, Lucis Trust, N.Y. 1951.

X
Conclusion

If I drink oblivion of a day,
So shorten I the stature of my soul.
— George Meredith

Man, if indeed thou knowest what thou doest,
thou art blessed; but if thou knowest not, thou art
cursed, and a transgressor of the law.
— Luke

A guide to living with other people, whether it be
psychological, astrological, or any other, cannot — if it is to
do justice to human nature — provide shortcuts. We have
lately had a surfeit of shortcuts, ranging from LSD to five-day
"enlightenment intensives", and none of them have solved our
relationship problems. The growth of a human being is slow; it
begins at birth and ends at death, and requires a lifetime's
nurturing. It cannot be hurried. The growth of a relationship
cannot be hurried either, particularly if it is to be a conscious
one. Nor can the process be made free of conflict by
psychological techniques and exercises, or even by horoscopes. We must all, in the end, accept the consequences of
our choices, and choices are never as simple as they seem.
Even the wisest of men makes poor choices, and it is these
very "mistakes", with all the pain of their consequences,
which enable him to achieve some wisdom. Unfortunately
for the facile seeker, the questions we ask can only be
answered by more questions. "Should I leave my husband?"
for example, cannot be answered by "Yes", or "No". Were it

that simple, we would have no problems at all, and would not grow. Thus the question can only be answered by other questions: "What does your marriage mean to you?" and "What do you feel it means to your husband?" and "What do you understand to be the main problem in the marriage?" and "What is your share in the constellation of this problem?" And to each of these questions, the answer is a dozen more. The astrologer or psychologist who answers "Yes" or "No" is a presumptuous and a dangerous fool; for no one can make another man's choice for him. And in every choice, however apparently black-and-white, lies a web of associations and nuances which ultimately, if one knows how to look and inquire properly, can illuminate its deepest meaning. Parzival, in order to redeem the kingdom, was not required to perform any heroic deed; he was required to ask the right question.

The path to greater understanding suggested in this book will not be a popular one, because it entails individual responsibility and offers no shortcuts. It is far easier to blame one's parents for one's psychological problems, conveniently forgetting that the power of the parents derives from what is projected upon them; it is easier to shout out one's anger at one's neighbour in an encounter group and then go home and forget about it, than to search within oneself for the anger's real source; it is easier to leave a relationship or a marriage because monogamy is "out of fashion", or because one's partner is obviously a beast and wholly responsible for the mess. The recognition of the element of projection is a burden many of us do not wish to assume; for if we *do* assume this burden, not a single incident — not a single quarrel, mood, fit of rage, secret suspicion or outburst of resentment — can pass without recognition of one's own motives. And many things must also be talked about, which involves trust of a kind we are not accustomed to reposing in our fellow human beings — because we do not trust ourselves. Not only are we completely uneducated in this inward way of seeing; we are also subject to a certain apathy, an inertia which shrinks from the effort of learning to see, preferring the refuge of unconsciousness. Yet there is no alternative to the long, slow, laborious process of self-discovery through living each day as oneself, to bringing into being a truly conscious relationship with another person. Inevitably, it hurts; any birth does. One must dare to suffer the death of illusions, and the dissolution of projections. One must dare to be mistaken. One must dare to be vulnerable, to be inferior, to be magnanimous enough to allow for the failings of others because one is prone to them oneself; and one must dare to incur (and inflict) pain and wounded pride, as well, at times, as a thoroughly bruised and battered ego which needs to be shaken out of its self-complacency. One must retain a sense of humour. And one must be willing to accept the element of unconscious collusion in all situations, however much they may seem the fault of the other. Nothing comes into a man's life that is not a reflection of something within himself. Nothing is ever wholly the fault of another, for at the deepest roots of our being we are all one psyche, and the same life stream permeates us all. We possess in seed form every potential in human nature, from the darkest to the lightest; within each of us there exists the saint, the martyr, the murderer, the thief, the artist, the rapist, the teacher, the healer, the god, and the devil. Individuals are different, but the collective psyche gives birth to us all.

Ultimately, one must acknowledge both the smallness and the greatness of the personal self in all matters of choice, and one must stand between these opposites of being nothing and being everything. If we choose to cooperate with the eternal flow of life, which is ceaselessly changing and becoming and seeking consciousness of itself, we cannot indulge ourselves with either self-abasement or unwarranted arrogance or inflation. Yet there is room for the neglected child in each of us, the child full of burgeoning potentialities which we perpetually condemn and repress because it does not conform to our self-image and the images of those around us. Valuing the child allows us to value ourselves as whole people, and it is only as whole people that we can value others. We need to educate ourselves to look behind selfishness, greed, dependency, jealousy, possessiveness and will to power, and discern the needs and the energies which govern them; and such modest, undogmatic discrimination will enable us to transmute the clumsy and ugly into something vulnerable and precious. We must all, in short, become alchemists, and the work of transmutation is synonymous with learning how to love. Christ's injunction is to love your neighbour as yourself. But if you do not love yourself, what will you be capable of doing to your neighbour, vindicated by the self-righteousness of your own judgment?

These are terribly simple principles, implicit in any fairy tale. Even a child is familiar with them, until we pound his wisdom out of him by busily educating him to "face life". But while it is easy to identify with the hero, it is rather more difficult to recognise that the enemy, the sorcerer, the dragon, the witch, and the evil stepmother, as well as the beloved, are all figures existing autonomously and wielding power within one's own psyche. Early in this book, we cited the inferior son who is scorned and ridiculed while the king and his two handsome progeny ride roughshod over him. Who is this inferior son within ourselves? What secret wisdom does he possess, what key does he hold, that leads him where no one else can go — into the heart of the earth where the treasure lies concealed? It is not easy to live with one's inferiority, acknowledge it, grant it sanctuary, nurture and value it for its own sake. We are all so terribly embarrassed about displaying it even to those we love, so much more comfortable seeming wise, capable and always right; and then we must make our lame excuses when, in revenge, what we have disowned reclaims its heritage and we perpetrate acts of violence upon others. To face the secret, transsexual side of one's own nature, to begin the long work of freeing and redeeming it, also requires courage. We prefer to let a partner enact it for us, so that if failure of some sort ensues, it is someone else's responsibility.

The *Zeitgeist* of our age is urging that we cease this unconscious hypocrisy — just as we ourselves ask a pubescent youth, who has outgrown childhood and must face the challenges of adolescence, to stop behaving like a five-year-old. While we do not always expect him to succeed, we expect him at least to try. Immaturity is forgivable, even appealing, in a child. But deliberate evasion of psychological adulthood, particularly at the expense of others, does injury to life itself, and is perhaps, in the final analysis, the true meaning of sin.

If there are no psychological shortcuts, there are no astrological shortcuts either, for astrology's great and ancient fund of wisdom, shrouded in eternal symbols, is a reflection of life, not a means of avoiding it. On some abstract level of cosmic energies, Cancer may be compatible with Scorpio, and incompatible with Aries; but in human relationships, such arguments cannot be used as excuses to shirk the responsibilities one commits oneself to assume. Living through and beyond the birth horoscope is the individual, who — so far as the consciousness he develops is concerned — is not bound by his astrological map. Anyone attempting to diagnose relationship problems from a supposed incompatibility of signs will be sadly disappointed. For in the end he cannot escape the fact that half the relationship is his own creation, and must be explored and handled through a recognition of his own nature, both conscious and unconscious — as well as by a recognition of the motives at work within him when he performs any action or makes any pertinent decision. If a man is to know and experience another, he must first know and experience himself; and to do this, as the fairy tales tell us, he must undertake a quest, a journey on which the unknown denizens of his own inner world will confront him in strange shapes and guises. And he must come to realise that they are not creations of the ego, but participants with the ego in a psychic totality — a totality for which the ego plays the role of the loving redeemer and servant of the gods, not of dictator or slave.

There are myriad paths along which the quest may lead. For all of us, in one way or another, it is the process of living which is the true therapist and counsellor; and only through living one's life with loyalty to one's whole self can one learn to understand it and make knowledge — whether in the language of psychology or astrology — truly one's own. At the appropriate time, however, some individuals can benefit from guidance, from counselling, or from participation in group experience; and it is only fear and senseless pride that convinces us we should always be capable of seeing and helping ourselves in tight-lipped solitude. Many of us can also benefit greatly from an understanding of astrology, but there are numerous way of expressing what the chart symbolises, and not everyone understand the same symbols. It sometimes happens, before any real understanding emerges, that a person must try many things, and wander for a long time in darkness, with only a vague intuition to guide him. And when understanding does emerge, it is less likely to do so with a thunderclap than with a very small, almost inaudible click, which shifts a mode of perception and reveals what we have always known, only in a slightly different perspective. At moments of greatest need, the unconscious psyche will offer to consciousness its own symbols of wholeness and of the next stage of the journey; and if we are not to travel blind, we must learn to read these symbols in our dreams and fantasies, as well as in the horoscope. It is into the realm of symbols, of dreams, of myths and fairy tales, the domain of the shadowland, the kingdom of the idiot son and the imprisoned inner partner, that we must journey, marking our map as we go. And if one is too busy measuring how far one has gone, one may never know if and when one arrives. One must simply embark, must lose oneself in the experience of journeying; for journey and goal are ultimately the same. And then, like Parzival, one may awaken to find oneself in the magical castle, perhaps once, perhaps many times. But unlike Parzival, one may have the wit to ask why.

None of us is in a position to define what love is. We experience it in many different forms, and it experiences us or lives through us. If we are to obtain any glimpse into its mystery, we must learn to respect it as a power, not as something that can be turned on and off like a water tap, or classified as a mode of behaviour. "If you really loved me, you would not have spoken like that/flirted with the waitress /neglected to prepare my dinner" is an attitude which has no place in the sanctuary of this god whose temple is the heart.

> Love is a force of destiny whose power reaches from
> heaven to hell,

says Jung. Since we are not in a position to define love, we
must simply allow ourselves to experience it in whatever form
it comes to us — even if we must later speak of "infatuation",
"illusion", "need", or any other rationalised appellations for a
failed relationship. Even the most distorted of projections, if
it has the power to move the individual to become greater
than he was — to strive, to aspire, to grow, to reach out
towards another — houses somewhere the daemon of love.
Although we must introject them, projections should also be
respected, for they are the emanations of our souls. It is not
wrong to project. On the cor.trary, it is very likely that we
ourselves are projections of the Self. It is only when we refuse
to recognise our projections that we are culpable. The
content of a projection is an aspect, an inseparable part, of
the individual's own essence. He must therefore reclaim it as
best he can so that he can give it freely another time, instead
of having it wrenched from him by fate.

We are both the prince and the princess; and the happily
ever after, although we are not likely to find it in any earthly
relationship, remains a real and living symbol of an inner
marriage which can occur at any time, within any person,
once, many times, or forever. This sacred marriage is one of
the undying symbols at the deepest level of the human
pysche, and constitutes both the end and the beginning of
the quest; for it is this marriage that gives birth to new life. It
is not a question of outgrowing childish illusions. It is a
question of learning to live in both the inner and outer
worlds, recognising the language of both and our share in
both — and that they, and we, are part of the same totality.

> Woe to the man who sees only the mask. Woe to the
> man who sees only what is hidden beneath it. The
> only man with true vision sees at the same moment, and
> in a single flash, the beautiful mask and the dreadful
> face behind it. Happy the man who, behind his
> forehead, creates this mask and this face in a synthesis
> still unknown to nature. He alone can play with dignity
> and grace the double flute of life and death.[1]

1 *The Rock Garden*, Nikos Kazantzakis, Simon & Schuster, New York, 1963.

Selected Bibliography

Bailey, Alice A., *Esoteric Astrology*, Lucis Trust, New York, 1951.

Bishop, Beata and McNeill, Pat, *Below the Belt*, Coventure, London, 1977.

Campbell, Joseph, *The Masks of God: Creative Mythology*, Souvenir Press, London, 1974.

Campbell, Joseph, *The Masks of God: Occidental Mythology*, Souvenir Press, London, 1964.

Campbell, Joseph, *The Masks of God: Primitive Mythology*, Souvenir Press, London, 1959.

Frazer, Sir James, *The Golden Bough*, Macmillan, New York, 1922.

Gauquelin, Michel, *Cosmic Influences on Human Behaviour*, Garnstone Press, London, 1974.

Gibran, Kahlil, *The Prophet*, Alfred A. Knopf, New York, 1971.

Greene, Liz, *Saturn: a New Look at an Old Devil*, Samuel Weiser, Inc., New York, 1976.

Harding, M. Esther, *The I and the Not I*, Bollingen Foundation/Princeton University Press, Princeton, New Jersey, 1969.

Harding, M. Esther, *Women's Mysteries*, Rider & Co., London, 1971.

Hartmann, Franz, *Paracelsus: Life and Prophecies*, Rudolph Steiner Publications, New York, 1973.

Jung, C. G., *Modern Man in Search of a Soul*, Routledge & Kegan Paul, London, 1961.

Jung, C. G., *Letters, Volume II*, edited by Gerhard Adler, Routledge & Kegan Paul, London, 1976.

Jung, C. G., *Psychology and Alchemy*, Routledge & Kegan Paul, London, 1953.

Jung, C. G., *Psychological Types*, Routledge & Kegan Paul, London, 1971.

Jung, C. G., *Civilisation in Transition*, Routledge & Kegan Paul, London, 1964.

Jung, C. G., *Aion*, Routledge & Kegan Paul, London, 1959.

Jung, C. G., *Two Essays in Analytical Psychology*, Routledge & Kegan Paul, London, 1966.

Jung, C. G., *Synchronicity: An Acausal Connecting Principle*, Routledge & Kegan Paul, London, 1972.

Jung, C. G., *Contributions to Analytical Psychology*, Kegan Paul, London, 1928.

Jung, C. G., *The Archetypes and the Collective Unconscious,* Routledge & Kegan Paul, London, 1959.

Kazantzakis, Nikos, *The Rock Garden,* Simon & Schuster, New York, 1963.

Neumann, Erich, *The Great Mother,* Bollingen Foundation, New York, 1955.

Robertson, Marc, *The Transit of Saturn,* The Astrology Center of the Northwest, Seattle, Washington, 1973.

Robson, Vivian, *Astrology and Human Sex Life,* W. Foulsham & Co., London, 1963.

Singer, June, *The Boundaries of the Soul,* Anchor Books, New York, 1973.

Watson, Lyall, *Supernature,* Hodder & Stoughton, London, 1972.

Whitmont, Edward, *The Symbolic Quest,* G. P. Putnam's Sons, New York, 1969.

Wickes, Frances, *The Inner World of Childhood,* Coventure, London, 1977.

Wickes, Frances, *The Inner World of Choice,* Coventure, London, 1977.

Wilhelm, Richard and Baynes, Cary F., translators, *The I Ching or Book of Changes,* Bollingen Foundation, New York, 1950.

Yeats, W. B., *Collected Poems,* Macmillan, New York, 1922.

Suggested Additional Reading List

Books on Astrology

Arroyo, Stephen, *Astrology, Psychology and the Four Elements,* CRCS Publications, Davis, California, 1975.

Hone, Margaret, *The Modern Textbook of Astrology,* L.N. Fowler & Co., London, 1951.

Mayo, Jeff, *Astrology,* The English Universities Press, Ltd., London, 1964.

Meyer, Michael R., *A Handbook for the Humanistic Astrologer,* Anchor Books, Garden City, New York, 1974.

Oken, Alan, *As Above, So Below,* Bantam Books, New York, 1973.

Oken, Alan, *The Horoscope, The Road and Its Travellers,* Bantam Books, New York, 1973.

Rudhyar, Dane, *The Pulse of Life,* Servire, The Hague, Netherlands, 1963.

Books on Mythology and Fairy Tale

Campbell, Joseph, *The Hero with a Thousand Faces,* Sphere Books, London, 1975.

Jung, Emma and Von Franz, Marie-Louise, *The Grail Legend,* Hodder and Stoughton, London, for Rascher Verlag, Zurich, 1960.

Von Franz, Marie-Louise, *Interpretation of Fairytales,* Spring Publications, Zurich, 1975.

Von Franz, Marie-Louise, *Shadow and Evil in Fairytales,* Spring Publications, Zurich, 1974.

Von Franz, Marie-Louise, *The Feminine in Fairytales,* Spring Publications, Zurich, 1972.

Books on Depth Psychology

Adler, Gerhard, *Studies in Analytical Psychology,* Capricorn Books, New York, 1969.

Assagioli, Roberto, *Psychosynthesis,* Psychosynthesis Research Foundation/ Viking Press, New York, 1965.

Assagioli, Roberto, *The Act of Will,* Psychosynthesis Research Foundation/ Wildwood House, London, 1973.

Harding, M. Esther, *The Way of All Women,* Rider & Co., London, 1971.

Jacobi, Jolande, *The Psychology of C. G. Jung,* Routledge & Kegan Paul, London, 1942.

Jaffe, Aniela, *The Myth of Meaning,* Penguin Books, Inc., New York, 1975.

Progoff, Ira, *The Symbolic and the Real,* Coventure, London, 1977.

Others

Jung, C. G., *Memories, Dreams and Reflections,* Fontana/Random House, Inc., London, 1967.

Van Der Post, Laurens, *Jung and the Story of Our Time,* Vintage Books, New York, 1977.

INDEX